Life
in
Flip Flops

Life in Flip Flops

by Sonja B. DeChene

iUniverse, Inc.
Bloomington

Life in Flip Flops

iUniverse books may be ordered through booksellers or by contacting:

iUniverse
1663 Liberty Drive
Bloomington, IN 47403
www.iuniverse.com
1-800-Authors (1-800-288-4677)

ISBN: 978-1-4759-1450-4 (sc)
ISBN: 978-1-4759-1451-1 (ebk)

Printed in the United States of America

iUniverse rev. date: 05/24/2012

What's Inside

Foreword

My daughter, Sonja DeChene, uses "flip flops" to describe the sandals she loves to wear while relaxing in the sand, sun, and surf beside the seashore.

As for me, I can't stand flip flops! Give me the sea breeze in the shade on a porch two stories above the ocean front in late September. That's relaxation to me. But no flip-flops! Oh well, to each his own.

I published my first book in 1998, over fourteen years ago. Currently I am working on my fourteenth book. It flatters me to know that two of my younger brothers have also gotten into book publishing.

But it is especially pleasurable to know that my daughter, Sonja, is working on her first book, *Life in Flip Flops,* a collection of short stories about many of her life experiences.

From the first time she mentioned writing a book, I have encouraged her and offered my comments and suggestions on how to be successful. She has come to me many times with questions about writing and publishing. From time to time, she borrowed my books on writing to help her do things right.

Many times she has called her mama and me so she could read to us her latest short story. It didn't take us long to realize that Sonja has an extraordinary and expressive way with words.

What a delight it has been to see her make progress in her writing. I must admit that she has a way with words that her daddy does not have.

Often I have advised her to always remember the three main rules of writing successfully. These rules are quite simple, but very effective when followed:

1. Revise
2. Revise
3. Revise

Sonja has a genuinely unique writing style. I'm sure you'll recognize and appreciate that style as you read her book *Life in Flip Flops*.

"Daddy"
Elmer C. Brown

Preface

As a high school freshman in the eighties at Alamance Christian School, I was part of the first Speech class offered there. Duane Manning, a fresh face just out of Bible college came in like a whirlwind scaring me and my classmates half to death. He introduced us to a new world of writing and delivering speeches. From him, I learned not only how to write a story, but how to *tell* the story in front of an audience with confidence and conviction.

Twenty years later, I found myself taking an Expository Writing class at Alamance Community College as part of a nursing pre-requisite. My first class and first story came just two weeks prior to 9/11. I fell in love with the class instantly and realized that I had much to say about a lot of different things and a unique way of saying it. I completed the course with a grade of 106.

Although my daddy published his first book in 1998, it wasn't until years later after my writing class that I started entertaining the idea of writing a book of my own. The notion was subtle and the resolve was inward and it took some time for me to put all the pieces together. Me, write a book? Why not!

In 2009, that inward resolve surfaced and blossomed into a full blown endeavor to bare my soul and pen my thoughts for anyone to read.

I'm honored to follow in the footsteps of my daddy, Uncle Joe and Uncle John. Collectively, they have written 39 books and counting covering a variety of topics and genres including Christian devotionals, Christian fiction, history, family history, cycling and poetry. And now, I join them with my first effort.

It has been said that writing is therapeutic. Well, it really is. Creating and compiling this collection of stories proved to be quite the journey for me.

I took the time to reflect on my life on the simplest level. I believe that I reinforced, to myself, who I really am at the core and who I am still growing up to be. And along the way, learned a little bit more about life and such.

I laughed, I cried, I did a lot of thinking and I gained a greater appreciation for life and all of its gifts.

My wish is that you find these tales and musings entertaining on many levels and that if nothing else it will cause you to pause, ponder and extract joy from *your* life in the most obvious and not so obvious places.

If one person laughs, if just one one person sheds a tear, if only one person takes a moment to be still and reflect on all the gifts God has blessed us with, then my book has been a success.

On April 26th, 2011, I stopped by Mama and Daddy's house to pick up a copy of Daddy's latest book entitled *As I Recall*. As always, a conversation about writing and book publishing ensued. My brother sat quietly, listening to the conversation, as he so often does. My daddy shared his words of wisdom, "revise, revise, revise!", and we traded ideas on the art of writing.

My mama's contribution to the conversation came in the form of subtle encouragement: "I just want you to get your book finished before I die." She's always had such a way with words.

Look Mama, *I did it!*

To my family:
My loving husband, David
My sweet mama and daddy
My dear brother, Jeff

I love you all very much and appreciate
your love, support and inspiration
during the writing of these memories
and always.

Eternal thanks to
My Lord and Savior Jesus Christ
For His unconditional love, grace and mercy
and
for His many gifts.

Introduction

Everyone experiences that comfortable point in life where a certain level of maturity finally kicks in and reflection is inevitable. It's a natural next step. So, here I am.

Sitting in my mid-forties now like it's a comfy chair, I find I'm looking around more. Not so much for what's next in my life but more so looking back at what's already been. And more importantly, what it all means.

People are in such a hurry these days. The interstate is filled with folks whipping in and out of traffic trying to get to the next item on their "to do" list. Others are killing themselves slowly by getting their nutrition at a drive-thru window rather than from a home-cooked meal shared with the family gathered around.

And still, others are putting so much of themselves into their career that the life that is truly the most important is passing them by. Common courtesy has shriveled and negativity is taking over like the weeds in my lawn.

I'm here to say it doesn't have to be that way. And it starts with me. I've discovered that it's no longer cliché to stop and smell the roses. It's vital to a full and meaningful life.

I'm a simple Southern girl who has finally realized that life is a smorgasbord of gifts that can be found in everyday livin'—past and present. And no matter how simple or complex your life may be, it's still unique but similar to everyone else's all at the same time. In other words, we can all relate in one way or another.

No matter who or what you think you are, one thing is for certain: you cannot take yourself too seriously in flip flops. First, they make that loud smacking sound every time you take a step. And let's face it, you can't really run too fast in them either. They sort of force you to slow down your pace and let life catch up with you. You see, we spend too much of our lives wearing running shoes trying to get to what's next; and we spend too much money on uncomfortable "status" shoes trying to impress everyone else.

A little bit of reflection is good for setting your inner butterfly loose. I find that it keeps you grounded with a healthy amount of vulnerability welcomed for some much needed balance. If you have no clue what I'm talking about or if you're the least bit curious, I invite you to pull out those flips flops hiding in the dark recesses of your closet and take a walk with me.

Because ultimately, flips flops do go with everything.

Fortress of Solitude

A weathered beach house on the coast, your very own rustic mountain chalet or maybe a beautiful meadow decorated by hundreds of yellow wildflowers begging you to skip through their midst. I think there are very few who would disagree with me when I say that everyone needs a place they can retreat to now and again. For me, frequent visits are a must. Somewhere far away from the busyness of life where you are able to relax, do your own thing and just be still. In this place, it's all about you; and that's okay.

The beauty of this musing is that you don't need a lot of money, nor do you need to travel far from home to find this sort of place. It's much closer than you think.

My husband and I are big fans of the show *Smallville*. *Smallville* is a television series about the growing pains of a young Clark Kent, a.k.a (the future) Superman. Now, I was never into comic books and I have never been a fan of the super hero variety, but this show totally captivated me. That doesn't happen too often.

Over a very short period of time, it became an every night viewing ritual for us and still is. We now own all ten seasons of the show on Blu-ray and have watched and re-watched each episode numerous times, each time with fresh eyes able to see deeper into each story.

In *Smallville*, Clark's dad, Jonathon Kent, once referred to the loft space in the Kent's barn as a "Fortess of Solitude" since this is where a teenage Clark Kent spent a lot of his time alone. True to the comic book series, *Smallville* also included Clark's Kyrptonian getaway which was also called "The Fortress of Solitude." For him, it was an ice castle in the Arctic that contained much knowledge and the essence (and voice) of his deceased father, Jor-el. When Clark needed answers,

1

when he was angry or confused, when he needed to be alone, he often would super-speed to this special place and re-group.

Still with me?

Suffice it to say, inspiration can come from the most unexpected places.

At this very moment, we have the series finale left to watch as *Smallville's* ten year run came to a close in 2011. And recently, after watching an episode one night, my thoughts began to wander a bit. I thought about how much I have enjoyed watching this show with my husband and how I cherish the quality time with him as we have shared this simple, mutual pleasure together. Lights out and sitting in our man-chairs, it's like a switch has been flipped and the world has been cut off for a bit while we escaped into total fiction.

With a smile and a shrugging of the shoulders, I drew my own conclusion that "this" was one of my fortress's. Who says you can only have one?

A true fortress of solitude is a place of security, of survival and of strength. Much like home, it's safe, familiar and comfortable. It's a place where you can be alone and remote from society or let only the most special of people in. You're in control. It is where you can be a free spirit long enough to regain balance and where happiness in its purest form can be found. And it doesn't cost a thing.

I recently added another candle to my birthday cake. Other than an increased fire hazard, it changed very little in the grand scheme of things. I can still go home to Mama and Daddy's and re-enter the world of that introverted, wide-eyed child and pick up where time left her behind. Lying on the couch under a cozy blanket while an overhead fan tickles my face, I can lay my head in Mama's lap while she strokes my hair gently. Daddy sits in his chair watching another episode of *Andy Griffith*. The cheesy dialogue and manufactured laughter lull me into a another place. With my eyes pinched closed softly, it's as if time has stood still. Yes, I can always go home. This is one of my fortress's.

Where most people have a guest room at home, I have something a bit more meaningful and off the beaten path. I whimsically refer to this space as my "Happy Room." Of course it's got a recliner, a television, a phone and a computer. But it's so much more. It is decorated with so many aspects of me. I guess you could say my individuality lives here and isn't afraid of what people may think.

Family photos, countless tangible references to the coast, a giant baby blue teddy bear, and an eclectic mix of colorful accessories soften a driftwood colored space that would only be four walls were it not for their presence. Sunlight streams in the bay window creating a sunspot on the carpet and a tiny fortress of solitude for my cats. Memories of my life freely flow through this room. For it is here that I pray, that I think, that I create, that I rest and that I just am. It is my fortress of solitude.

A fortress of solitude can even be a bouquet of moments held closely together by a pretty ribbon and your desire on the fly to throw that predictable schedule or "to do list" out the window-temporarily of course-and just switch to autopilot. You see, it's not so much the place you're physically in as it is the sheer determination and secure, happy optimism that is with you in that place.

In case you're wondering, I'm not at all disconnected from the real world. I just realize the need to take a break from it; I have learned that I don't have to have an itinerary in place or a hotel reservation to do so. It's not a vacation, but rather a life time-out. God has provided me with everyday gifts that allow me to drift away for a bit without skipping a beat in the dance that is life. With Him orchestrating the melody, the sound is sweet and the message is not lost. You just have to be able to read the music.

Writing, I have found, helps me to harmonize. It too is a fortress of solitude as it has prompted me to think about my life and the people and things in it on a deeper, more emotional level than I ever have before. It has also helped me to not take myself, or others for that matter, so seriously. Life can be treacherous while being victorious while being downright humorous. Hey, I'm no Erma Bombeck, but I'd like to think that every now and again a little "Erma" seeps out of my writing.

I've found that I have a lot to say and frankly, I've never met a goose bump I didn't like. This collection of stories is proof that even the simplest moments, part of the simplest life, can over shadow money, possessions, power, trials and self imposed entitlement. It keeps me humble and suggests that my daddy's prayer for me whispered to the Lord when I was just hours old lying in the baby room was not in vain. "Please don't ever forget where you came from and keep your faith in the Lord strong."

The idea of a "Fortress of Solitude" might be pure fiction in the comics, but I think a kindred spirit was thinking outside the box when they brought that concept to life. It's that magical but real place where you are perfectly content, no strings attached; where much is accomplished or nothing at all. It's there already, you know, embedded in your life. It's sort of like one of those visual pieces that if you stare at it long enough, you eventually are able to see the message.

Going Coastal

A sign should be posted, "NO SHOES ALLOWED". How can you possibly be there if you aren't feeling the soft, silky sand caress your feet? As I walk closer to my destination, the cool grains of sand squeeze between my toes like Play-doh in the tight grip of a child's hand. The tall, limber sea oats line my path like a welcoming committee and tickle my skin playfully as I pass them by.

And though I have been to the coast many times before, catching my first glimpse of the ocean is always as if I am seeing it again for the first time. I stand humbly in awe.

The water sparkles in the sun like a thousand exquisite diamonds. For a moment, I close my eyes so I can take in all it has to offer. I hear the musical white noise of the waves crashing the shore and they are decorated with the frivolous laughter of the families who now inhabit the sand like seashells.

At times, the ocean breeze dances across my face and body like a feather, and at others, it lunges at me as if to remind me of its awesome power. I inhale deeply and smell the sea air, though I never really thought it smelled like salt. And that familiar scent is intertwined with the strong fragrance of tropical tan lotion.

I exhale, as if full, and open my eyes to see a beautiful seagull gracefully flying by. With feet tucked securely behind and under its belly, my feathery friend polices the beach for morsels of food that might have escaped the hungry masses.

My spirit too, begins to take flight as I walk to the glistening waters and the lukewarm ocean touches my bare feet. It is both cleansing and refreshing. I stand there now at water's edge trying to take it all in. It is truly a feast for the eyes, ears, nose, and skin.

More than that, it is heaven for my heart and soul. A place of refuge and an arena of release for many emotions held deep inside. Here, I am at peace. All that saddens me, stresses me, or angers me is far away when my feet are one with the sand, and the ocean waves talk to me like an old friend.

I have never been in another place that not only stimulated my senses so breathtakingly, but set my spirit free like the beautiful seagull whose home is this place.

Accident Prone
or
Target of an Evil Plot

I could be wrong, but I think it's possible the whole plot manifested itself at the tender age of two weeks old. This is when my mama first popped me on the side of my chunky, little thigh.

Some of you may gasp at the thought of this, but really, it's ok. I don't remember a thing. I only know what my mama has told me—that I had been changed, fed and had already had a nap. I had no reason to be crying so defiantly. Though my mamaw never agreed with her course of action, maybe, just maybe it set me on the right course for life; but what course was that?

There are many objects found in typical homes that, when crossing paths with the wrong individual, can become a weapon of sorts. Take for instance homemade ice cream. You laugh in disbelief. But haven't you ever made a frozen treat with layers of Kool-Aid and ice cream in one of those old, metal ice trays? The memory, even now, causes me to pause and aggressively brush the chill bumps from my arms as I recall biting down into a chunk of this home-made concoction only to find that when I pulled my mouth away from it, I had left a tooth behind. Imagine my surprise. It was a yummy orange and vanilla dessert. To this day, I can't look at a dreamsicle without reliving the entire event all over again. *shivers*

You wouldn't think something as seemingly harmless as food could cause one to be calling on the tooth fairy so often. But oddly enough, french fries, chocolate chip cookies and yes, even the all-American hotdog, seemed to have it out for me. I might let the hotdog off the hook because in all honesty, the hotdog might have chipped my tooth, but it was my dear mother who saw the need to pull it. Again, it's okay. I do remember this event but it didn't scar me for life. I mean, the fact that my tooth bled for three days until it built up a blood clot in my mouth as high as Mr. Everest that dissolved in my sleep scaring the life out of me when I woke up—was really a minor detail.

All of my traumas have not been isolated to food alone. There are evil props outside of the home as well. Let's consider an innocent looking swing. You remember-the older ones that had a bench seat on each end and you entered it from the side? Fun little contraptions until the smallest rider (that would be me) falls off the back of the seat onto the ground. This is where the story should have ended. However, being a little one who was taught to get back up after you've fallen down, I found this little nugget of wisdom to not be true 100 percent of the time.

Enter an older brother who thought it was fascinating to count the number of times his little sister sat back up only to be slammed in the head by this speeding death trap. His logic was that I shouldn't have kept sitting up. My logic: I was, like, four years old. Cut me some slack already. And what saved my little melon from permanent indentations? Of course, my loving mother, who stood in horror watching from the kitchen window as this horrible drama unfolded. Maybe she didn't have it out for me after all . . .

While we're talking about my sweet mama, I have to add that Mama not only taught me valuable life lessons, but she also taught me how to play "patty cake". You remember this delightful, childhood game, right? It's the one where Mama sings "Patty cake, patty cake, bakers man; roll 'em up, roll 'em up, toss 'em in a pan" . . . . and slaps her child's tender cheeks knocking out yet another loose tooth. What? That's not how it goes?

The plot thickens . . . .

Let's get back to items in the home. A pencil is a no-brainer. It can be a very dangerous weapon, especially when freshly sharpened. Just ask my brother. He stabbed me with one once. No, really, he did. The whole scene almost resembled an old western standoff.

8

There I stood, six years younger than my brother, at one end of the hall; and there he stood, being my older brother and supposed protector, at the other end of the hall with a pristinely chiseled #2 school issued pencil held tightly in his grip. The evil grin on his face may be a detail I have chosen to make up in my mind rather than fact, but the lead mark that exists to this day in my lower lip is 100 percent real. Ask him about this confrontation, and you are sure to get a different pile of . . . fiction.

What role does the father play in all of this, you might ask? Was he the quiet mastermind sitting in the shadows as Mama and brother carried out his evil plot? Apparently it was his plan all along to play mind games with me. Only, it backfired.

I have been told by my mama how I talked back to my daddy once. I asked them both what I said, but they conveniently don't remember. And what was his course of action? He made me write 50 times, "I will not talk back to my daddy." Was this a subtle form of discipline or mind control? Being that I am writing this book, I would say that his plan failed, especially after I finished my task and exclaimed to both my mama and daddy proudly "That was fun!"

Ah, the joys of youth sometimes shattered and scarred by such horrific events as these. But the question still remains . . . was there an evil plot devised against me, even before birth, or am I just that accident prone?

Let me give you a piece of solid, heartfelt advice. Don't ever use wire clothes hangers. They may be good for helping to unlock your car when you have forgotten your keys but they have a very dark side. Not only do they leave awful looking lumps in the shoulders of your shirts but if you are ever on the phone with your daddy having a pleasant conversation and you try to yank a shirt off the hanger from your closet, that piece of monster metal will contort itself until it has succeeded to fly up your nose and cause quite the commotion.

With that being said, I think we have our answer. My mama didn't slap me on the thigh 43 years ago just because she was instigating an evil plot against the child who kept her in labor for three days. No, she popped me out of sheer embarrassment because she knew that someday I would end up with that darned wire clothes hanger up my nose.

Cats and Children

They say having only one child causes that child to be spoiled and to miss out on the fun of having a brother or sister. Does that same thought process apply to felines?

He was born on September 1, 1993. At Christmastime that same year, the golden-eyed, tiny puff of black fur came looking for his new mom. She feared a name change at such a tender age would cause confusion for her new baby, so the name "Cougar" was adopted, as well.

As a kitten, Cougar seemed to be your average size fury bundle of cuteness. He liked to play and chase strings, as most kittens do, but more than anything he seemed to love to wrestle with his mom's hands. He was a ferocious little fighter with very sharp teeth.

But she was determined for him to know how much she loved him, so she picked him up and cuddled him a lot. He knew he was loved. He returned the sentiment by developing into a devoted lap cat at an early age. He was mischievous, too. His favorite holiday tradition for the first two or three years seemed to be lying in the Christmas tree. That was until he had that transforming growth spurt.

Apparently, the human food delicacies of pizza, popcorn and fruit loops, that his mom so lovingly shared with him, proved to be the catalyst for Cougar's inevitable obesity. Now, years later at age eight, Cougar weighs in at an astonishing 24 pounds. Restrictive diets have failed and the added weight has started to affect his lungs and cleaning habits. Even the simple task of sitting down or leaping onto a loved one's lap requires premeditation and precision. He is not poetry in motion. But rather an oversized fellow that moves with more calculation and unsureness in his steps than he once did.

Despite his limitations, he is even more loving and dedicated than ever. Ask him what his first love in life is and he would probably proudly bellow out, "food!" His purr is now replaced by a crackling wheeze, but it sounds loudly proclaiming the happiness and love he feels in his heart for his home and his family. To be convinced of that contentment is to observe the handsome mass lying in his favorite chair propped against a pillow with an apparent smile on his perfect, chubby face.

She was born on March 6, 2000 and came to live with Cougar and his family in May of that year. Once the decision was made to add a little girl to the family, the search led them to a very shy and scared kitten with luxurious fur that resembled a timeless patchwork quilt of grays, peaches and whites. Her inward beauty beamed from her exquisitely outlined eyes of yellowish-green. She was named after a new age poet, "Rumi". Time would tell whether she would live up to this name synonymous with poetry.

Rumi far surpassed her older brother's level of mischievousness. She made this apparent by not chasing strings, as Cougar did, but by chasing his tail. Though Rumi's parents thought this was so cute, Cougar seemed to be quite annoyed with the ritual and the new feline in his house. That old habit has died hard and given way to greater feats such as climbing into garbage cans, any empty box she can fit in, and mad dashes from room to room with lightning speed while playing fetch with a paper ball.

For Rumi, the drug of choice has not become food, as is the case for Cougar. Her addiction seems to be licking the skin right off of her mom and dad's bones. It's as if her body is lacking a nutrient and a pleasure that only the noisy, little lick of human flesh can provide.

Still in her youth, the epitome of cuteness remains lean and swift of foot. To see Rumi drop to the floor, with paws curled demurely, and like an actress overacting a dramatic scene, is to realize her name reflecting poetry was properly chosen. Raised with as much love as Cougar, Rumi has also grown into a loving lap cat. Her moments of intimacy, however, are of her choosing only. But there is never a doubt when hearing her motor running like an idling sports car that she is happy to be where she is.

Individually, they are as different as night and day. Together, they complete an already happy home that has been enriched beyond dreams with the laughter, loyalty, love, and affection that only a feline nurtured into a treasured member of the family can bring.

Warriors

I still remember sitting in the den of our ranch style home on Cocoa Drive in Greensboro. Daddy was announcing that we would be attending Alamance Christian School once we made the move to Graham.

I laugh as I recollect how Daddy told us this school even had a "gym". I laugh because somehow I thought that meant gymnastics or ballet. Yeah, I still scratch my head about that perception. What can I say; I was eight years old and didn't get out much at the time.

I would spend the next nine years receiving a quality education in a safe, Christian atmosphere. It was an education my parents sacrificed to pay for. There was no funding or help from the state. But my parents did not waver in their decision to provide us with more than the government could. The education they wished for my brother and I went far beyond reading, writing and arithmetic.

From birth, I was in the midst of a loving, Christian home and in church many times a week. A Christian education seemed only natural to me. I had no clue what the alternative was. I was too young and too immature at the time to grasp the extent of the gift I was being given. But as a somewhat seasoned adult, it has all become crystal clear. Being called "sheltered" by public school kids more times than I could count never bothered me. Now that I understand why they said it, I can honestly say it still doesn't bother me. As a matter of fact, I'm thankful.

Let me make it clear, however, that the school as a whole was not perfect and neither were the students. But God was (and is) the foundation on which this school was built. The goal was simple: "Pursuit of excellence through Christ."

Prayer was a part of everything we did. Class did not get underway until every student had been seated and the teacher had opened with prayer. Giving thanks for our food did not fall by the wayside just because we were at school. I remember prayer being said at the end of class each day before the lunch bell rang and we invaded the gym for our midday eats.

Of course each grade had a Bible class as part of the curriculum. We also had chapel one day a week where several grades were blended together for a short time. It was just like being at church. There would be announcements, special music and of course a great lesson from various faculty members or visiting speakers, beginning and ending with prayer.

Many would surmise that a Christian school was all about a strict environment. But for me, it was an extension of the environment my parents were giving me at home. And I did not see it as strict. And looking back now, I am grateful beyond words.

ACS was a small, tight knit community. The campus, still growing at the time, consisted of an elementary wing, a high school wing (yes, one high school hallway), a larger room (sort of like an auditorium) and a gymnasium where lunches, sports, plays, concerts and everything else pretty much took place. There was a soccer field, a playground and a school bus or two. Doesn't sound like much but we had everything we needed back then.

Despite the small size, there were still plenty of opportunities available at school such as sports, music and the arts. ACS is where I first learned to play team sports. I played four years of volleyball and five years of basketball while lettering in both. I even snagged a 2nd team all tournament trophy in volleyball one year.

I have such fond memories of pep rallies, spirit week and the rides on the bus to away games. I was so proud to wear my letterman's jacket and represent the red and blue! I still recall the attack of the nerves as we would wait to take the court for any game. I've always heard that if you didn't get a little nervous, it was time to stop playing. Well, the amount of butterflies in my belly proved I had a long career ahead of me *wink*.

Back then (and still today), Alamance was known for a good sports program. While I ended up playing volleyball for many years after graduation, I'm sad to say that I did not get to experience too many milestones or success while I was in school. Come to think of it, the last memory I made as a high school volleyball player consisted of me spiking the ball into the net to lose the game against Wake Academy, dashing our hopes of making it into the state tournament. I cried like a baby.

Basketball, on the other hand, was a different story. We girls loved our coach, Mr. LaTour. Practices were tough and how I hated running those suicides. But the hard work paid off. We won our district championship my junior and senior years and went on to be runner's up in the state championship. Cutting down the nets was so cool . . . and I still have my pieces tucked safely away with other school keepsakes.

Some would say that being a runner up two years in a row was a letdown, even after achieving a record of 18-3 my senior year. What made the difference is the emphasis that Coach LaTour and the school placed on FINISHING. We can't all be winners, but it is our effort and attitude and how we finish the task at hand that make us winners, even if the score does not reflect a victory. Putting forth our best effort while maintaining our stand as Christian ladies, giving God the glory for our wins and losing with grace were principals instilled in us as young, Christian athletes. Without a doubt, it was always a team effort that started with each one of us. All of these were philosophies I have always remembered and will never forget. Did I mention that practices and games began and ended with prayer? One-two-three-FINISH!

I enjoyed being a spectator in the stands as much as playing. We always had an impressive guy's soccer program, also coached by Mr. LaTour. We won many state championships during my years at ACS, and it was so special making those memories surrounded by other Christians students and parents who understood that this experience was so much more than the final score.

But Alamance Christian was about so much more than sports. Music and the Arts were an area of expected expertise. And that was never more evident than when concert or competition time rolled around. Our reputation preceded us when it came to music and speech, both headed up by the one and only, Duane Manning.

He demanded perfection from our varsity chorale and (smaller group) Agapes. Whether practicing to perform in front of our student body, the spring and fall concerts for hundreds of family members, or in front of our peers in state competition in Charlotte, he never wavered in his work ethic or what he expected from us.

And while there was certainly resistance along the way from the students from time to time, we usually came out on top by glorifying the Lord with our song. It was, after all, because of Him and for Him that we sang. I will never forget the year Mr. Manning presented us with the task of attempting and eventually succeeding in a stellar performance of "The Hallelujah Chorus" in state competition. I get chill bumps even now recalling the performance and eventual first place finish.

Drama and speech also yielded our school many trophies and ribbons during competition time. I even snagged a couple of awards myself by delivering speeches and performing readings in the April competition. Those awards reside with other keepsakes I hold very dear. We also excelled in art and many other categories, as well. And I never got tired of the exhilaration and pride I would feel when the competition drew to a close and the overall school winner was announced: Alamance Christian School.

Like I said, we were a small, tight knit group. And I never felt smothered by the dynamic. If anything, it felt like a large family: lots of brothers and sisters with a few extra parents keeping a close eye on us. And yes, there was even a boyfriend or two along the way.

Christian school kids had their own brand of mischievousness back in those days: wet willies in the ears and rearranging a class room while the teacher was out of the room are just some of my favorite goofy memories. Lame, I know. But I never had to contend with vulgar language, bullying, and weapons or anything of that nature like some public schools fight with every day. And I can say without a doubt I loved and respected my teachers. Well, I didn't like them all, but I appreciated every single one of them for their choice to share their gift to teach in our Christian School.

I will never forget Mrs. Smith, our sweet Bible teacher who wore her hair in a round, little bun and taught us that not going to the bathroom when we wanted to would build character. She also taught us to "Pray for tolerance, not patience." Mrs. Cardwell, bless her heart, taught us awkward girls how to sew and do other girly things in Home Economics class.

Then there was Mr. Manning who, unbeknownst to him, gave me my start in writing; I just didn't know it until almost twenty years later. He also scared me senseless by volunteering me to sing a solo in front of a concert crowd. Yes, I lived to tell about it. And of course there was Mr. LaTour, my basketball coach, who liked to refer to me as "Downtown Sonja Brown" for my long range perimeter shots. He turned me into an athlete that could win and lose like a lady Warrior.

It was about 16 years after I had graduated ACS that I found myself and my family by Daddy's bedside in a hospital preparing for surgery to remove his colon cancer. But we were not alone. Duane Manning and Bob LaTour joined us that morning and had prayer with our family. A Christian education is truly a gift that keeps on giving.

And I doubt you will find anyone back in those days who did not simply adore Mr. Blalock, affectionately referred to as "Mr. B." He was a fairly young man who, in addition to being a fantastic teacher, wore a pretty good comedian hat on the side. He made learning fun! But like any human being, he had his limits inside and outside of the classroom. Inside, if you had pushed him too far, his usually quiet demeanor would take on an uncomfortable sternness that made his point. Of course, that point usually had a tension breaking comical blurb at the end and then we would move on.

Outside the class room, his limits would be tested by something far more destructive than a bunch of teenagers; cancer. Many years after graduation, I found out he was losing the battle with a melanoma found on top of his head. I felt compelled to arrange a visit with him at ACS where he still taught. It was surreal. I remember walking down the hall to meet him and thinking how small these hallways seemed.

I had a nice visit with Mr. B that day, not as teacher to student, but as two adults. He still maintained that adorable humor all of us kids loved way back when as he talked about a Yoo-hoo one of the current students had left him on his desk, to lift his spirits. I can only recall one statement he made to me during that visit: "Sonja, this cancer is just eating me up inside." And it was said in such an incredulous tone. It's not a conversation I would have ever dreamed having, yet, here I was. Somehow, having this conversation in one of my old classrooms made this harsh reality pill easier to swallow.

He died a short time later. You know, God gave us the ability to laugh and to enjoy a sense of humor. And I feel certain Mr. B is keeping heaven in stitches these days . . .

Now, some might think that going to the same small, Christian school for nine years might have caused me to "miss out" on things a kid and teenager "should" get to experience growing up. On the contrary; I received the education I needed and made straight A's throughout the process. I excelled in sports and was a member of the first group of "Finishers"; I participated in the singing groups at school and even enjoyed the experience of recording an album with the chorale at Bob Jones University in 1982. I was inducted into the National Honor Society and enjoyed my place on the Homecoming and Valentine Court my senior year.

Every bit of those nine years at Alamance Christian School built on the foundation that my mama and daddy had worked so hard to create for me at home. I missed out on nothing, and was given the opportunity to achieve everything. At ACS, the Fruits of the Spirit were cultivated. Integrity, character, and a life centered on Christ were in full bloom. I believe that life at a Christian school gave me what a public school could not: Pursuit of excellence through Christ. It was openly nurtured every day, unapologetically. It was the focus then and still remains the focus today.

Not too long ago, I met an ACS alumnus at the school parking lot to exchange an exercise video. We were acquainted from Facebook but didn't really know each other as she was an upper classman at the time I was in school.

As I waited for her to arrive, I sat in my car in front of the school and my mind began to drift. I could almost hear the bell ring and see my classmates scurrying down the halls; I could almost see the high school student body packed on the front steps of the school cheering on our teams that would be playing later that day. I could almost see my life at ACS over 25 years ago happening in front of me; almost.

My years at ACS might have been a long time ago, but many memories are still fresh in my mind and refreshing. When I pause to think back to those school days, I am reminded of a simpler time when life seemed less complicated. And as a kid and teenager, it should be. For me, I remember very little drama that I had to endure. Yes, I had to wear skirts and dresses to school every day and our sports uniforms were ultra conservative, but did that scar me for life? Of course not.

What I received from my life at Alamance Christian has always been and will continue to be part of what helps me to weather the storms of life. Words will never be enough, but they are all I have. At age 45, I am still proud to be a Lady Warrior.

Yard Work

Growing up, I never would have believed anyone who told me yard work meant anything more than unnecessary hard work. I recall summer days being swallowed up by hours in the hot sun mowing the lawn and picking green beans. That way of life was not a choice of mine, but it was expected of me as a strong, healthy kid living at home.

Little did I know that what I felt was a direct violation of child labor laws actually had deeper meaning to my parents. It would not be until at least 15 to 20 years later that I would discover that the yard work I loathed so much as a teenager would actually mean more to me than I could have ever imagined.

I didn't view a crystal ball, I didn't call "Cleo" to read my tarot cards; I didn't even ask my mama or daddy what value yard work actually had. I simply acquired a beautiful landscaped home attached to a mortgage. I cannot give any other explanation for the behavior to follow than the fact that I was finally growing up.

I soon found myself looking forward to the weekends so I could mow our lawn or trim our shrubs. The madness escalated when I started daydreaming at work about what I was going to do in my yard when I got home. I could not wait to get out in the fresh air and be stimulated by the visual ecstasy of God's flowers in bloom. A flower had never looked so beautiful to me until it was one that I had planted myself.

The hot sun, sweat and sneezes from the blowing grass didn't upset me at all. In fact, I finally knew what living was. I could finally relate to my parents as an adult. Weekends of sleeping in and mall runs had been replaced by road trips with my mama to any greenhouse we could find. My daddy's years of hard work and gardening experience had finally found a place in my life, too.

Do I still think gardening is hard work? Let's just say that I am a Licensed Massage Therapist by trade. I know what therapy is and it has a new friend. I think I'll call it yard work.

Delirious

It was October 29, 1985.

This could never happen to me. It's just like in the movies. These things always happen to someone else. It was all like a bad dream.

We've all heard these clichés, never thinking they could or would come true. But for me, the words played themselves out at 12:30 on a sunny, Tuesday afternoon in 1985.

I was 19 years old working my first job at the mall. What could be more exciting than spending your days in a video store in the eighties? There was so much anticipation with all the new technology. I still remember all the excitement when the movie *Ghostbusters* was released on VHS and sold for a mere $89.95!

I was assistant manager at this video store which sat safely in our local mall in Small Town, USA. Being assistant manager meant that I would work low traffic shifts alone. No big deal. It's daytime. It's a mall. It's safe. It was all subject to change.

The store was empty. This was typical for an unsuspecting Tuesday afternoon. Empty until one purposely, sharp dressed man entered the store from the side entrance and began to browse our large selection of movies. After strolling around the store for a bit, he approached the counter holding an empty box in his hand for a video he was looking to take home. Or so I thought.

I was raised by two loving parents in a Christian home, went to a private school for all 12 years of my education and went to church whenever the doors were opened. I didn't run with the wrong crowd or find myself in questionable situations. Violence or aggressive behavior was something I had only seen on television. So I can't even begin to describe to you the complete shock that swallowed me as this man leaned across the counter grabbing me by the collar. And what's harder to put into words is my unwelcomed view of the barrel of a Derringer that peered from the hand of this man. I had only seen guns on TV. It's not a situation I was prepared for by any means, but nevertheless, this was my life at this very moment.

To say that something didn't seem real is not a cliché once you've lived that moment. Even now as I try to relive this event on paper, I feel as if the details add up to a poorly written "B" movie with actors none of us have ever heard of before, much less, care about. He wanted money. It was as simple as that. And I was going to give it to him. I didn't have any kind of hero complex or preconceived plan to rid my store of a would-be thief. I was a scared and naïve 19 year old who had been ambushed and couldn't comprehend what was happening.

Did more happen than the robbery? Thank God, no. But the fact that a physical assault didn't take place has never prevented me from knowing that it could have. I was shoved into a bathroom in the back storage area of the store and told not to come out. Naturally, I was going to heed his warning. But I knew that he would quickly be on his way in order to elude capture.

After a matter of minutes, I emerged from the bathroom to find that the closest phone line had been cut. I walked slowly from the storage area to the door leading to the front desk. Peeking around the corner without any real concept of what I was doing, I could see the violated cash register. It was empty. And so was I. Standing there in total shock, it was incredulous to me that the UPS guy was waltzing up to me with a delivery as if this was an ordinary day. Saying it out loud made it real to me. "I've just been robbed!", I muttered. You can't imagine the weight those words carry until you hear them coming out of your own mouth.

The next few hours were a flurry of activity from calling my manager to tell him what had happened to taking my first ride in a police car down to the station to give my testimony. I only remember three things about my experience at the police station; that someone gave me a can of Coca Cola to drink while I rattled off a description of the suspect so the artist could draw the composite; that trying to give a description of someone you had never met who had just threatened your life was a lot harder than it looked on TV; and, I really had to go to the bathroom. I guess life is just strange like that sometimes.

The next several weeks and months were a roller coaster ride of events and emotions. In the immediate days following the robbery, I remember that there were nights where I would literally sleep by the bathroom, sick to my stomach from the stress I was dealing with. There were line-ups to view and regular meetings with the detective handling my case. And much to my relief, there was the eventual capture of the one who shattered my illusion of human nature. How pathetic that this man, who was so invincible with a gun pointed at an innocent young girl, should be gassed out of his own home by the police while hiding underneath a sofa.

Eventually, I testified in court against this man in a trial for another crime committed locally. But as time went on, my life that was before the robbery picked up again and I found myself moving to another state, preparing for my then-husband's return from his first naval deployment. But I wasn't free from the grips of this unresolved crime. I began receiving crank phone calls in my new apartment where I was living alone, warning me to not testify in the upcoming trial. Was this for real?

At last, the day had come—September 4, 1986.

The calls didn't deter me from doing what I had been waiting to do for almost a year now. My day in court finally came. Surrounded by family, I was nervous but confident that justice would be served again, just as it had in the local case I had testified in previously. While waiting for our trial to begin, I remember the disgust I felt as he sat in his seat *pretending* to read the Bible. It was palpable. He was manipulative and calculative. He knew what he was doing then just as he knew what he was doing when he walked into my video store that day. He had cased the place, obviously and came at a time when he knew I would be alone and that there would be few, if any, customers to get in his way.

The trial and its outcome are something I don't like to relive. The defense attorney put on the performance of his life and the jury from my own community bought it. The verdict was read and the words "not guilty" slapped me in the face. I felt so discarded. I lost more than the trial that day. I lost a certain measure of innocence. It changed my view of the legal system and it was also the beginning of my trust issues.

I don't see myself as racist or prejudice, but from the day of the robbery on, I would shrink back in fear anytime a male fitting the description of my assailant walked into the video store, even on a crowded Friday night. I even recall a day about five years ago where this whole nightmare rushed through my memory again.

During lunch one sunny afternoon, I was covering the front desk of the medical office I worked at. Our clinic was empty and I was alone. I remember seeing this man, again, fitting the "description" of *the* criminal, walking across the parking lot. I recall the feeling of my heart crashing to the pit of my stomach. To my dismay, he entered our office and I could feel my body tensing up as he stood before me inquiring about employment. For a moment, I stereotyped this man based on my past experiences. But fortunately, that moment was brief and I snapped out of my momentary visit to the past, knowing that even after 20 years, those scars were still there and able to control me involuntarily.

But, there is another popular cliché: "Time heals all wounds." I believe this one to be true, to an extent. It has been over twenty years since I lived through my own little nightmare. I don't feel broken by the robbery any more like I once did, but I haven't forgotten.

My detective confided in me once that this man was one of the most evil individuals he had ever encountered during his time on the police force. I know without a doubt that God was watching over me that day. I will never forget the fear I felt or the name of the criminal who held a gun to my chest and robbed me of so much. Yes, the wounds have healed but there are definitely scars that have affected my life permanently.

The store was empty. This was typical for an unsuspecting Tuesday afternoon. Empty until one purposely, sharp dressed man entered the store from the side entrance and began to browse our large selection of movies. After strolling around the store for a bit, he approached the counter holding an empty box in his hand for a video he was looking to take home. The cover of the box featured a red leather-clad comedian at the height of his popularity. The video was a raucous and offensive stand-up routine. It was Eddie Murphy's *Delirious.* Isn't it ironic, don't you think?

What Kind of Daddy Will My Father Grow Up To Be

When a baby is born, she comes only with a slap on the butt and a piece of paper that states who her mother and father are. But only time will tell what kind of daddy that father will grow up to be . . .

Call me a late bloomer or a slow learner, or maybe, just maybe it's been God's timeline all along, but it has taken me my lifetime to this point to realize the treasure that is my daddy.

I'll admit that as a kid growing up, I wasn't sure that Daddy and I had much in common. He has always been hardworking and serious, and I always walked on the more lighthearted side of the road, hitting ever mud puddle as I went. My favorite line, one I will never forget was "You'll be surprised at how much I learn from you in the next 5 years . . ." Of course that jewel was always delivered with a twinkle in his eye and a teasing grin. I'd like to think that fortune cookie comment has something to do with why my daddy is so smart, but I tend to believe the knowledge came from a higher place.

It is well known that a child does not come with an instruction manual; but a Christian does . . . the Bible. And Daddy's wisdom and inner strength to raise a family and care for them and love them with all the love in the world came from his faith.

Daddy worked hard to provide what we needed as a family. In addition to his job, he nurtured a large garden so we would have fresh fruits and vegetables. I loved those watermelons but how I hated pickin' those beans! We didn't have the bells and whistles that some families have today, but we always had everything we needed: a nice home, food on the table and lots of love. Because we didn't get all the newest toys and latest gadgets, we learned to use our imagination and made our own toys that would keep us busy and happy. I am certain I didn't miss out on anything because I value my creativity more.

One of my most treasured facets of childhood was the unconditional sacrifice that allowed me to attend a Christian school from 1st grade until I graduated high school in 1984. That twelve year journey was instrumental in shaping my life. Over the years, I have been called "sheltered" more times than I can possibly count, but I have never for one minute ever wished that it had been any other way.

Through the years, as I look back now, I was given the world and all that I ever really needed . . . a Christian home, a solid education and as an added bonus, I got to travel with my family and see our beautiful country at a time when life was so much simpler and peaceful. I can still see all the beautiful places in my memory . . .

There is no doubt I am blessed. I have had Daddy with me for over 42 years now and still going strong. His bout with colon cancer in 2001 gave me the wakeup call I needed. It's been like I was taken back to childhood all over again and I have no intentions of ever growing up! I see Daddy through different eyes now and realize that it wasn't that we didn't have much in common, but more of I hadn't yet grown up to be the woman my daddy prayed I would be someday.

Is Daddy still a hard worker? You betcha. Is he still the serious man I remember as a child? He's serious about what counts. But once you've seen him grin as he throws a toy rooster to the ground so it will start cock-a-doodle-do-ing, you realize he's finally sitting back and mellowing just a bit 'cause the hard part's over.

I have Wednesdays off from work now and so my favorite part of that day off is going to see my mama and daddy. I soak in each visit like a sponge. When I see Daddy tending to his tomatoes or riding his John Deer, it's almost as if time has stood still . . . except that the large garden has morphed into a smaller raised bed and the tiller has been retired and replaced by Daddy's straw hat, long sleeves and big sunglasses.

When I go upstairs to his "office" I see that familiar scene of him sitting behind his desk and a mountain of paperwork along with his trusty adding machine and those ledger books he uses in accounting that I used to make my toys out of. The business suit and fancy hat have been hung up and exchanged for a white t-shirt, Bermuda shorts and bare feet, but boy, does he look as happy living his life now as he ever has.

Daddy, we have never really sat and had heart to heart talks, but I believe our hearts were always silently connecting; when you put your cheek next to mine or call me "baby", all I have ever needed in a daddy is contained in those simple gestures because you laid the foundation for my life when you prayed that first prayer for me as I lay in the baby room on February 6, 1966.

On this Father's Day, 2008, I don't want there to be any doubt about how much I love my daddy. I thank God every day for choosing you for me and I respect you and your walk with the Lord more than anyone in this life. No matter how old I get, I will be always be your little girl, and just for the record . . . on paper it says my father is Elmer Clyde Brown, but I'm proud to say you grew up to be the best daddy ever!

Love,
Me.
Xoxo
Written June 13, 2008

Old Soul:
The Original Buddy

Life is filled with "firsts". There are some firsts we want to remember and some we would like to forget. Let me tell you about one of my firsts that I will always remember . . .

This was one of the best gifts I had ever received from a boyfriend. Even though the memory of the boyfriend is long gone like this morning's deodorant, the gift has left paw prints on my heart that will last forever . . .

He was a Christmas gift that came a little early one year. And trust me, there are some gifts you don't want to box up and put under the tree for too long. He came to me as a tiny puff of black fur that would fit in the palm of my hands. I "oohed" and "ahhed" as us women do—you know, with that cutesy high pitched tone that could crack even the finest glass. He also came with a name—"Cougar". Well, I wasn't very fond of the name even though it was probably logical to name a jet black fierce looking ball of fur after an animal that could probably rip it to shreds just by sneezing on it . . . but I digress.

So, without any hesitation, Cougar became my first indoor pet; and come to think of it—my first roommate.

I guess you could say that Cougar had a normal kittenhood. I taught him how to use the litter box and nursed him when he had worms; I taught him how to wrestle like a fierce fighter and how to chase a string for hours. He was a little ball of energy that kept me laughing and kept my heart warm on even the coldest and loneliest of nights.

Now, apparently I am a slow learner or too optimistic for my own good because even though Cougar sat in the bottom branches of his first Christmas tree, I kept putting those trees up each year. Yes, sometimes the decorations would end up on the floor and sometimes broken; most years it would sound like a lumberjack had entered the living room and was cutting down a forest as the limbs would break under the pressure and the tinsel—well, we just don't even need to go there. But as time passed and Cougar grew into a young cat, well, the tree couldn't handle the emotional trauma anymore and the decision was made for me.

Tell me, when you think of a fat cat, you think of Garfield, right? Let's just say I think Cougar and Garfield must have been distant relatives. I mean, I don't think the fact that I fed Cougar fruit loops, popcorn and pizza could have possibly made a difference. Do you? Remember, I said he was my first roommate and don't roomies eat junk food together? We were no exception.

Cougar grew strong and sleek. Well, the sleek part didn't last long once those fruit loops kicked in. But he was more than a happy cat. And he was my best friend. Through all my joys and all of my heartbreaks, he was there for me. He didn't have to say words to comfort me. I could see it in his 14 karat golden eyes. He knew when I was hurting and he stayed right by my side no matter how loud the sobbing would get. He let me pour out my heart to him and he didn't judge me. He just loved me unconditionally.

It's not to say that we didn't have our share of disagreements. Cougar was better behaved than many kids I see running around these days, but he did have his moments. He was taught that there was certain furniture he could get on and others he could not. If he ended up somewhere he wasn't allowed, I would simply grab him by the scruff of the neck and with a firmly pointed finger in his face, speak in a stern voice of the crime he had committed and how he could not do it again.

Of course this was followed by a firm smack to the side of his hefty thigh. Now don't go calling PETA on me—I firmly believe in disciplining your children. And Cougar was my furry child. And you know what? It worked. Imagine that . . . spanking my child didn't kill him and he still loved me the next day and rarely committed his crimes a second time. Again, I digress.

Finally, my single years came to an end (thank goodness) as my husband, David, came into our lives and of course grew to love Cougar as much as I did. He was something of an "old soul". And what wasn't to love? Sometimes a lap cat, sometimes a paper weight, but always love.

And always hungry! Did I mention that?

He seemed to have a love affair with food. The one and only time we ever took Cougar to be groomed, we were told it would probably be best to forego this sort of activity in the future due to his weight and the enormous stress this sort of event must have been putting on his heart. You know, if we had thrown in a little mud, it would have made for an amazing mud wrestling event. And Cougar would have won that match hands down.

Over the years, Cougar's weight became an issue. At 25 pounds we knew he was severely overweight, but nothing we attempted seemed to make a difference. "Put him on a diet", they would tell us. But Cougar had something inside of him; something part of who he was that drew him to food 24-7. I just think it was his destiny.

And let's face it; his size was also a large part of his charm. The way he would waddle rather than run across the floor or the way he would lean on a pillow and readjust his belly just to be comfortable—the way he would sit politely by my side when I enjoyed a meal, and would quietly lay his paw on my arm or shoulder just to let me know he was there, and that he wanted.more.food. Now. All of this was his charm.

Somewhere along the way, Cougar also acquired a second name, or nickname, if you will; "Buddy". In our daily interaction with him, it just flowed from our lips and seemed to fit this fat cat that related to us more like a "dude" than a feline. It was clearly a term of endearment.

But you know, I didn't see it coming. And one day as if someone had taken the blindfolds off, David and I had a discussion about the fact Cougar looked a lot thinner. I'm not sure how much time had passed before we made this discovery, but we decided to get him checked out at the vet, you know, just to make sure he was okay. After all, he was only 12 years old and cats usually live to be much older, right?

Looking back now, I can't believe we didn't realize there was a problem sooner. Our once robust boy of 25 pounds had wasted away to a mere 10 pounds. I truly felt like I had failed him in some way, like I was a bad mother.

The news from the vet was upsetting, to say the least. Cougar had a liver disease. He was my first indoor pet and I didn't know cats could suffer such maladies as humans do. That was just cruel to me. He couldn't tell me that he hurt or didn't feel good. He was dependant on me to know that he was sick and to make him better. And I had let him down.

Nevertheless, Cougar had a new destiny now and it was one I was in denial of. I was eager for the vet to keep Cougar for a few days. I figured that they would find out a way to fix him, put him on an IV or something and that Cougar would get better in no time and be back at home with us where he belonged.

Every day after work I would visit Cougar at the vet to check on his progress, only, he wasn't making any. The staff at the vet's office was not able to get him to eat and the IV's were only buying me time. I just didn't realize that at the time. I knew Cougar loved me but his eyes were empty now and he hardly had the energy to venture to the front of the cage for me to love on him. I was sure that I could get him to eat, and then he would make that turn I knew was coming and all of this would be behind us.

It was at this point in Cougar's care that I decided to get him a real meal fit for a king . . . a McDonald's hamburger and French fries. I can't explain what was going through my head when I made this decision but those caring for my boy thought it was worth the try. Cougar had always loved people food and if anything was going to help him get better, this was sure to do it.

Going through the drive thru for the reasons I was going for relocated my emotions, as if I were in some sort of tunnel. What I was doing and why I was doing it made no sense at all but at the same time, made perfect sense.

I walked into the vet's office to visit Cougar happily carrying his edible treasure and with every fiber in me, was convinced I would lay this feast down before him and he would devour it, just as he had all his meals before. But it just wasn't meant to be. I had broken up the food for him; the way a mom does for her young children. With unfounded optimism I was ecstatic when he attempted a nibble or two

38

but that joy vanished like an extinguished flame when he retreated to the back of the cage.

It was at this point in the story where there is a void. The decision to be made—the decision my husband saw coming but I was oblivious to—the only decision that could be made at this time is not a memory I choose to retain.

What I can tell you about is what most would consider as the end. Once we had made the inevitable decision to put Cougar down, I knew immediately that I wanted to hold him in my arms for this moment. Why? Because I wanted him to know and feel, one last time, how much he was loved and how much he meant to me. I wanted my love to be the last moment he experienced before he rested peacefully forever.

Sitting in "the room" where Cougar would go to sleep was actually a pretty disturbing scene. When Cougar was brought in to us, he looked frail and disoriented, hardly able to stand and walk on his own. Memories flooded my mind of this once larger than life cat that made us laugh, who lay down by my side to take naps, who made me smile every day and who, without knowing, was such an important thread in my tapestry.

David and I were told of the procedure and what to expect. So I gently picked up Cougar and as we stroked his disheveled fur we whispered our goodbyes in his ears. He wasn't able to respond to us anymore as he always had—just slow, quiet blinks as he waited for his pain to end. All I knew is that I would hold my Cougar and we would love on each other one last time.

What I didn't know was how I would react to this seemingly straightforward process. With my husband by my side, I held Cougar tightly, but gently while a thousand memories flooded my brain. As the vet set Cougar free from his pain he laid his head down across my arms with a weight that felt like 1000 pounds.

The moment had its own crescendo and it was as if every emotion in my being went into overdrive. I honestly could not control myself. I loved Cougar with all my heart yet at that moment I could not bear to hold him any longer. The weight of his lifeless body in my arms was too much as I quickly handed him to the caring doctor who had put our Cougar to sleep. The tears flowed like a raging river and the sobs ruled my body like a seizure. But my loving husband was right there to hold me and cry with me as they took Cougar out of our site for good.

It's been four years since Cougar went to sleep. His picture is on one of our walls and I often stop to take a moment to remember and to smile. We had him cremated and his ashes remain in our home, his home, as a reminder of a family member lost—our broken chain.

I've come to realize that the hardest part of loving an animal and making them a part of your family and your heart is letting them go. Cougar has never been forgotten, nor will he ever be forgotten. He was my first, and some firsts you never, ever forget.

Loving Breezes

Waking up in the morning before sunrise and feeling so peaceful in my bed with the love of my life by my side, sleeping soundly. I hear his gentle breath as he rests and the soothing hum of my cats purring as they sleep with us. The ceiling fan nudges the lightest breeze across my face. At this very moment, life is beyond perfect. Well . . . maybe a little more snoozing would be nice.

Two of the sweetest sounds I know—the giggle of my mama and hearing my daddy say to me, "My baby."

Birthdays, anniversaries, Christmas—without fail, I can open my mailbox and find a card from her patiently waiting inside. In a world that lives online, her genuine sentiment is innocently offline and I love it. I wonder if she knows how much her thoughtfulness means to me? Thank you, Carolyn.

Love is a cold, wet nose brushing your arm before a sand paper tongue gives you a lick. A head butt ensues and the purr is as loud as your heart can take. The moment may not last for long, but you know it's real, and she will not let you forget. She will be back for more. How genuine.

To feel like a child again, with all the peace in the world and not a care in the world, all I need to do is lie my head down in my mama's lap as she strokes my hair until I fall asleep. That is something I will never outgrow.

Finding the Answer

"What do you want to be when you grow up?" I'm sure we all heard that question over and over again when we were in school. For many, the answer to that question came easily after high school. For myself, I started to wonder if I would ever have the answer. Upon graduation from high school, I got my first job and started community college. I was good with math and figured I would follow in my daddy's footsteps as a CPA. I couldn't have been more wrong.

The next ten years were laced with numerous office and retail jobs. Though none of those endeavors ever inspired me, I did learn that I had a touch of creativity and a way with people. But how could this take me to where I wanted and needed to be? I didn't have the answer. As frustrating as it was, I continued my walk through the white-collar world. Armed with both the hope that someday I would uncover my professional gift and the fear that I would never amount to anything professionally, I landed a job in a health club. Having a love for sports and fitness I thought, "This is more like it." And the journey began.

Through acquaintances at the club, I was introduced to massage therapy as a potential career. I cannot tell you what moved me in that direction. Was it my sixth sense telling me this was it? This will be the answer to the question "What do you want to be when you grow up?" Or was it just another mile marker in my long journey of unfulfilling jobs with no passion or meaning?

The process of finding the school I would attend was short and rather easy. A member of the club graciously retrieved a list of potential schools from the Internet for me. The only school I ever researched would be the school that would change my life.

I decided I would visit the school at an open house and make sure this would be my next move in my unfortunately lame professional career. The impact of the school on me was immediate. The school grounds were full of wide-open spaces with nature's treasures. The aura inside the school was fresh and exciting. I left with an incredible sense of hope and determination. In the weeks following, I completed necessary paperwork and preparations to secure an interview for admission to the school.

Finally, the day of my long-awaited interview had arrived. It was an absolutely beautiful and sunny winter day. The drive in was about forty minutes long and was saturated with scenery that seemed to take you far away from where your journey had began. As you crested the entrance of the school you were greeted by the most amazing tree. It stood proudly and firmly with its limbs outstretched as if it were an umbrella or safe haven for all who passed under it. I drove slowly on the gravel drive, as to not stir up too much dust, while enjoying the unfamiliar tranquility that came over me.

I was nervous about the interview. This would determine if I would be accepted into a school that was unlike any other college or university around. Yvonne, the admissions director, was kind and very personable. She was quick to put me at ease and made my experience so simple it didn't seem possible. Up until that point, I was going through the motions of my next venture in the professional world. My life changing moment came when I walked out of the office trailer back into the beautiful surroundings. It was if I were stepping into my future. I knew I was going to be accepted as a student at the Body Therapy Institute.

Within minutes, a feeling came over me that still to this day I can hardly put into words. As I got into my car and started back up the long driveway, it was as if God touched me on the shoulder. I cried amazing tears of joy because I finally knew the answer to that question I had longed to put to rest, "What do you want to be when you grow up?"

The answer: What God wants me to be. I was finally realizing I had been looking in all the wrong places for the answer. I was trying to figure it out all on my own. God intervened and was leading me to where He wanted me to be: a health care professional. And it was only the beginning.

Embracing the Elements

You know, I really think I should have been a storm chaser. In actuality, it just may be my alter ego; or at least one of them. The "weather station" and cloud chart that my brother and I played with as kids could have been an early indication, don't you think?

I am both intrigued and fascinated by the weather. Who doesn't fancy a clear blue sky, a steady stream of warm sunshine and a gentle breeze? A scene like that is easy to accept and even easier to love. But the weather is so much more than a perfect scenario. There is a darker side saturated with mystique; one that I am in awe of.

For as long as I can remember, I have kept my eye on the sky. As a kid, I was extremely scared of storms; especially at night. But as an adult, that fear has turned into respect and a cautious curiosity that needs to be recognized. I've never ridden out a hurricane nor have I experienced a true tornado. But I still get a bit of a knot in the pit of my stomach when the forecast is predicting a thunderstorm. And I will be the first to admit that if I knew it wouldn't kill me, I would be front row for one of these events in a heartbeat. But that is a guarantee that simply doesn't exist.

What does exist is meteorology. While it helps us understand and predict the weather, I have my own unique take on things to add to the mix. Beyond the undisputable facts and math, there lies more. I see personalities.

Let's face it: I don't do cold. Winter is painful to me and as beautiful as a fresh dusting of snow can be, the dead grass and lack of vibrant colors isn't. My teeth chatter, my appendages go numb, and it takes forever to warm the chill that sets in my bones. Don't get me wrong; I understand the necessity of winter and the purpose it serves. And I am thankful for the season in that respect. I'll admit, it does have some cozy qualities. However, my interest resides with the warm weather events. Give me a hurricane, a tornado or an intense thunderstorm and you've got my attention.

Of the three, thunderstorms are the most abundant and experienced by more people in more places. A staggering 2000 thunderstorm cells are estimated to be present over the entire planet at any given time. They're flashy, they're noisy and their bark is usually worse than their bite. But don't be deceived. They are often ignored and overlooked when in reality, they can be quite dangerous. With updrafts and downdrafts, microbursts and supercells, a thunderstorm is no lightweight.

An approaching storm can create an amazing display of cloud cover that is rather mesmerizing. With light and airflow, clouds project colors and textures that evolve as the storm travels. There's a heaviness and darkness in the sky that is daunting. And with that presence comes the potential for gusty winds and torrential downpours. The rain can range from light and prickly to heavy and soaking. Put the wind and rain together and it becomes quite the inconvenience if you are out in it or trying to operate an umbrella.

Though the sky gets your attention, it's nature's fireworks that steal the show. But as beautiful as the lightning can be against an evening sky, if you happen to be in its path, the outcome can be painful and even fatal. The thunder that accompanies the strike can pierce your ears with a deafening crack or reach in and stop your heart with a powerful rumble. The whole production on any given day can range in severity and display. And though a classic summer afternoon thunderstorm can be a soothing backdrop to an otherwise uneventful day, a severe one can stop you in your tracks while keeping you on your toes. I love the simplicity within its complexity.

A tornado, on the other hand, has practically no redeeming qualities. And while we have *The Fujita Scale* to classify tornadoes by the amount of damage they can produce, an EF-1 is about as comforting as being told you've had a "mild" heart attack. It is what it is. And what it is is frightening. Like a parasite within a thunderstorm, it's a temper tantrum in action that gives very little warning of its arrival. Most folks spend a few panicked moments trying to hide and protect themselves from its wrath. A twister moves with a vengeance so violent and unpredictable that those in its path are often left bewildered and speechless. It is fast and furious, utterly chaotic and wastes no time devastating land and lives.

From a safe distance, given the right conditions, it can be spectacular to look at. Storm chasers and unsuspecting onlookers could confirm my claim. But get close enough to be sucked in to its insanity and your fate is simply unknown.

Unlike a thunderstorm with its almost poetic voice, a tornado is pure audible evil. Most who have heard its wail say it is unlike anything they have ever heard before or want to hear again. The wind is a slave to this beast and ravages the land and manmade structures making sure it leaves its mark. And while hurricanes receive a "name", the deadliest tornados are not known by their EF rating, but simply by the name of the town they destroy. I think one that will be remembered and talked about for years to come will be Joplin, 2011.

And then, there is the intense, rotating oceanic weather system with cyclonic circulation. That's a mouthful simply because there is a lot going on in there. The hurricane is a very complex phenomenon. It forms deep in the Atlantic far away from people or land but knowing it's eventually headed towards both. But it will have to earn its name. So it is patient and it is calculating, changing its course to keep us guessing. Along the way it will gain more power, and more fury. As you follow its journey, you will see conditions deteriorate as it moves over the water teasing land, almost taunting it because it demands respect.

Call it having mercy because it gives you fair warning of its approach, or call it ego because it wants to make the grandest entrance; a hurricane of any category, is to be respectfully feared. You can't help but marvel at its power and organization and ability to shape-shift at will.

I believe a hurricane has multiple personalities. And what side you see of one depends on where you are when it finds you. Living in North Carolina, three hours inland, I have seen my share of the softer side of these storms. And even if you had pulled a Rip Van Winkle and were just waking up, you would know what was going on. The wind plays puppet master to every tree, every flower, practically every blade of grass and the sound it makes is almost like a hypnotic white noise.

The sky is an empty grey with a parade of clouds quickly moving "in the wrong direction." And this is just one scenario.

But should you be looking a hurricane in the eye, what you see is very different and far more intense. Unleashing its fury, a hurricane has the unforgiving ability to change the landscape of our coastline permanently; but God's earth is resilient. And more importantly, so are we. A hurricane changes people. Some lose everything they own and choose to rebuild. And some lose life itself. Those who have made the coast their home, those further inland who may experience a different level of the storm and those who lose a loved one tragically—they too find a way to survive and rebuild.

With all of these diverse characteristics, I find it only fitting that a hurricane should possess a name. And Hazel, Hugo, Fran, and Irene are just a few of the names that have scooted across our beautiful state and devastated our unique North Carolina Coastline over the years.

But what's in a name? Well, aside from identifying a storm by something other than a number, it's simply therapeutic. And hurricane graffiti is proof of that. Years ago, folks started spray painting messages on the plywood they would use to board up the windows of homes and businesses they were protecting and leaving behind. Messages of defiance, humor, desperation and prayer were just some of the emotions displayed on wood for a violent weather event that affected folks deeply and hurtfully.

Obviously, the storm can't read, but I believe that assigning a hurricane a name just gives folks an outlet for dealing with the disaster. They can lay blame to a name. They can be angry at that name. And they can better deal with their anguish and frustrations when there is "someone" to channel their emotions to. I don't know if this is actually the case, but I can only envision it to be a possibility.

I've entertained a lifelong relationship with the weather that has evolved from being terrified of storms as a child to having vivid dreams about them as a young adult to nurturing a tremendous respect and acceptance of all of these events as the "me" I am now at 45 years old.

From my weather station to *The Weather Channel* it's been a personal journey of discovery. While Hollywood can portray an interesting replica of a weather event, such as the 1996 film *Twister* which has grossed nearly $500 million since that point, there is no substitution for actually being there and experiencing the elements first hand. And even though I did not discover *The Weather Channel* which launched in 1982, until some years later, it has been my eyes, my ears and my heartbeat for such events.

Jim Cantore, chief meteorologist who has been with *TWC* for 25 years now, is a name and personality synonymous with the weather itself. He has been on the front row for numerous hurricanes, he has sifted through the aftermath of the deadliest tornados and he has told many storm stories along the way.

I guess you could say that my alter ego as a storm chaser lives vicariously through him and the many others who have a true passion for the weather. For some, it isn't enough to tell the story but to be there with their cameras and equipment in place as the story is being written.

Chasing tornadoes since 1999, Sean Casey—Professional Storm Chaser and Film producer—is driven not only by seeing a tornado the way no one else can, but by capturing the ultimate shot: from inside the tornado. And after four season's on Discovery Channel's *Storm Chasers*, he finally realized that dream and later shared it with us all.

October 29, 2011, a modified version of Sean's IMAX film, *Tornado Alley*, christened the brand new WRAL Theatre at the North Carolina Museum of Science in Raleigh, NC. But even more exciting for me was the fact that Sean Casey and his "TIV" (Tornado Intercept Vehicle)—15,000 pounds of fearless metal on wheels, were there to greet the fans.

Yes, fans. There were oodles of "us" there, young and not so young. This self proclaimed weather nerd was completely giddy by meeting Sean, who was very pleasant. I landed an autograph and a photo with the famous storm chaser. To top off the experience, I was able to get inside the famous TIV and sit in the seat where the first footage inside a tornado ever was captured. I think the little girl that sat in front of me in the theatre said it best when she exclaimed to her daddy, "Best day everrrr!"

Hurricanes, tornados and thunderstorms are just three of the potentially violent and deadly weather events that we face here in my little part of the world and elsewhere. For me, the allure of these weather events is not too difficult to understand. I find their design, behavior and visual display amazing. There is a certain beauty in each storm. You just have to have the eyes to see it.

But I also firmly believe that these same events have the ability to bring out the best in people. When forces of nature and the human spirit collide, the result is often a pulling together in ways that you don't see on an average day. We hurry about our business, cutting one another off in traffic or speaking a harsh word for the simplest inconvenience. Yet, when disaster strikes, we somehow find a way to unify. That is another kind of beauty.

I will never be able to fully explain what it is about the weather that I connect with; I just know it's there and it's a part of me. And on the heels of Hurricane Irene, who devastated the east coast in September from North Carolina to New England, a little reflection and introspect is always good for the soul. It is simply an irrefutable fact of life that these storms are going to happen and it is beyond our control to prevent them. But it is our individual choice in how we deal with them. This story tells of my choice.

Mama

"Patty cake, patty cake, baker's man, roll 'em up, roll 'em up, toss 'em in a pan." And as Mama playfully patted my cheeks, out flew a once loose tooth. Not a painful memory, I assure you, but one I am quite fond of. And there have been many.

I have always loved my mama dearly, but as I've grown into an adult, I have learned to appreciate her many unique and wonderful qualities. More than anything, my mama is loving.

Family means more to her than any material possessions you could ever bestow upon her. One walk through her home would easily convince you of that. Family photos, past to present, decorate every available wall space. Trinkets from our childhoods and beyond are carefully placed on both shelf and table. No item, no gift is too insignificant to her. I think a memory that will always warm my heart is the time I was going to visit Mama, and as I walked down the sidewalk, I picked a fluffy, yellow dandelion for her. To this day, that same dandelion is pressed under glass with a simple note that says "Sonja gave this to me March 9, 1992."

My mama is also very giving. She has always been a homemaker and got an "allowance" from Daddy regularly. And even now, she will empty her change purse for me if she thinks I don't have enough money for a drink or for lunch. Some may say I am a little spoiled. I just believe I am loved a lot.

All the love and kindness of my mama is not displayed without emotion. She has shed many tears over the years, both tears of joy and tears of sorrow. And you don't have to be a professional comedian or tell a funny joke to make her laugh. She giggles like a kid at everything. I believe this comes from her sweet, child-like spirit trying to get out.

I cannot speak of my mama without sharing how much I respect her example as a Christian woman and mother. Her testimony has always been strong and true. It has given me a goal. And it has showered me with the kind of love I believe is rare these days. My mama is my best friend and I cannot imagine life without her. But if she were gone tomorrow, she will have left behind a true legacy of love.

The Art of Montaging

One of the perks of getting older is being able to look back on your life and entertain a bit of reflection. I may only be in my mid forties, but I have lived long enough to have an epiphany or two. And I find that the decision to write this paperback collection of experiences and musings has been somewhat of a catalyst in this journey of expression.

Free will, given by God, and freedom, fought for by man, has made it possible for me to enjoy all aspects of the creative process. What follows is the luxury of sitting back and taking great pleasure in the finished product. Will I ever win a Pulitzer Prize? Will my name ever be synonymous with award winning photography? Will Stephen Spielberg ever call me up begging me to be part of one of his cinematic wonders because of my montaging prowess? The answer is easily no. And that's okay.

The real prize comes from within; pure and simple, utterly sincere and genuine satisfaction. God made me one of a kind. And He gave me gifts. Some will be realized and some will not. And looking back, I now can see the development of my gift to create.

Let me give you a brief tutorial about the timeline. As a kid, I made a lot of my own toys and played outside until the light from the sun had been replaced by lightning bugs. The pre-electronic age did have its advantages. In high school, I was involved in art class, speech class music and sports. It was there that I was introduced to not just being a competitor, but being a FINISHER, win or lose.

Beyond high school, I really discovered music; all kinds. I continued to play sports competitively and if you don't think volleyball is an art form, you have never been an athlete, rather just someone sitting in the stands on one of those portable cushions. Once I started strolling the information highway on the net in the late nineties, my eyes had widened at all the possibilities. Still, I was not ready. That was to come.

My husband, whose face might as well be next to a photo of Bill Gates (in my eyes at least), introduced me to the finer points of the internet's possibilities followed by an enormous "etc." There is certainly a plethora of it within the click of a mouse.

A few classes at our community college for a major that I never pursued unwittingly lit the fire under my pen and keystroke. And a career that I did pursue for a short time served its purpose by giving me the unforeseen realization of balance and how I needed it in my life. And how it fit into my life would be a learning experience for me down the road that would have its role in the most unique places.

From age nothing to something there were people, experiences and a multitude of other factors that cultivated the growth and eventual blooming of my creativity.

Do you see where I am headed with this? All of these things I've mentioned that seemed so individual, so random and taken for granted at one time or another were tools. And tools are useless without a purpose.

But for all of these elements to come together and be something beautiful, you've got to have more. There must be vision, organization, inspiration, ambition, passion, expression and a determination for more while staying focused, grounded and realistic. You have to be open to criticism and suggestions from others. Who knows, through letting others in, you might gain that one fleck of gold that makes you say "Yes, that's it. That's how I saw it in my mind."

You have to be willing to fail. Not quit. To fail is to not get it right the first time. To quit is to never know what it's like to succeed. The beauty of it all is that ultimately, this project is mine. I call the shots. And at the end of the day, I cherish both the journey and the destination; for there is nothing like it.

Throughout my life, I have noticed, but not necessarily understood, a common thread running through my tapestry: the need for balance. To this day, when I eat, I will eat a bite of this and then that, with the intent to take the last bite of each food together. Balance. It's hard for me to listen to a single CD all the way through because I like the variety of many artists and genres. Balance. I love my job and I love to be at home doing my own thing. But if I didn't have a job to go to every day with purpose, I would be lost. If I stayed home every day without a place to go to utilize my skills and come in contact with others, I would be missing something. Balance. For me, it's all about a delicate balance. And that is where I achieve the greatest satisfaction.

I understand now. And I understand the role that balance plays in the creative process, hence, the finished product that you cling to with pride and a sense of accomplishment; a finished product that is yours forever and that is always there to be shared, relived and enjoyed, again and again.

So let me tell you about my coveted genre of creativity. It's montaging. Montaging is a collection of audio, video and still images that are put together in such a way as to tell a story, express a thought, or relive a memory while evoking a wide array of emotions.

My love affair with montaging began in 2003 when I was a fan of a particular Raleigh, NC native who came in 2nd on some show called American Idol. Being a part of the message boards was a first for me as was so much during that time. The message boards were where I first came into contact with "homemade" montages. The attraction was instant and I was captivated. I was intrigued. I was moved. I wanted to make one myself. The key was that I believed I could.

Because of the (ahem) ingenuity and dedication of some of the fans, I had access to all of the video and photos I needed to create one of these things myself. I had no training and no guidance but I found it very easy to sit down and create. It felt natural to me and with a few montages under my belt; I had a pattern, a routine. Little did I know that my process actually had a name. It's called storyboarding.

My quest always started with a song. What music would I use? What kind of tone did I want my video to have—fun and lighthearted or dramatic and touching? Or did I want it to cover the gamut of emotions? This decision was the biggest ingredient to my videos and once I was comfortable with my choice, the rest was cake; albeit, that cake consumed me for weeks on end and kept me up late at night because I couldn't turn "it" off.

During my early years of montaging, I literally watched thousands of clips from concerts and TV appearances. I couldn't deviate from my routine. I would download every video I could get my hands on. Then I would start the most mind numbing ritual of watching every clip from start to finish, weeding out videos whose quality wasn't good enough to make the cut. Then, I would watch the videos that made it through the first round again while making notations in my notebook with time stamps of sections I felt might be useful in my montage.

Once this part of the process was complete, I literally had pages and pages and pages of clips to edit. Editing and rendering those segments weren't nearly as painful as my eyes drying out from the no blinking for hours that had already taken place; nevertheless, still a tedious part of the process.

Now, I am sort of a realistic gal and I knew my job would be much easier if I could whittle down my pile of clips. So, I started multiple rounds of watching each individual clip and deciding if it would stay or if it would go. I closely observed for clarity, special effects, anything that made it stand out from other similar clips. What came next was more of the same. Next round was watching again and thinning out the playing field just a little bit more. I had to get the number of clips that I would be working with down to a reasonable amount, lest my eyes lock in place and my brain die from a lack of oxygen.

But really, the best part was on the horizon.

After three, sometimes four rounds of watching the same snippets over and over, I finally had my premier group of clips that would be used in the creation of my montage. This collection of media along with photos, audio and other extras were organized on my computer and ready to be transformed into a work of Art. Time for that horizon to shine!

Now, for the fun part: piecing all of these little treasures together in such a way that my vision is realized and it captivates, tells a story and touches all those who may watch it while fitting it into the span of 10-20 minutes. Definitely a challenge I am always up for. This was my Everest. I would spend endless hours on the computer buried in my editing software and moving clips around like puzzle pieces. I would watch and rewatch segments and observe the blank spaces on the timeline fill in. The process was truly magical.

Now, I love photography, but motion always seemed to be the spirit of the project. And when each clip is blended perfectly with the music, it's beautiful thing. Matching the beat of the music with a physical movement in the clip results in a poetic expression (at least for me).

Still being a "newbie" in terms of my knowledge or use of special effects software, my videos were simple and straightforward to some extent. So I had to, again, rely on my own imagination to smooth out the edges and make it "pop." Just as when I was a child, my creative edge came from within; it was intuitive and somewhat of a vision in my head and heart. I found that slow motion, freeze frames, and fades were dynamic segues, while photos, text, and snippets from "outside the subject" added an exclamation point to the visual.

Along the way, I found it impossible to turn off the creative process once it had reached a full gallop. At the height of any project, I would sometimes wake up in the middle of the night with a new idea and find myself running to my desk to document my thoughts. That's the point when I knew I had a gift.

Finishing touches were usually an intro and a closing bookending the contents. Sometimes the title of the montage came easy and came early, and at other times, it just came when it was ready. I learned to welcome it, rather than force it.

But once it had all come together and I had watched it innumerous times, the point did come when all the tweaking had come to an end and it was time to let it go and share it with the world; or at least a tiny fraction of it. And with every presentation, my heart pounds awaiting the reaction to my labor of love. At the end of the day, my work being accepted, understood and appreciated by others is important and so gratifying. But it's not the reason I do it.

In the span of eight years I have created 17 music montages celebrating various musicians, 7 personal montages dedicated to my husband and family, and 2 montages (hopefully the first of many) for my church's Vacation Bible School. I approached every project in the same fashion with my strict set of self-imposed guidelines and an anticipation that I can't even begin to articulate.

Plain and simple, I love to montage. It fulfills something in me that I can't explain. And though each piece has a story to tell, there are times I think I am enamored by the process as much as the subject matter. It's a gift a lifetime in the making. I don't try to over think it any more. I just embrace it.

For me, montaging is an art. And I am simply an artist.

It Was a Good Day

It's been a good day; a very good day, actually. It was warm, like you would expect for late September. The sky was free of clouds except for an occasional drifter which resembled a cotton ball that had taken flight and was floating across the exquisite blue heavens.

With my cheaply stitched, half-priced beach umbrella and colorful sturdy chair, I had made my home on a tuft of sand just out of reach of the crashing waves. This is where I would spend most of my hours for this day. Occasionally I would stretch my legs by taking a slow stroll down the beach, inviting the cool water to invigorate my warm, sunburned skin. It was so refreshing and exhilarating. When hubby would venture with me, we would take along a couple of slices of soft bread. No, not a snack for us, but for my feathered friends that glided above me. This aided in the perfect luring technique for a photo opportunity.

Back under the shade of my personal splash of nylon on the beach, yes, this is where I desired to be. Many things could be accomplished here. I could observe the activity of the variety of beach goers. Let's see; there is the weathered gentleman who is doing a little fishing with his son. This seems to be a ritual with them every day. There is a young couple, obviously a young love, walking hand in hand down the beach smiling and talking, not really noticing the activity going on around them. And over here, there is a gaggle of middle-aged women donning straw hats and chatting with much animation as they clamor down the beach. It's a foregone conclusion that they are enjoying themselves immensely.

And I can't miss the attractive older lady who is walking her beautiful golden retriever, Claire, who just might be her best friend.

She talks to her casually as they stride down the beach. And as waves get too close to her beautiful golden coat, Claire pulls back and looks up to her mom as if waiting to be saved. She pets Claire vigorously, with reassurance and splashes her fur with a small amount of water, and with tail wagging, Claire bounces on.

And over my shoulder, I see a proud grandfather standing on the boardwalk, holding his little cherub. She's wearing a tiny white bonnet to shade her ivory, flawless skin from the rays of the sun. With squinted eyes, she smiles a goofy smile larger than her newborn self at all of the colors and movement going on around her. Oh, to see the world through those eyes again . . .

Content and secure in my surroundings, I dig my toes into the sand, allowing myself to slip down in my chair and prepare for a bit of a siesta. The ocean sings me a lullaby and as the breeze collects under my sanctuary, I find myself drifting easily into my own personal dreamland.

My thoughts begin to mix like oil paints on a canvas, waiting to be turned into a new, beautiful scene. For me, it's a time of resolution. Like a summer new year, if you will. It's a time of reaching towards new goals and letting go of vices that interfere with my "Life is good" mentality. Because life is good. And I'm ready to build on that.

What do the next few months have in store for me? I don't know. But God is in control, and if I remember that, my journey will most certainly be a smoother one. Within His control, He allows me to make choices. That is where I must place much thought and purpose. There is no better time than sitting on the beach in a setting such as this to realize just what you've got. And where I go from here—the possibilities are endless. Dream big. Because if you don't dream, you can't achieve . . .

With eyes closed, my subconscious wonders and wanders. My stress melts away and is replaced with the positivity and hope of a brighter tomorrow. I'm blessed, of this I'm sure. Opening my eyes again and taking in the beauty before me is clear confirmation of this. I take in a deep, cleansing breath and absorb the energy from these few stolen moments in a world that has lost its way. But none of that—the world and its problems—seems to matter right now.

For a few days, I'm a beach bum. I have no job, no alarm clock, no worries, and obviously, no diet. I'm free to be free spirited. That in its self is both nurturing and cleansing; and necessary. The hustle and bustle of everyday life with its routine has to be balanced with the sort of existence only a week at the coast provides. It's a time of reflection and projection. Without it, I feel I would wither up like a flower that has been cut off from the sun.

The chatter of a seagull passing overhead brings me back to the here and now. Opening my eyes once again and stretching my arms and legs after what feels like a 20-year sleep, I feel refreshed and rejuvenated. I look around as if I have been away for a while, looking to see what might have changed since I took my soulful journey. Kids are still playing and laughing, the waves are still rolling in and the coastal breeze lightly pats me on the cheeks as if to say "welcome back."

With renewed spirit, I stand to my feet once again and collect my belongings. For some, this was just another day at the beach. For me, it was moments spent in much needed solitude and reflection. With arms full, I begin walking slowly back to our rented home away from home. I pause for a moment and look over my shoulder catching one last glimpse of the day at my safe haven. Yes, it was a very good day.

Be My Valentine

Some ladies love the traditional flowers and candy. Other more modern women prefer a fancy dinner and jewelry. And then there's me.

My thoughtful hubby knew how much I wanted to add one more to our beautiful little family. And in 2000, he made that wish come true. On Valentine's Day that year, he presented me with a lovely card, a beautiful rose along with a stuffed animal holding on to that vase for dear life. It made sense only after I opened the card and his gift was revealed.

He was giving me his blessing to adopt another kitten. For just over two years it had been David, Cougar and I. But our family needed one more bundle of love to be complete.

And finding the perfect fur ball didn't take very long. A friend of mine had a brother whose cat had recently had a litter. And as soon as they were old enough, he invited us over to pick out our favorite. Amidst the heard of fuzzy kitties running around and clumsily falling over the way little ones do, we couldn't help but notice one that was a bit stand-offish, staying away from the litter. She was standing by a wall, practically snubbed by the others. When all of a sudden she darted past us and her beautiful markings caught our attention. She stood out in the crowd; not only by her beautiful motif but by personality as well. There was something about her that was calling out to us. She was the one.

Rumi came into our lives nearly twelve years ago. And she has most definitely impacted our lives. I bet you are wondering how we came to name her after a thirteenth century Persian poet. There really is no deep, mystical answer to how we came about this name. I happened to have a book of poetry by Jelaluddin Rumi that I had picked up while in massage therapy school. And one day while at work, my mind drifted a bit as I was searching for the perfect name for our latest addition. As I glanced over to my desk where this book innocently laid, it was an easy affirmation.

Rumi is a bit of a diva; a "Miss Priss", if you will. She's every bit as finicky and demanding as a classic cat, yet unique in so many ways; at least to us. Her markings of peach, charcoal and white are only enhanced by what almost resembles eyeliner encircling her golden, almond shaped eyes. The silky white fur around her nose and mouth make those features appear to be so pink, so delicate and ladylike. Her paws are petite, yet very expressive. For it is with these paws that she regularly reaches out to gently touch my face when she's feeling especially loving. And with those same paws she will not hesitate to smack you down at the speed of light if you have succeeded in irritating her. It really is a gamble on which paw you will be greeted with.

Her tail is long and stately. It typically stands straight up in the air, sort of like those poles attached to shopping carts you see in department stores so you can keep track of them while they move about. But when she is being held and is perfectly happy, that same tail will curve slightly and swish to and fro in total contentment.

Rumi is not only a beautiful cat to look at but she also captivates you with her endearing qualities.

She rarely drinks out of her water bowl. She prefers the faucet at the bathroom sink instead. And since she hasn't figured out how to turn it on herself, she will let out a screeching meow specific to what she needs. She will literally sit on the bathroom counter patiently until you pass by and then she will blast you with her request until you give in. She will test the water with her paw first, before putting her face under the gentle stream of H20. And once done, she simply walks away. It would be so convenient if she could turn it off herself. I can't tell you how many times we have come back to the bathroom only to notice we have left the water running for who knows how long. What we do for our children . . . .

Remember when I said Rumi was a diva? Well, this girl can dish it out but she cannot take it. Sage, her sister, rarely takes the straightforward approach when trying to interact with her. Really, she prefers the element of surprise. Needless to say, Rumi is not too fond of this tactic. We don't have to see what's going on, because we know she has been ambushed when she rolls out the growl/hiss/snort combo. Yes, our dainty little princess will respond with a dog-like growl, a classic feline hiss, and a snort-something I'm sure she's picked up from me-all in one breath. That one is always good for a belly laugh from us.

David and I have also determined that she speaks many languages. After all, a meow doesn't have just one meaning, so why should they all sound the same. And if you lived in our household, you would totally understand what I am talking about.

I believe I have mentioned the screeching water meow. Well, there is also the demanding "you've closed the door and I can't get in" meow. One of my favorites is definitely the pathetic and weepy, stuttering "I didn't know that was wrong but I'm sorry" meow. You can hardly discipline her after that sound because she sounds so darn remorseful plus you're choking back a giggle.

There is also the bellowing, decibel drenched "where are you mommy" meow when she is in another room and we have failed to share our whereabouts with her. It's loud, it's shrill and it hits our ears with great force. And when she is feeling a bit European, Rumi will project a meow that rolls off her tongue as fluently and sophisticated as a spirited Italian.

Then we have what I like to call the "yawnus interuptus" meow. There are few visuals as adorable as when Rumi is trying to talk to us (meow) while yawning. It's a squeak that resembles a baby's hiccup. It's fast and if you don't catch it quickly, the moment is gone. What she was trying to say is simply a mystery.

But no meow is as full and genuine as the smooth and gentle resonance of the meow expressing love. If you don't think it's possible to know the difference, then you have never been loved by a cat. Her face is intent and expressive; her eyes are fixated—all powered by a purr with so much tone and purpose that it tugs at your heartstrings. And the pitch is high, practically imitating a question mark.

And when she softly nudges her head against mine or reaches her paw towards me to make contact, I know we are sharing a moment. And that moment is sealed with the gentlest lick to the end of my nose or my cheek. They call them sandpaper kisses.

Did I mention just how much this cat licks? It's almost like she's got a salt deficiency or some kind of no lick/no pass zone. Maybe it's just feline OCD. As annoying as it can be sometimes to have the freckles nearly removed from my body by a cat's tongue, the licking fetish does have its benefits. With that same passion, she bathes more than most humans I know. And when I pick her up to get my "Rumi love" as I like to call it, an inhale ensues. Her fur is fragrant and soothing to the senses, which would also include the sense of touch. A rose petal has nothing on the silkiness of her fur.

Of all of her many apparent gifts, caretaker seems to one of the extraordinary ones. I recall being really sick a few times where Rumi stayed right by my side. I would move from bed to the floor and from room to room and there she would be. Looking at me with obvious concern, the feeling that she cared was overwhelming. I have heard how pets comfort their humans when they sense sickness or pain. I have witnessed it more than once, and the fact that I indeed felt comforted is quite amazing to me. And though this trait may come imbedded in many animals, it's still just another reason to love my Rumi.

While she was quite active and playful as a kitten, constantly amusing us, Rumi has definitely settled into the personality she was always meant to be. And that's what I will cherish the most about her. She is simply our girl. And her latest ritual seals the deal.

She now climbs onto the bed with us at night and ends up sleeping between our heads on our pillows. Now and again I will be briefly awakened during the night by a toenail digging into my arm as she stretches out in complete comfort. Or, David will be pulled out of a deep sleep by a Gizmo/Gremlin-like sound coming from her as she sleeps deeply. It's a cat snore. Who knew? Often I find that my pillow has become Rumi's and my head is dangling off the side because she has moved in during the night.

But it's okay. She's earned the right to share our pillows. We are her humans, after all, and she has stolen our hearts; why not our pillows as well. And as long as I live, my heart will always have her imprint right there. See, she's more than a cat; more than a pet. She's family. And will forever be my Valentine.

Changed Forever

I could never have imagined being a 35 year old college student sitting on my sofa and reading an article in my writing class textbook about terrorism while watching that article come to horrifying reality on my television. But like so many Americans, I am now changed forever. For my generation, September 11, 2001 is the day that will live in infamy.

Pick up a dollar bill or a coin and read, "In God We Trust." Our country was founded on a faith and belief in God and a life lived accordingly. Over 225 years ago, many men and women in various acts of courage, fought and died for the freedom we now enjoy.

Yet we have become complacent and have begun to take for granted our freedom, the only life we have ever known. We are a confident and prosperous nation. We are blessed and we are free. But as freedom came at a price for our forefathers, I believe we are now living in a time where it will come at an even higher price.

Terrorism, in any capacity, no matter the motive or the source, is inexcusable, inhumane, and unforgivable. It used to stem from a purpose and a goal; now, it breeds out of pure hatred for a united nation such as ours. It strips a people and a nation of its dignity, freedom and precious life. Its core is a society scattered worldwide that has become infested by evil minds, souls and intentions. No matter the claims, it is not of a loving God, but of an evil beyond what we have ever witnessed before.

But this is the world in which we live now. Terrorism is no longer a terrible thing we see on television going on in lands far away. Previous events such as Pearl Harbor, the first World Trade Center bombing and the Oklahoma City bombing were precursors to the rude awakening that the United States is no longer immune to terrorism, but actually a target of choice.

No one knows exactly what will happen now, but we all know what must happen in retaliation to the unthinkable and horrible events that took place at the World Trade Center and our nation's capitol on Tuesday. We must make it clear that our country was founded on and still stands on a firm foundation, In God We Trust. The price of freedom has now gone up.

Throughout this tragedy, we have seen up close and personal the ugly face of terrorism, maybe clearer than we ever have before. We have witnessed sickening and devastating moments and we have embraced the incredible acts of courage and love from fellow Americans for fellow Americans. We are seeing what we are truly capable of when united in tragedy. God help us to never forget these moments and to unite as strongly in times of peace.

My heart broke as I watched the horrible events unfold before my eyes while at work that day. The emotions that course through my veins both now and then overwhelm me and they hurt deeply. I can't fully comprehend all that has happened. But I am a Christian and an American and I have faith in my God and my president that our country, though devastated in loss of life will not be devastated in spirit.

We have so much ahead of us. We must recover bodies and give closure to thousands of families who are grieving and to a country that is angry. We must clean the wreckage and find a way to rebuild both businesses and lives. We must seek and achieve justice for this deplorable act of hatred. No matter the timeline, we will overcome this tragedy and once again be the sturdy monument of pride, prosperity, unity and freedom. God Bless America!

What She Saw

Growing up as a self-proclaimed introvert was not the most fertile soil for planting ones professional seeds. As an up and coming senior at a Christian high school in the eighties, I vaguely remember discussion and choices to be made regarding a college versus non-college route after graduation. For me, the choice was easy though the embarrassment behind it wasn't. I had no plans for a four year college or university. I was afraid of the whole concept as I felt I wouldn't fit in. I had no idea what I wanted to do with my life after high school. But I'm sure my parents would have found a way to make college a reality had that been the natural next step for me.

Instead, I made plans for taking classes at my local community college. How did I choose the curriculum of Accounting, you might ask? Simple, my dear Watson; my daddy was a successful CPA and I aced my bookkeeping class. I loved numbers and adding machines so this must be it. Makes total sense, right?

Again, that logic proved I had no clue. But I was trying in my own indirect way to fit in and grow up. There was no pressure from my parents, but I was intelligent enough to know that high school was over, and it was time to move on and make something of myself. Lord knows I had a great education, thanks in part, to the sacrifice and vision of my parents.

I had a fantastic educational experience as I was blessed to receive twelve years of education at a private school. Being a Christian, getting an education from Christian teachers who cared about not only my growth as a student, but who were also personally invested in my growth as a young Christian, was priceless to an impressionable young person in a quickly changing world.

My parents gave me the firm foundation at home that I needed, that the Lord required of them; my teachers and the administration at Alamance Christian School were committed to building on that foundation.

Allow me to digress for just a moment (or two). In school, I wasn't confronted with drugs, foul language, or violence as most kids are these days on a weekly and sometimes daily basis. There was the occasional misfit who enjoyed giving classmates wet willies (Google it if you are too young or too "cool" to know what I'm talking about). No, we weren't perfect and there were those who ended up in the principal's office on occasion for disciplinary action.

As "Christian School Kids", we were often labeled as "sheltered" by public school kids. I'm not really sure how others felt about this, but it really never phased me. I treasured my existence in this environment. It was all I knew, but deep in my heart, I knew it was the best opportunity I could have been given.

Being an introvert, you might find it odd to know that I sang in chorales and ensembles as well as played sports during my high school years. I wasn't pushed into these activities; yet, the choices came very naturally to me. That doesn't mean I wasn't afraid. It's clear to me now that there was some sort of inward battle between the introvert in me and the part of me that knew there was some kind of potential. I also seemed to excel at numbers and the arts. It was in high school that the creativity in me began to surface as I excelled in both art and speech classes.

One term I would use to describe life at a Christian School would be "close-knit". Many of us that went to school together also attended the same local churches. We saw a lot of each other. So you can see how our lives intertwined on a different level.

Our entire school, K-4 through 12th grade consisted of maybe, in a good year, 450 students. Yes, I can hear the gasps from here. Here's another fun fact for ya—25 in my graduating class. Not one of us was a small fish in a big pond. We all mattered; and no one was invisible. We were like a big family. Was it the right fit for ever child? No. But with all my heart, I know it was the best fit for me and one of my most treasured blessings in this life.

I still recall, as if it happened yesterday, my last day in high school. As was customary, the high school student body would meet in the gym for a final send off for the seniors. I remember how our senior class stood in front of our peers and teachers, holding hands as the principal prayed for us and our futures. This was it. The experience I had clung to safely for 12 years was about to come to an end. It was bittersweet. The tears in my eyes are as real now as they were over 26 years ago. That, my friend, is a foundation that should stand the test of time . . .

Eventually, it happened. I started to grow up. I say it that way because even at age 44, I still see myself as a work in progress. Over the years I've had many jobs in my quest to find where I belong professionally. On a resume, those jobs may just look like data with locations and dates and job duties. To me, I see a journey; a path leading somewhere, growth.

Through a sequence of choices and circumstances, I found myself in dire need of a job in 2005. I had worked at a physical therapy clinic as a massage therapist for over six years and found myself miserable and ready for a positive experience in the workplace. God answers prayer. He provided me with what I thought was an excellent opportunity to get on at Duke through their temporary services. Little did I know, that job that lasted only one day was the decoy and wake-up call I desperately needed. Thanks to an incredibly supportive husband and a family that has never once ceased to be there for me, I was able to be unemployed briefly where I could commit to finding a new job.

Committed to not blowing this genuine opportunity for a fresh start professionally, I spent eight hours the next day on the computer searching and applying for jobs. Well, not just jobs, but career opportunities. I applied for a few, but none of them felt as promising as the one at UNC Healthcare. Being a small town Christian school kid who was still an introvert on the inside, the prospect of a job at such a well known and large healthcare facility both excited me and scared me to death. I had only worked for small businesses, most of them local. And even though I had brief contact with physicians at my last job, I had never worked directly with one or with a public population with such diversity. We are talking about Chapel Hill. I have to admit, on a non-professional note that landing a job here as a lifelong Tarheel fan would tickle me blue!

Not to self deprecate, but I was actually surprised when I got a call for an interview. With virtually no college credits and only six years of experience in the medical field, I was sure they could do better, but this wasn't a dream. They had called me. And I was going to make the most of it. I had never really been on the UNC Campus myself, so I was quite nervous at the prospect of finding where to go for my initial interview; so, my mama and I drove down the day before so I would be totally prepared the next day. This is where the overwhelming began.

OK, thanks to the drive-by the day before, I found the parking deck without getting lost. And for a non-local driving on campus for the first time, that's quite the feat. Finding the Orthopaedic clinic in the hospital was more of a challenge. I mean, have you ever been inside UNC Hospital? I found it a bit intimidating, but somehow, I arrived at my destination unscathed. I felt the interview went well and left feeling pretty good about myself. Not in that I felt that I would get the job, but more so that I had conquered some of those introvert demons that seemed to be giving me a run for my money. I'm pretty sure I drove home that sunny day with a big silly grin on my face.

Caller ID is a wonderful thing. About a week and a half later, THE call came. I'm not entirely sure, but I believe my heart might have stopped for a few beats as I picked up the phone to say with my best, unsuspecting voice, "Hello?" Trish, the clerical supervisor back then, was on the other end and wanted to let me know herself that they. had.picked.ME! She didn't say it with that kind of emphasis, but it was definitely how I heard it. ME!

Once the call ended, pandemonium ensued. I was mega skipping through the house with a giggle as innocent as that of a baby just learning how to laugh. I was delirious and flabbergasted. I am going to work as a Patient Business Associate (front desk) in the Orthopaedics Department at the University of North Carolina at Chapel Hill. Had such a nice ring to it! I hadn't just landed a job, I think I might have just landed a new career.

So you're probably thinking this is about where the story ends. Not hardly. In fact, this is where it really begins. For the next six months, I would battle fear, self doubt, regret, stress and a knot in my stomach that I was sure had taken up permanent residence.

Every day I dreaded getting up for work and every day I was sick to my stomach until I punched out at 4:30pm. What had I done?! I just knew I had bitten off more than I could chew. What was I thinking; that someone like me could survive in a professional world like UNC.

My husband helplessly watched me struggle and he supported me with all that he had. Along the way, I had half-heartedly started job searching again. There were times I literally considered throwing my hands up in the air and seeking a greeter job at Wal-mart. I wanted to give up.

At one point I had an interview near my home with a small, medical facility that looked very promising. Very little benefits, no time off for a while, but . . . you got it; I was rationalizing and willing to settle in order to avoid facing my fears. But you know, it's interesting how God will intervene when He's given you the opportunity to trust Him, but you've been so consumed with your own short comings that you've failed to do so. God had a bigger plan for me. And He was going to make sure I didn't miss out on it.

The tide seemed to change for me when our department made our big move from two locations to a newly renovated space at the Ambulatory Care Center. Our department was beginning its evolution, the first of many changes. And who do you think the powers that be positioned at the front desk as one of the first faces you came to when you entered the department? That's right: the girl that was on the verge of throwing up every morning before coming to work. The girl that some in the department thought wasn't going to make it there.

As time passed, things started to change. But it was subtle. That army of butterflies that once used to rule my stomach had all but been defeated. Yes, there were setbacks along the way, but my will to overcome them seemed to be getting stronger. Could someone like me, one who seemed to always be fighting the confidence battle, really survive in a fast paced, ever-changing and diverse environment like Orthopaedics? Unbeknownst to me, there was someone who thought so . . .

Brenda, our clinic supervisor who was flying solo for a while without a clerical supervisor, started inviting—no wait, recruiting me to various committees. Again, this was new territory for me, but I respected her and if she really wanted to go out on a limb and let me represent our clinic, she must have had a good reason.

Either way, I found that I really enjoyed these new opportunities. It was different than the usual grind at the front desk and I got to meet and mingle with other UNC employees throughout the hospital. I also got to spend some one on one time with my clinic manager;

someone who I had always seen as a smart lady with a tough exterior that really didn't seem to have a "softer" side. I couldn't have been more mistaken.

We frequently had seminars at the Friday Center and the Rizzo Center and it was encouraging to feel at times that I was someone more than just an employee. I was learning how to feel a little more comfortable outside of that box I had placed myself in all my life. But, I always knew that no matter what, I could dive back into that box anytime I needed to.

My confidence continued to build and after Jessica was hired as our new clerical supervisor (love her), she and Brenda recommended me for the position of Lead PBA at the front desk, a position that up until that time, did not exist in our clinic. Granted, I had worked hard, but this sort of thing just didn't seem real to someone like me who often didn't feel like she fit in with mainstream society and who had confidence issues. Nevertheless, I became the "go to" gal at the front desk, and it felt good.

I can't recall now if it was during an annual review or when I (finally) applied for a new position at work (and got it). But it was at this moment that a light bulb finally flickered on in my hard head.

During a meeting with Brenda, she made the comment to me, "Just wait until you see what I have planned for you in the next three years." I guess you could have knocked me over with a feather. It was as if all the self doubt and stress I had dealt with since being at the clinic, the "closed doors" when trying to seek another job—suddenly it all made sense. God DID have a plan for me, and Brenda had been instrumental in the whole thing, whether she realized it or not.

What I realize now is what she saw—potential. I don't know at what point, but somehow, she saw potential in me that neither myself nor anyone else saw, but my Lord. I walked out of her office that day feeling pretty good about my future. God was definitely in control and He had most certainly placed Brenda in my life and kept me at that clinic so that His plan for me would continue to be carried out.

Fast forward a couple of years to a Wednesday morning staff meeting complete with breakfast. We were enjoying the yummy Panera's pastries and chatting amongst ourselves about what this shin dig could be about since we had already had our monthly jam session. Perhaps it was about the new location that was being built and the new batch of changes our clinic would be experiencing, yet again. As we were munching on our goodies, an uncharacteristic fidgety clinic manager stood before us. Brenda, who was always cool as a cucumber and business as usual appeared as if some alien had been by to swipe her swagger and all that was left was a bucket of goo.

As she was searching for a starting point, the uncomfortable silence was broken by one of our nurses who blurted out, "Are you leaving us?" When her head nodded a shakey "yes", the breakfast I had been enjoying suddenly turned to gravel. I looked around the room at the totally bewildered faces and the gasps from various employees solidified the apparent fact that no one saw this coming; least of all, myself.

She had been sought out and offered a position from another department at UNC. Brenda is a phenomenal professional. Her hard work and vision had transformed our Orthopaedic Department into an exceptional and well respected clinic at UNC. Apparently, she had wrestled with the decision to leave us as she had actually turned them down two times prior to finally accepting their offer. That alone spoke volumes coming from someone who never let emotions get in the way. Indeed, Orthopaedics had been a very special experience.

I was trying with everything I had to hold back the tears. Sadness and disillusionment were my initial emotions and they were 100% genuine. And they caught me by surprise. I was having a hard time processing why I was so overcome with emotion. I don't get attached to people that often.

Having time to think would help me to understand that she had been an instrumental piece of this professional journey I had been on for the last four and a half years and it had obviously meant more to me and had more of a lasting impact on me than I even realized. Not ready to acknowledge the bombshell, I quickly left the mob scene once the "meeting" was over, as she continued to receive hugs and well wishes from my co-workers.

I knew I couldn't avoid her for the rest of the day, or the next month that she would still be our manager, so I pulled myself together and decided to go to her and get it over with. I knew I would be a blubbering mess and that's not something I liked for anyone to see.

We ended up in the hall near her office at opposite ends and it was obvious she had noticed that I had avoided her. As a matter a fact, I think she said as much with a grin. Feeling the tears trying to escape before I was ready, I pointed to her office and followed her in shutting the door behind me. We immediately embraced and the flood gates opened.

My words weren't the most audible, but she knew what I was trying to convey. She was my professional mentor. What she saw in me and what she did with it is something that I will never forget. God used her in my life and that is not something you take lightly. To step back and see how the Lord had it all under control truly had an impact on me. And she was at the center of it, because of what she saw. And when she quietly and sincerely told me that watching me grow had truly been special, it was as if the ends of the circle had finally met.

So where do I go from here? I don't know. What I do know is that God is still in control and He's not through with me yet. Brenda was just part of my journey. Maybe our paths will cross again. But if they don't, I don't intend to forget just how far I've come because of what she saw.

E.T.A. An extension of Brenda's mentorship emerged after her departure. It was lying quietly within my immediate supervisor, Jessica. Together, they were what I like to refer to as the "dream team" of bosses. One was strong, highly intelligent and carried much vision for our department; the other was a quick thinker, energetic and totally compassionate to her employees. You don't find that kind of chemistry often in the corporate world. Well, at least it was a first for me.

And with Brenda's departure well in my rear view mirror, I find that Jess's farewell is on the horizon. This will also be a great loss for the department and for me personally. As a Christian in the workplace, having a supervisor who is also a Christian is an amazing blessing.

Not only did Jess pick up where Brenda left off as a professional mentor, but she has walked side by side with me as a sister in Christ. She has constantly been a source of encouragement, optimism and positivity that, I believe, have come from her walk with Christ. That is an aspect of my job that I have cherished and will greatly miss once she moves on. And I hope she knows this.

As always, I know the Lord will continue to provide. He always does. And I pray that I will use every bit of that provision to become stronger in my professional life but more importantly, in my spiritual life.

Once again, I find that I'm asking myself, "Where do I go from here?" It's in pondering this question that I realize now that maybe all along, it was what He saw.

The Semi-Colon

He hadn't been feeling well for some time. Nothing major; just low energy and a general under-the-weather demeanor. Eventually, a visit to his primary care physician for a physical resulted in a "poop smear", as my daddy called it, which indicated blood in his stool. A blood test also showed a low red blood count. The doctor put him on iron pills while he awaited his appointment with the GI doctor. So in February of 2001, at age 66, it was determined that Daddy needed and would have his first colonoscopy.

At the time, I was a massage therapist at a physical therapy clinic adjoining the hospital where my daddy would be having his procedure. My brother was at work, so I sat with my mama in the waiting area as long as I could before having to return for my next patient. This was around 4pm on a Tuesday.

My last patient of the day was someone I had known from school and had been seeing regularly in the clinic. The door was closed, the music had started playing and I had just laid my hands down on her back to begin her session when a purposeful knock came at the door.

"I'm sorry to bother you, but your mama is on the phone and needs to talk to you", said my concerned co-worker. Something didn't seem right. So I excused myself from the room and quickly made my way to the office next to mine to take the call.

In no way was I prepared for what I was about to hear. In a slightly broken but controlled voice, Mama uttered the words that Daddy had colon cancer. The news was delivered to me as straightforward as the doctor had delivered it to her. It's like instant cobwebs. I wasn't processing what I was hearing. And Mama was holding it together as best as she could. I couldn't believe I had left her alone to hear this kind of news.

I informed my patient what had transpired. I apologized, and thankfully, she understood that being with my mama was necessary at this time and I left immediately to head back over to the hospital.

Mama was sitting all alone at that 2nd floor waiting area as I approached. I don't remember tears but rather a wave of incredulousness. This was simply unchartered territory for all of us.

Daddy did not want to leave the hospital that day. He opted to be admitted after his procedure on Tuesday and was scheduled to have surgery on Thursday, March 1, 2001.

Everything seemed to happen so fast. I remember only bits and pieces of the rest of that day and the next day prior to Daddy's surgery. And you can call it denial if you want, but I recall feeling in my heart that Daddy would come through this and everything would be okay.

One moment I do remember very vividly is how Duane Manning, my speech teacher from high school and Bob LaTour, my basketball coach from high school, came by to visit with Daddy and to have prayer with him (and us) before he was taken to the operating room. That visit spoke volumes to me.

Daddy came through his surgery as well as anyone could under those circumstances. And we thanked God for that.

Another vivid memory I have is seeing Daddy in that hospital bed after surgery. He had a tube going through his nose down into his stomach to keep fluid drained. It hurt me to see him like that. My daddy who had always been so invincible and strong suddenly appeared vulnerable, small and scared. But that's what cancer does. It strips its victims of who they once were. And whether they become that person again or not is where another journey and battle begins.

The doctors 'believed' they had removed all of the cancer. But along with removing the tumor, they also took away one-third of Daddy's colon. It was obvious he was starting to feel a little more like himself when he came out with the unexpected statement that he now had a "semi-colon" rather than a colon. That comment sparked hope in me that soon life would be back to normal.

Things are never as simple as you make them out to be in your mind.

A third vivid memory I have of Daddy's bout with cancer is how I would visit him at the Cancer Center every Monday while he would undergo his chemo treatment. The staff were so caring and friendly. And Daddy really seemed to be coping pretty well.

But only Mama and my brother know the full extent of the transformation that occurred following Daddy's ordeal. Though I lived just up the hill from my family and would visit almost every day during that time, I only got a surface view of what was really going on. And though Mama and Jeff lived with Daddy day to day, only Daddy and the Lord knew the struggle within himself to cope with such a devastating circumstance. Life would be different from that point on.

My daddy survived the surgery and the cancer and for that I am so thankful. He has been cancer free for over ten years now. But one thing I have learned is that with cancer, there are no guarantees. Half of the battle is surviving the cancer and the other half is coping with life and who you have become because of the cancer.

If I recall, it took about a year before I saw glimpses of "my" daddy again. But there was no doubt in my mind that he was changed. Who wouldn't be? We are all different in how we handle what life throws at us. We can say we would do this or we would do that, but the truth is we don't know until we walk in those shoes. And with that being said, I would rather be barefoot.

On May 18, 2001, Daddy walked in his first "Relay For Life". It was a milestone for him and a proud moment for Mama, my brother, my husband and I as we joyfully joined in a lap with him. I recall three things about that evening: One, Daddy looked healthy. Two, there were those at this event who were obviously in the midst of their cancer battle. And three, the makeshift lanterns that lined the track were a dramatic reminder of how many lives had been touched and taken by this terrible disease.

Every year, every month, every day that I have my daddy with me is truly a gift. Cancer threatened to fracture our family but I believe the Lord replied, "No, not yet." I have always and will always look up to my daddy more than anyone on this earth. He is a true man of God who has given so much to our family and doubled those efforts in service to the Lord.

And though I recall another true man of God who was so young when stricken and taken by cancer, I know that the Lord has a plan for each of us and He makes no mistakes. Whether it be in our death or in our life, as Christians we have a responsibility to trust in the Lord and welcome His will. That is where the greatest victory can be found.

Bare Feet and Breezes

Life is busy. I know this. But if you're too busy to enjoy some of the simplest pleasures in life, are you really living?

Take a few moments to step outside on a sunny spring day. Invite the warm breeze to dance across your face like a feather teasing you with each brush. As you feel the welcomed tickle, you notice that your ears tingle from the delicate "ting-ting-ting" of a nearby wind chime. Joining the entrancing tones are the rustling leaves that seem to applaud as you give in to the sunshine that warms your soul and feeds your senses.

You look up to witness the bluest of skies so crisp and rich with color. There is a cloud here and there, fluffy like cotton balls, with a tint of color, each one randomly placed in the sky like a watercolor painting. You begin to drift away and with each step, the bottom of your bare feet come alive as your skin communicates with the fresh grass below and catches up like old friends after a long separation.

Sit and close your eyes, if even for a moment, and you will hear the songs of a choir of birds as they travel from tree to tree speaking of the brand new season that has just emerged after its annual hibernation. Everything is new and fresh again . . . a beginning.

Close your eyes and lean your ear in to hear the determined buzzing of the bumblebee as he too moves from place to place exploring the new in the familiar. His lively chatter is so electric that you feel your back arch and the hairs on your neck stand at attention from the vibration of his efforts.

As you open your eyes again, find a vast field of flowers in bloom and let the vivid colors saturate your dreams. Reds, yellows, lavenders, pinks . . . your eyes widen with childlike wonder. Nothing is out of reach.

Lean down and join the delicate butterfly in her quest; inhale the intoxicating fragrance of a pristine pink rose in bloom. You can't get enough. It's okay to want more. The sweetness is stimulating and causes you to exhale, letting go—just letting go. You pause for a moment to contemplate what you are feeling inside and a smile decorates your face like a rainbow spreads across the sky after a refreshing rain.

Your soul is alive and your feet say it's time to run. Going nowhere and everywhere all at once, your energy is transforming your body into a song in motion celebrating life and God's exquisite details of the masterpiece we know as creation. With a childlike giggle you stop abruptly, catching your breath, while looking over your shoulder to absorb the subtle peacefulness of the water flowing over the stones in a nearby brook. It sings a different tune and you are happy to sing with it. It has rhythm, just as life; lows and highs but each part of the song, part of the journey. You dip your hand into its cool, refreshing existence and feel the cleansing effects exhilarate your soul yet again.

Still kneeling by the smooth stones that are sprinkled throughout the water like stars illuminating a midnight sky, you notice the wind dancing with the silky grasses perched on a hill in the distance. The sun peeks through each strand and its twinkle is so bright it almost blinds you. But its movement calls to you and you eagerly run to it until you rest by its side atop the hill. You sit with a sense of ease and reflect while the grass sways generously and dances like a free spirit. You want to feel that free. And if only for these few stolen moments, you are.

The Hummingbird

I've never really been able to blurt out the phrase "Let me tell you about my big brother." Even though it wasn't a literal statement, it still just didn't fit. So, I guess I will tell you about my only brother, Jeff.

He's always been six years older than me but I guess I never thought that much about the age difference because we always saw eye to eye, literally. He was picked on in school for his small stature and even nicknamed "peanut". I still remember how a bully on the school bus once dropped a Planters peanut on the floor of the bus and squashed it flat. I'm sure he was attempting to make a statement with that act of violence, but I never figured it out. We'll chalk it up to 70's style bullying.

Honestly, there's not much to tell. And I don't mean that in a negative way. With my brother, what you see is what you get. Jeff doesn't hold back much in terms of opinions. You will always know where he stands on political issues and religious issues. And there will never be a doubt about how he feels about his family.

He's meticulous, a bit stubborn and very gifted artistically. I like to think that our originality is our most shared attribute. As kids, we would sit and draw for hours or create make believe countries where every detail was thought out, documented, and exactly the way we envisioned it. Our imaginations were twins, even if we weren't.

But when it comes to getting inside to see what makes him tick, I'm not sure that's ever been done . . . or is even possible. He reveals very little while holding so much inside. I'm not sure if he's aware, but he's not fooling those who love him most. We see what's in his heart because it's written all over his face.

My brother loves hummingbirds. He thinks they are unique and unlike any other bird; and how fitting because I see my big brother as a little hummingbird. Did you know that hummingbirds have proportionally the largest hearts of any living animal? As much as I admire my mama's heart, I have to say that my brother seems to have inherited that heart—not me. He is always willing to give, to do, to be there. He rarely says no and he rarely complains. He doesn't ask for much. And he really seems to put his needs and wants in the shadows of everyone else's.

While I don't think my brother's life turned out the way he might have envisioned it when he was younger, I hope he knows his life holds tremendous worth as is. And maybe, just maybe, the Lord handpicked him for the path he is travelling on now.

Christmas Past, Christmas Present, Christmas Future

It was almost like a classic Christmas story playing out before my very eyes. This was last Christmas. But let me tell you how we came to be a part of our very own Christmas miracle.

I grew up in the south, born and raised in North Carolina, and born into a family where the home cooking was so good, it'd make you lie on your back after a meal and beg for your belly to be scratched; and where family was all you ever really needed growing up.

As a child, Christmas meant many things to me. There was always the excitement of the Christmas program at church; and Christmas also meant lots of gifts including my first real baby doll at age one. *She* is 41 now and sits in the corner of my room wearing one of my baby dresses. She serves as a constant reminder to never forget the kid in me.

But one of the most treasured essentials of Christmas for me has always been Christmas Eve spent with my mom's side of the family. From my very first Christmas in 1966 until my thirty-fourth Christmas in 2000, we would make the long drive up into the foothills with the anticipation of seeing our family and all the night would entail causing us to nearly burst at the seams.

And although as I got older and no longer gazed up into the sky on the drive home looking for Santa and his sleigh, the special feeling of being a child and a grandchild at Christmas has never left me.

Over the years, the location of our gathering changed from Mamaw and Papaw's house to their barn until our family had grown so big we had to move on to other relatives' homes. Eventually, we had to relocate our festivities to a local church nestled up in the mountains.

Regardless of where we gathered, the scenario was always the same. It was tradition. The tables were always overflowing with the most delicious home cooking (Paula Deane would be so proud) and the beautifully decorated Christmas tree always seemed to get lost behind the mountain of gifts that were awaiting eager hands.

Little ones would be running around burning off energy and the older kids and adults would mingle about engaging in various conversations and even doing a little bit of reminiscing. Oh, and we can't overlook the blinding flashes of 30 cameras taking pictures of the family. Of course this meant that Mamaw and Papaw were always the most photographed. They were never too fond of that kind of attention.

There was never a shortage of laughter, love or hugs—another tradition in our family—with the biggest hugs always reserved for our dear Mamaw and Papaw, the foundation of this special family. Almost sounds like a Norman Rockwell painting doesn't it?

It was. This was our Christmas past.

Papaw was 86 when he passed away about a month after Christmas, 2000. None of us really saw it coming and we were devastated to say the least. And although all forty plus of us practically lived in the hospital during Papaw's last days, we weren't prepared for the loss and we were now in uncharted territory.

Our family was no longer whole now. How do you carry on such rich family traditions once you have lost one of the pillars of your family? Right away, we realized that you just dig deep and find a way to do it. You do it for Mamaw, you do it for Papaw, you do it for each other, you do it because the tradition is part of who you are and life goes on . . . and so does the love.

Life did go on and five more Christmas' came and went. Traditions were altered a bit, but still had a strong presence in our family as they always had.

That was until August of last year. Mamaw's body had gone about as far as it could go in this life and though she had always wanted to live to be 100, at age 96 she left us abruptly within one week's time of falling ill.

Suddenly, the frailty and shortness of life was more real than we could handle. Our family was forever changed and the traditions that had always held a certain security for us, for me, were now in danger of vanishing.

As Christmas and the holiday season approached, so did the angst and uncertainty of what our first Christmas without Mamaw and Papaw would be like.

To deal with the loss of Mamaw and Papaw and the presumably realignment of family traditions, I found myself engaging in self-therapy when I made the decision to create a montage about our family and our rich traditions. I began collecting photos and Lord knows, there were millions. I had some grainy snippets of video I had taken with my first digital camera back in 2000, our last Christmas with Papaw.

Along the way, I obtained 8mm footage from the '60s and more video from my brother from the '90s. I spent hours and hours reliving the past while creating what I thought just might be the band aid this family needed. We were hurting and we were a bit lost.

I was hoping this video capturing so much tradition and love through the years would once again bring to the surface for each of us of just what we have had all these years, all our lives, as being part of this family. We didn't have Mamaw and Papaw physically with us now, but we had their legacy of love and so many special memories.

Christmas Eve, 2006 was here. The tree was decorated, the tables were full of home cooked dishes and we were all there in body, but our spirits were struggling.

It had been decided that after the meal and before passing out gifts, I would share my video entitled "Family Heirlooms" with my family. There was apprehension on the part of some, afraid of opening up fresh wounds by reliving the past. It had been almost six years since Papaw's passing but only four months since losing Mamaw; were we ready for this kind of walk down memory lane?

I remember as I had been creating this montage that I prayed that the Lord would use it to help our family heal, to keep us strong, to keep us together—to carry us from Christmas past to Christmas future—from what we had always known to what we were going to be. But it was out of my hands now and time to watch.

We all gathered closely around the small TV and turned down the lights. My heart was literally about to beat out of my chest as the video began and the song "What A Wonderful World" began to play. Images of Mamaw and Papaw with their whole lives ahead of them graced the screen. Giggles could be heard as we saw Papaw in his striped swim trunks, which closely resembled present day Speedos.

Through the course of the video I looked around and saw smiles emerging and my heart began to relax again. The laughter, well, it was easy and pure and as if the grief had been erased from our hearts for just those few moments. Picture after picture faded in and out on the screen as the music played. Maybe, just maybe, we would be okay.

As the latter part of the video began, I knew I was taking a risk as the first notes of "I Can Only Imagine" began to permeate the room. As video of Mamaw and Papaw rolled, recalling the life we knew, so did the tears roll down our cheeks like a spring rain cleansing a delicate rose petal. Soft cries could be heard yet somehow, I knew it was going to be okay.

And it was.

As the video ended and the lights came on, one by one my aunts, uncles and cousins came to me with tears and hugs and gratefulness. The band-aid was on and the healing had begun. I had never felt closer to my family in my life than I did at that very moment. This was a gift. This was our Christmas present.

Christmas, 2006 was a miracle of sorts as we started a new chapter in our family. And though no one knows what Christmas future holds for us, I expect the home cookin' to taste just as good, the laughter to sound just as sweet and the hugs and love to be just as warm and strong as ever.

This is my Christmas wish!

Pep rally at ACS . . . I'm the one on the front row
with bad hair . . .
Wait; we all had bad hair in the eighties

Mama, Daddy, and me . . . taking a little nap

The Huff Family, Christmas Eve 2000

My daddy participating in his first Cancer Walk in May, 2001

Cougar, the original Buddy

Rumi, my little diva

Taken for Granted Breezes

I love to drive through our neighborhood on a Saturday evening during the summer. The smell of fresh cut grass, the mouth-watering aroma of hamburgers on the grill and the sounds of folks just settling in. Suburbia provides me with all the nightlife I need.

The cozy yet invigorating aroma of an outdoor fire on an overcast, fall day. It's like an old friend and I can't decide whether I want to curl up next to that fire or leap over it celebrating the beginning of another football season.

Going into one of my favorite stores to see what treasures I can find while sipping on a yummy smoothie. I don't have a schedule, so I can spend as much time as I like just browsing and shuffling through merchandise that others have passed over. Ya gotta move stuff around a bit, and maybe, just maybe you will find a great deal for a few bucks. I may only walk out with one item, but if it catches my eye or screams my name, if it causes my face to light up like a Christmas tree, I feel like I have come away with a priceless treasure. I am rich!

There is a lesson hidden behind the common cold: don't take your sense of taste or smell for granted. If I couldn't smell the salt air at the beach, if I couldn't smell the familiar fragrance of my husband or taste one bite of food ever again . . . it would be like a song without music, a painting without color, life without breath . . .

It's All About Balance

Where did the battle begin? I couldn't even begin to tell you. I wasn't predisposed to media brainwashing as a kid. I watched *Hee Haw, Scooby Doo and Happy Days*; and despite the busty blondes in denim cut-offs and girly-girls in poodle skirts and ponytails, it never occurred to me that I should look a certain way.

I didn't buy the teen magazines so I didn't really know how everyone should look and that thin was in. I was just me. What I do remember is that my waist measured 26 inches in 8th grade charm class and that I weighed 105 at graduation. At the time, those were just numbers to me with no real feelings attached to them.

I remember a photo taken of me one summer while on vacation at the Grand Canyon. I was wearing a cranberry colored short set made of decade appropriate terry cloth. I was perched on a rock and the sunlight caught the side of my thigh just right and you could see the presence of cellulite even then, at age 16. Of course, looking at the photo then, I didn't see what I see now.

I also remember writing my senior term paper on eating disorders. I think we've all binged at one time or another, but I had never purged or fallen into that kind of vicious cycle. Somehow, I felt some kind of distant connection with these people whose lives seemed to be ruled by food and *more*. I believe the real story is in the *more*.

It was only a few short years after these memories that "it" happened. I realized I was part of a power struggle between me, my body and food.

Food is a necessity of life. But for some, maybe even many, the role food plays exists on a much grander scale. For me, it's a bitter-sweet symphony.

Take for instance, a piece of chocolate cake. Simple in theory, but what I see before me is so much more. I get excited about the prospect of a yummy dessert. It's something I look forward to; it brings me joy. My chocolate dessert of choice is the "Chocolate Obsession" that can be found at TGI Fridays. Aptly named, the anticipation alone of the first bite is the crescendo of the experience. Before I have even picked up a spoon to begin my conquest, saliva rushes through my mouth like a tidal wave. The first bite hits the inside of my mouth and before my teeth even meet, my mouth comes alive with tingling and almost audible giggles. Euphoria ensues.

The irony of the moment is the inevitable guilt that crashes the party. A dessert infused with generous amounts of Ghirardelli chocolate and sweet caramel is destined to provoke the demons in my psyche. Remorse creeps over my body like a dark shadow.

Each dessert exhibits a different scenario. Sometimes the guilt reaches me before I have swallowed the last bite, cutting the experience short. At others, the shame delays just long enough to allow me to enjoy the sweet treasure for a moment, providing me with an artificial sense of bliss that is gone within seconds. Sounds a little dramatic? When put on paper, yes. But isn't this what many of us experience on a day to day basis when we're dealing with food and more?

As a kid, I don't recall spending a lot of time thinking about food. Mama was a country cook and most of what we had came from our garden. Potatoes, beans, corn, tomatoes, and watermelons would decorate our dinner table rather than casseroles and fancy steaks and the like. I don't recall special rules about sweets and snacking, nor do I recall abusing the privilege.

But nighttime was always a favorite part of the day for me. Daddy would be working in his study and Mama, my brother and I would watch TV and eat our usual snacks. Some nights I would eat a bowl of cereal and other nights I would settle down with a bowl of dry fruit loops and some Dr. Pepper to wash it down. Didn't seem like a big deal at the time. For me, it was a great way to end the day.

Somewhere along the way, family get-togethers became an outlet for me to unknowingly showcase my growing affection for food and the need to have a certain fragment of control. I had to be at the front of the line when the dinner bell rang. I can't say what was going through my mind when this little tradition started, but looking back, I can only surmise that I had a hidden fear that if I didn't lead the way, that I would miss something.

My twenties brought on a new revelation: body image.

"Sonja, meet mirror. Mirror, meet Sonja." And so the ever-evolving obsession with my waistline began. Catching profiles in the mirror became my daily ritual. I would check out the thickness of my waist and the flatness of my stomach anytime I was near my reflection. I knew exactly how my side should feel when I would cup my hand around it. It's hard to explain, but in my mind, I knew how thin I should feel. But why? On what basis was I drawing this conclusion? And if the difference was palpable, I was either eating too much or not exercising enough; sometimes both. I was hard on myself.

When it came to exercise, I was meticulous and at times, a bit excessive. I even remember a time when outside factors kept me from making my five miles at the walking track one night and I literally found myself on the verge of tears. My fixation on my flat stomach escalated when I heard that the Pro Football player, Andre Rison, completed a thousand crunches a day. Well naturally, I saw this as a challenge, even a call to duty so I began my quest for delivering the same quantity of abdominal work with every workout. And you know what? No sweat. That was a goal I met easily and maintained for a while.

Subtly, over time, my world of food and my world of fitness crossed paths and a love triangle emerged. Boundaries became fuzzy for me. I could be eating one meal while thinking about what I would have for the next meal while exercising relentlessly in-between; and how fitting that I should be working full time at a health club. This would be a great way to keep a balance between my two loves.

Yes, as a single gal, by day I was a gym rat, and by night, you could find me tucked away safely at home alone downing a whole pizza-pizza. And for a little bedtime treat, a pan (yes, the whole pan) of chocolate chip cookies with a couple of stadium cups of ice cold whole milk. After all, I was young and the next morning I would be up bright and early working it off; remember—life is all about balance. And I had it down to a science.

Well, we all know science is based on facts, and for years I had them all wrong. Finally, a little wisdom snuck up on me as I got a little older and I was soon seeing clearly for the first time that I was in a battle—a battle of wills.

On the one hand, I wanted to be healthy and fit and I wanted to be thin. Now granted, I have curves, and they aren't all in the right places, hence, my obsession with my stomach and waist. That was one area of my body that I had going for me. I could never seem to tame the thighs so I focused the bulk of my attention on what I thought I could control. Everything else, I maintained as best as I could. You know, for balance.

On the other hand, I wanted my food and what it did for me. I'm not an adventurous eater so I don't think there's a lot of truth in saying I love food, although I enjoy what I eat. What I can confess is that food serves a greater purpose for me. That is where the love is. It's there for me when I am sad, when I am stressed, when I'm bored, when I want to celebrate. It's part of a ritual; Sunday night cookies or Friday night milkshakes . . . and of course, it's there when I am truly hungry.

I guess the most dominate part of this battle is my will power . . . or more truthfully, the lack of. This is where I struggle the most. I know a bit about nutrition and what I should or shouldn't eat. And in my forties, I have learned more and more about portion control and making healthy choices; that's where it's at.

I also know a lot about fitness and exercise. I have played sports competitively since I was 15 years old and exercised regularly in gyms since I was 21. Exercise is such an important part of not only physical fitness, but mental and emotional fitness as well. And, I enjoy it!

What I haven't even begun to master is how these two loves can coexist in my life without constant tug-of-war. I'm not a psychologist, but I am intelligent enough to know that my struggle goes beyond food or exercise. Food isn't the problem. Exercise isn't the problem. I may have not discovered the root of all this strife or understand it all, but I do know one thing; it's all about balance. And I don't have it . . . yet; but I'm striving for it.

There are days and sometimes weeks and months where I feel like I am in control and that balance, permanent balance, seems to be within my reach; that is, until I allow myself to get derailed and the fight to get back on track is at the forefront . . . again. It's a roller coaster ride, a vicious cycle. It can be so frustrating to want to starve yourself and eat everything in sight all at the same time and know neither is possible; to never want to make the effort to exercise again but knowing that you couldn't and wouldn't want to live without it.

I'm older now. And though my goals are still the same, I seemed to have lost the focus I once had. Bad knees, every day aches and pains and a slower metabolism are just some of the factors now that play into the equation along with waking up each morning saying "I'll do better today" and going to bed each night thinking "I'll do better tomorrow." When did it all get so complicated?

It's a lifelong battle and I don't plan on retreating or surrendering, though there are days when I truly want to raise the white flag. Those are the days when I have hidden a container of cake icing in a drawer so my husband won't find it, and then when I am alone, I eat half of it in one sitting, along with some diet soda, of course. Those are the days when I grab a bag of potato chips and shove them in my mouth, hardly chewing what I have before stuffing more in, savoring every bite and at the same time not tasting it at all. Those are the days when it takes every ounce of energy I have to get in a workout because if I don't, I am taking yet another two steps back in this journey. Those are the days when I check my profile in the mirror, still, as I have for so many years, only to find the reflection to be so different than it once was and knowing the battle still rages on.

Not a day goes by when I don't wish at least once that I didn't have to worry about food or exercise and I could just be happy with who I am and that the battle would end. But letting go of obsessions you have carried with you for so many years without really knowing why you are the way you are is not an easy task. And really, is it even possible? I just don't know.

Playtime

F.A.G. Schwartz wouldn't be impressed; and I'm pretty sure you wouldn't see them on the shelves at Toys R Us. Our toys were unique and they were handmade; adolescent craftsmanship at its best . . . a lost art in the new millennium.

Growing up in the 70's meant that toys were still somewhat in that pre-electronic stage unlike today where very few traditional toys survived modernization. Crayons and Play-doh seem to have nine lives but beyond that, creativity seems to lie within the deep pockets of the manufacturer, and not in the little hands that are meant to play with the toys.

My parents made sure that my brother and I had everything we needed growing up. We had a roof over our head, clothes on our body, food on the table, a Christian education and lots of love. Although toys are a necessity for children, they weren't the focal point of our existence. However, every growing child needs playtime and some toys. We were no exception.

I don't recall a lot of sleepovers and play-dates with other little girls in the neighborhood, only a few; but rather, I remember sitting in the floor for hours playing with my older brother. There was a "Barbie" here and there and of course a "Ken"; life-sized baby dolls and little matchbox cars littered our floors like every other household at that time. But the bulk of our playtime came from our own creativity; something I feel has been lost in today's younger generation.

My daddy has been a CPA for as long as I can remember. So growing up, his profession provided us with many wonderful tools for creating original replicas of store bought toys that didn't fit into the family budget. And to be honest, I didn't know the difference. Once

Daddy finished using the paper on his ledger pads, the cardboard was very useful in creating the next new doll for me. A little crayon and magic marker and voila!—the face of a rosy cheeked doll. And what's the beautiful face of a new doll without the long flowing locks of hair to complete the look. All I had to do was retrieve the miles of curled up adding machine paper from Daddy's overflowing trashcan and tape them to the cardboard, uh, head of my new friend. And when I got bored and thought she needed a new look, all I had to do was give her a trim or add some new fabulous curls! The possibilities were endless!

Other everyday items found in the home came in handy for creating new toys. For instance, you couldn't even think of throwing away an empty Kleenex box or the cardboard spool leftover from a roll of toilet paper. With a little ingenuity, these cardboard finds could be carefully crafted into cars and trucks. And if you stacked the Kleenex boxes on top of one another and grabbed an ink pen, you could draw up the floor plans for a cool new condominium.

Our toys were more than for shaping us for future careers as such as hair stylists and engineers. Why, they needed to be functional and provide the basic necessities such as footwear. When telling of my affectionately named "wooden shoes", it has often been received with bellows of laughter. I happen to think it was an idea ahead of its time; but that's just my opinion.

You see, all you needed were a couple of those little building blocks, some more of that nifty cardboard, some tape and a variety of sizes of rubber bands all of which could be found in Daddy's office. And with a little measuring and a few revisions, within the hour I would have a new pair of sling backs or flip flops! Of course, this invention preceded the ever popular family of "Jellies" and "Crocs." Unfortunately, my wooden shoes never caught on in the mainstream.

As normal healthy kids, fresh air and outdoor activity were a must. So, when we took playtime outside, it involved various activities such as making mud people on pieces of plywood, a killer kickball game for two, and chasing and collecting lightning bugs while Mama and Daddy made homemade ice cream with a crank-style freezer. I think that might have been one of my favorite things to do. To me, there was nothing like running barefoot through your yard just as the sun was going down and the dew was just enough to cool your feet while chasing these little wonders of light with a glass jar in one hand and the lid in the other. The only problem I found with this activity was that the excitement was short-lived. Because the next morning, the lights had disappeared and those little suckers were lying on their backs with their feet stuck up in the air. What a shame!

We also loved to ride bikes like other kids. Mama and Daddy did manage to save up for those. But that's where it ended. We didn't get all the bells and whistles for our bikes. They came however the blue light special at K-Mart offered them. So naturally, we improvised. Like any other kid in our day, we created "flappers"; you know, playing cards or pieces of multi-use cardboard clipped to the fork of your bike with wooden clothes pins. This nifty invention allowed the cardboard to be smacked around by the spokes every time the tire rotated. The faster you pedaled, the louder the pop. It was noisy but so awesome! And yes, I said clothes pins. You honestly think we had a clothes dryer back then?

As growing children, we weren't just developing physically but also mentally. Creativity in our playtime also took the form of thinking outside our own little neighborhood. Why, there was a whole new world waiting to be created. So, Jeff and I came up with our own little islands where we were king and queen. My brother named his island "Charity Island" and I named my little piece of paradise "Pleasure Island." We would sit for gobs of time writing up the structure of our make believe worlds. This was a lot of work, you know. Every island needs medical facilities, law enforcement, restaurants, schools . . . and the list goes on.

I specifically recall as I was looking through our phone book to get ideas for names of the town's people that the name "Geo" sure seemed to be a popular name. I didn't like it much, but it was clear someone did. It was only years later that I realized the name "Geo" was just short for George. Funny, I don't like that name any better.

Yes, play time with my older brother suited me just fine. Who needed a bunch of silly girls who wanted to play mommy and dress up and scream at painful pitches. I got along just fine being a bit of a tomboy and exercising the artist in me alongside my brother. We could sit and "Van Gough" for hours. We understood each other and we never, ever fought.

Well, there might have been a few altercations. My brother tells me that he had rendered a drawing of "Astro Boy" once. Naturally,

Astro Boy was meant to fly so my brother was running up and down the hall with this piece of paper flapping furiously. Apparently this annoyed me, so with swift hands I ripped it from his grasp and tore Astro Boy in half. My brother won't admit whether he cried or not, but rather, "he wasn't happy about it." Of course, the tattling came next. That always came next.

And, well, there was the incident regarding the monkey. You might be more prone to believe my story if I support it with a piece of evidence—the letter my brother wrote to my mama when he was only seven years old. I was only one at the time and really don't recall all the details. It went something like this:

> Dear Mamy,
> I sorry for what I did. But I should say this;
> Is it too late to give Sonja the car to play with?
> Put it in the box . . . yes or no . . .
> If yes, I'm going to keep her in my room with it.
> I'll have to play with her monkey.
> Your mean friend, Jeffey B.

It was obvious my big brother was still working on his penmanship as some of the letter was written in lower case and other parts were written in caps. The spelling needed some work as well. But you get the point.

Looking back now, I wouldn't trade what I didn't have then for what kids do have now. I have the absence of hi-tech electronics and my mama and daddy to thank for that. They knew what we needed most and made sure we had it. Everything else would be icing on the cake. I don't recall having a trampoline in the back yard or the coolest "must have" toys of the season, but to me, we had everything we needed and that was each other.

At an early age we knew the meaning of family and fun and I think those impressionable years full of imagination sculpted me into the creative adult I am today. You know, maybe I will just write a book about it someday.

As Long As I Can Dream

It's called a "bucket list"; simply, a list of things you would like to do before you die.

I've never really given much thought about this kind of thing and therefore, never made a list. Lists and I actually have a love-hate relationship. While I operate off of lists on a regular basis and they tend to lead the charge to keep me organized and productive, lists also make me crazy.

Being a bit of my own brand of perfectionist/control freak, I tend to feel I have no choice but to complete a list only to go on and make a new one.

You can see where I'm heading with this. I would most certainly over-think a bucket list and obliterate any joy that might arise out of the experience. With this mentality, I find it easier to dream. And this bucket dream is strictly geographical . . .

Wearing my ultra comfy shoes, faded jeans and a cozy cable knit sweater, I run through the lush green meadows, hill after hill, as the cool, damp air gently bounces off my face. The colorful wildflowers sway to and fro as I run like a child towards a dream. The sound of the waves crashing over the rocks creeps up over the cliffs; it's almost as if the sea is applauding my frivolity.

Still, I find a way to pause and rest on a beautiful stone, a piece of ruin of an ancient castle. The texture compliments the silkiness of the emerald grass. This place is so rustic, so picturesque and so welcoming. My eyes nor my camera have ever seen such beauty. Thank you, *Leap Year*, for the inspiration. This is my Ireland . . .

The painted rocky landscape is rugged and dusty yet poetic in a way that demands your attention. With majestic mountaintops, wildflowers in the valley and abundant water features, everything you could want is right here. Rest under an old tree, find a shady spot next to an enormous boulder or simply sit on the ground in the vastness that is the western United States. With a big sky and an even bigger spirit, it's a great place to think and explore. This is my Colorado . . .

Laidback and friendly—I can certainly relate. What lifestyle suits the white beaches and azure blue waters better? I want to sit at water's edge forever, while I gently wiggle my toes through the warm grains of sand.

I want to soak in the warmth of the sun and breathe in the cleansing salt air. I want to imprint the beauty of this place in my memory forever. That's all. I just want to be still and do nothing else but take it all in. This is my Australia . . .

Tropical paradise, it truly is. History and beauty—I want to see it all. The colorful foliage is happy and flirty. Even the palm trees project a certain lightheartedness you can't find anywhere else. Its undeniable mystique draws me in.

Crowded? I'm sure it is but I imagine that all who are lucky enough to find themselves here for even a short time feel as if time stands still; and there is room for everyone to enjoy a slice of heaven. This is my Hawaii . . .

With no schedule, nowhere I have to be, I relax at a curbside café table in a quaint part of town. The colorful structures gather around me as the charming music both calms me and entertains me. I slowly savor a bowl of authentic spaghetti as I remember the movie *Under the Tuscan Sun,* my inspiration for this quest.

I don't understand the chatter around me, yet somehow, I feel at home. It is a simple moment really, one that I don't want to end. Maybe I'll do a little window shopping later. This is my Italy . . .

You know, one day, maybe someday, I will see my dreams become reality. Visiting any one of these places would definitely be icing on the cake of my life that has been sweet so far.

Until then, I'll enjoy the vision I carry around with me, hidden in the far corner of my desires. But don't look for me to make a list and definitely, don't wake me. This is my dream . . .

To be continued . . .

Kumquat and Kiwi

After Cougar died, I was inconsolable and knew without a doubt that I wanted another male black cat. We had often called Cougar "Buddy" as a nickname and knew this would be the name of his successor. It seemed only natural. Of course we still had Rumi, and believe me, we loved her with all our hearts, but there is something indescribably unique and special about a male black cat. I was well aware that Cougar could never be replaced, but somehow I just knew that adopting a new kitty would ease the pain and fill the void left by the death of my first indoor pet. Everything would be back to normal again. It's funny how things work out sometimes.

Free kittens are usually easy to come by. All you have to do is check your local newspaper or put the word out and via a friend of a friend—voila, you have oodles of kitties waiting to steal your heart. In the meantime, I had expressed to a co-worker my search for my next boy kitten because I just couldn't imagine our home without one. She mentioned that a local vet had adopted two black kittens, a brother and sister that were brought to them by a Good Samaritan. Apparently, some heartless individual had abandoned these two furry cherubs by the side of the road all alone which right away, spoke to my heart. There was no time to waste.

David and I visited the vet's office and were formally introduced to Kumquat and Kiwi. Yes, you heard me right. These poor little kittens had not only been separated at birth from their family and left on the side of the road to die, but some strangers actually rescued them and named them Kumquat and Kiwi. Really, did they actually think these two looked like fruit?

If there is such a thing as love at first site, this was it. The two were perfectly adorable and somewhat inseparable. They were barely three months old with so much personality that the cage could barely contain them. Right away one attribute caught our attention; one of them had a larger-than-life purr. I have never heard a cat purr at this decibel. Of course this little feature was endearing and though they both were two cute for words, not to mention identical, we knew we could only adopt the boy. We were on a mission, remember?

As fate would have it, the audible wonder was the boy of the siblings and our decision was not only predetermined, but effortless. Leaving his sister behind was not easy, but we knew our home was only big enough for the four of us. So, we completed the paperwork, gathered up our brand new addition and quickly headed home.

We're going to skip introductions between Buddy and Rumi. Let's face it; if you have ever had cats, you know what I am talking about. It really is some big drama when you introduce a new feline to a home where another feline already resides. Suffice it to say, we're *still* in transition.

Evening number one with our little baby Buddy was quite eventful and full of fun. I just adore kittens and getting to know them and their unique personalities. To no surprise, even at three months old, Buddy was already full of mischievousness and adventure. He took quickly to chasing strings and balls and the other toys we had lying around the house. He liked to hide, too; another favorite activity among furry youngsters.

The first night at home with Buddy went off without a hitch. We got up for work the next day and prepared his room for our absence; his room being the guest bath. Call it animal baby proofing but we had the room stocked with a fresh litter box, food bowl, water bowl and plenty of toys. Oh, and we hid the toilet paper as well. All of this was prepared with love behind a securely closed door. You do not want a three month old kitten to have full reign of a home when you are not around to supervise while his claws and curiosity are in charge.

So, I went to work with a smile on my face knowing our little boy was safe at home and our family was once again, complete. We would love him with all of our hearts and play with him and give him everything a growing boy needed. Did I say boy?

I received a phone call at work about mid morning from the vet where we had adopted Buddy. Naturally I assumed this was a courtesy call hoping to find that Buddy's transition had been a smooth one. However, my assumption couldn't have been further from reality.

The staff member on the phone cut right to the chase and blurted out in sheer embarrassment and uncertainty (of my reaction, I'm sure) that they had failed to give us the male kitten. Translation: they had sent us home with a female kitten that we had named "Buddy." Ok . . . time out . . . how does a vet's office, responsible for the care of our furry young, give someone the wrong gender? I know they were tiny little specimens, but really?

Back to reality, and my unexpected phone call, I was obviously caught off guard and honestly do not remember how I responded. All I know is that bottom line, it would be totally heartless for us to return a kitten to a sterile and totally not cozy cage in a vet's office after teasing her with one night of what every pet longs for . . . a home. She would not be an orphan because of us. And, this news also meant I still needed that boy kitten I had originally set out to adopt.

So, with only a minuscule measure of hesitation, we picked up the "real" Buddy and brought him home to join his sister. Inside, I was elated beyond one's daily recommended dosage. On the outside, however, I had to maintain a certain degree of forethought and essentially keep my husband from freaking out at the reality of one cat and two kittens in our home.

I had to stay focused as there was much to do now with two little ones to raise. And since the bathroom was already kitten proof, the obvious next step was picking out a name for our little girl.

I found myself standing in front of the kitchen sink one day rinsing some things out and gazing out the window that gave me such a nice view of the beautiful trees in our back yard. My attention fell to some décor I had sitting on my window sill; some small, artificial greenery that portrayed the herb *Rosemary*. "Rosemary", I thought. "That would be a lovely name . . . wait, no, that would remind me of an old horror movie." My eyes shifted to the left of the window to see another small pot of greenery. "Sage. That's it!" I called out to my husband in the other room sharing my ingenious choice in names. We decided it seemed fitting for our girl and so she became "Sage."

For the next three months or so, this dynamic brother and sister duo would steal our hearts beyond our expectations and turn our home upside down all at the same time. Their antics were priceless and no longer did having three felines in the home seem like such a conflict.

We started out seeking a baby boy to fill an empty space in our homes and hearts left by a difficult death and came home at last with double the trouble and double the love. As a matter of fact, we just couldn't imagine our home without Buddy or Sage. They were a set. Funny thing about life though; it has a tendency to make you see things you never thought possible and make the unexpected, reality.

Mama's Museum

What does a dandelion pressed under glass say?
I didn't particularly care for Merriam-Webster's definition of the word sentimental so I decided it needed a little tweaking. I think a picture of my mama next to the word is far more accurate.

Mama and Daddy still live in the house I grew up in from age 9 until I left the nest at 19. On paper it sounds like such a short time. But back then, I'm sure it seemed much longer; and I'm talking in a good way. And with my husband and me living a mere two minutes away, just out of the valley, I am able to visit often. Heck, it's not really visiting. It's just going home again . . .

Over the years I have seen the décor evolve. From scarcely furnished to so many plants you felt like you lived in a jungle to the country flavor it is now, with a twist of course. Every inch of that house is now a reflection of a family that has been truly blessed. The family photos and the little trinkets that many would have not given a second thought to didn't just jump into place all by themselves. They were arranged with great thought and with lots of love by Mama. It's those little details, along with a loving family, that make a house a home.

Walking into Mama and Daddy's house is like walking into a museum. And at times you feel like you are sitting on the pages of a virtual scrapbook. It really is quite impressive, but I'm a little partial. And while seeing is believing, you're just going to have to trust me on this one and sit back while I tell you all about this family treasure chest.

I guess I should warn you that the sheer volume of family photos seen here is staggering. It's like our home is ground zero for a Kodak film factory explosion. Adorable baby photos, old enlargements of grandparents, great and great-great grandparents, sisters, brothers, cousins and entire family trees make an appearance in a variety of ways.

On one shelf you will see a frame with a logo "The Boys" across the top. It's home to a photo of Mama's two brothers. Another frame with the logo "The Girls" contains a photo of Mama with her two sisters. And on top of an armoire is a collection of snapshots of my brother and me including the only cameo Mama has of me in my bassinette. In the midst of these little gems is a plaque of baby shoes that reads. "The journey of a thousand miles begins with one step." Yes, that's life.

Two tiny, dainty frames sit side by side on another shelf. "Princess" is engraved on the top of one of these and it holds a photo of my mama as a young lady. Papaw called her princess and she's never forgotten. Because home, family and memories are not just words etched on the frames holding these photos; they are the essence of what Mama holds closest to her heart.

The den, where family time is unified and abundant, is a great place to begin this tour. And one would expect the presence of a china cabinet to exist for the sole purpose of displaying fine china. But not in a den and not by my mama. She found that it had a more meaningful calling.

Keepsakes from Mama and Daddy's silver and golden anniversaries in 1984 and 2009 respectively live inside this cabinet. One of those keepsakes is a poem Daddy wrote for Mama for their 50th which is displayed in a stylishly appropriate frame. "It's hard to believe but yet it's true, these fifty years I've spent with you . . ." You can't help but smile.

On both sides of the brick fireplace are shelves built by Daddy many years ago. I'm guessing he knew that someday, those shelves would be filled with memories, and of course they are.

On one of these shelves sits a piece of wood. The wood itself has no significance except for who gave it to them and the message written on it. During Papaw Brown's later years, he started nailing photos and other various things to the walls of his home. He also liked to label them in his own special way.

So, on this piece of wood written in black, permanent marker by an unsteady hand reads this message: "Elmer, Jery. I love you. God bless you. J.C.B. 1994." Papaw died alone in his hospital bed in

January of 2000. But not before taking one last Polaroid of his view from that bed.

Sitting unassumingly on the coffee table in the den is a clear glass insulator that once lived on a light pole who knows where. With a love for the nostalgic, Mama purchased this from the famous Godsey's store on Walton's Mountain several years ago. What a story there must be behind that simple piece of glass.

Seashells of different shapes and sizes presented in different ways stream throughout the house commemorating the beauty of the coast and our many memories made from our family trips. A whole clam shell still intact and opened wide sits in one room. Mama, with her beautiful, creative vision, has placed a single pearl inside like a hidden treasure that has been found. It sits delicately on a small piece of driftwood that she rescued during one of our many sea shelling walks on the beach.

That little room just inside the back door of the house was always referred to as a utility room, housing the washer and dryer and other miscellaneous items. It now has a more distinctive title: Mama's scrapbooking room. No one really visits this room except for Mama and the dirty laundry. Yet, its walls and empty spaces are filled with memories just like any other room in the house.

In this small space is where you will also bump into a towering mountain of scrapbooks assembled with great care. Included is one devoted to Mama and Daddy's first fifty years of marriage. I recall attempting to scrapbook once. But after seeing the amazing job Mama did with hers, I was intimidated and gave it up quickly. This was her area of perfection, and rightly so. It's a hobby that is a sentimentalist's calling. She's even managed to display a small photo of herself sporting a scrapbooker's sweatshirt.

And though Mama has never typed (that I know of), perched high on top of a cabinet is a vintage "Remington" typewriter used by my daddy some fifty years ago. I can imagine him sitting at his small, wooden desk in a dimly lit room typing this or that. It's a simple yet sobering reminder of how life used to be. But then again, walking through this home is like stepping back in time. It's a trip more of us should make.

The walls are covered in cross stitch pieces created by Mama's hands; old country homes and poems about family live here.

Cross stitching; wow! I recall how Mama loved to sit and cross stitch for hours. And while the arthritis in her hands makes it difficult for her to engage in that old past time now, it doesn't seem to take away from the joy and pride that came from all of those finished projects. Many of those pieces appear throughout the house even now, each one holding its own special memory. Cross stitches of Bible verses, replicas of family photos and beautiful flowers and nature; and some as simple as Mama's first cross stitch, a 3x3 inch framed message of "Home Sweet Home" which sits in the dining room. Those three words really tell the whole story.

You will also see a couple of pieces crafted by the hands of Mamaw Huff. In 1990, at age 80, she completed a large piece which still hangs on one of the walls in the front bedroom. "But they that wait upon the Lord shall renew their strength . . ."

Aunt Hilda even got in on the act and now has her place in this museum of our family history. "God made us sisters, hearts made us friends." A trio of photos of Mama and her two sisters hangs below this piece. I have always adored their close relationship with one another.

The kitchen has a country diner feel with an old stool from a Burlington Soda shop sitting off to the side. Other trinkets lay around blending in with the decor and taking you back to another time. There's an old wooden sign advertising Royal Crown Cola on the counter leaning against the wall. And on top of the fridge is a ceramic cake stand and cover decorated with pretty pink flowers that was made by my great aunt, Kathleen, in 1969. Some pieces are just timeless.

Also in the kitchen is a rack of hanging plates from the years of 1954, 1959, 1960 and 1966. Respectively, those plates commemorate the years of Mama and Daddy's first date, the year they were married, the year my brother was born, and the year yours truly made her entrance into this world. But Mama is like that; she will buy a piece of jewelry with colored stones in it as long as they represent special dates such as our births and such. And she will always point them out to me when she wears the piece. Pointing at each stone, "This stone is for . . . ."

In a corner cabinet, built by Daddy of course, is a collection of pottery pieces. Some are gifts from Mama's old friend, Carolyn. Others are little treasures she picked up on our many visits to Oak Island. She only purchases pieces made by local artists. Because going to a small shop on the island and buying a piece of pottery with a label "Made in China" would make no sense at all.

By the front door, there is a small table where two old cameras sit; a Marksman and a Dick Tracy, both belonging to my daddy and used back in the day. Who knows just how old they are or what memories they captured.

Probably one of the pieces with the most tragic history hangs on the wall by the staircase. My great grandpa Winters hand carved a set of embracing hands into wood. It used to hang in his son's room. But the young man fell victim to a horrible accident.

One night while smoking a cigarette in bed, he fell asleep. His body was found by the door where his attempt to reach for the handle to escape the flames had failed. Sadly, he perished but the wooden piece emerged with obvious scars. The fingers of this beautiful carving were blackened by the heat of the fire. And though it was a grizzly reminder of what took place, Mama wanted to leave it as is because it was part of our family's history.

Nearby is a photo of Papaw Huff on his riding lawn mower and one of Mamaw Huff surrounded by all of her beautiful flowers that she loved so much. In each frame, Mama has punctuated the memory by including a sample of each of their favorite flowers, mums. Once vibrant and full of life, the blooms are now dried and faded. But it's important to understand that these flowers haven't died; they just took on a different meaning once pressed under the glass.

Easily the most impressive and by far the most beautiful room in the house would be Mama's pink room (formerly known as our living room). Aside from the vintage pink theme throughout this space, what really stands out are the memories carefully placed within.

Visually, this room could easily pass as one of America's most charming bed and breakfast finds. But for its level of history, a red velvet rope protecting its greatest treasures would be most appropriate. Even the bed has special meaning. Mama explained how she slept in this bed as a young lady in her childhood home, so many years ago.

And decorating that well preserved bed is a delicate pink bedspread. At the foot of the bed lies a quilt that was cross stitched by Mamaw Huff, Mama's mom. Folded up neatly, it has a note pinned underneath one of its corners which reads: "Mama made this and gave it to me in 1990."

Lying casually on a cabinet is a small book from my brother's childhood. Its title is "What would you do with Charlie?" My brother is 52 now. I remember looking at this book when I was a kid. Most would have thrown it away or put it in a yard sale so many years ago. But Mama is endearingly different from most.

In the corner sits a grandfather clock built by Papaw Huff in the sixties. It was his first of many crafted by his own hands. In other rooms of the house you will see a mantle clock and a corner clock as well. He loved his wood working. And with all the clocks in the house, including the grandfather clock built by my daddy also in the sixties, you might think time had some kind of hold over us. Touché.

On a small table next to Mama's Victorian style chair is a glass coaster. It has a photo inside of my brother and me. I'm barely a few months old wearing nothing but a diaper and a confused look. Jeff, who is six years older, is sitting on the steps next to my carrier, by force I'm sure, with a similar look on his face.

Yet another china cabinet holds no china, but rather two of Uncle Gene's treasured collectible model cars along with some other items. He passed away in 2011. But his memory is always close by. His wife, Aunt Brenda, gave Mama and her two sisters one of his old shoes for Christmas in 2011. It sits by a piece of furniture in Mama's pink room. Sentimentality does run in our family.

Next to Mama's small but adequate TV lies a book that I gave her as a gift in 1987 entitled "Mother, I love you forever." Lying on top of it is a smaller book that I gave to Daddy in 2005. It's title is "World's Best Daddy." The sentiment hasn't changed.

On that same TV stand hiding behind a recent purchase from TJ Maxx (an oversized vintage alarm clock) sits our only failed beach trip craft project. Despite it's shocking appearance, it holds a photo documenting the craft tragedy in progress; and then, as if to dull the visual impact, Mama has a strand of pearls emerging from the top and oozing over the side, as if it too, is trying to escape.

In the far corner is a stand that seamstresses, back in the day, would use to display a dress. No dress hangs here, but rather a scarf that is held together by a couple of Mamaw's old cameo pins. On top of this piece is an old hat that she wore as a young lady. Bringing the memory together is an old pearl necklace of Mamaw's lying around the "neck" resting peacefully on the scarf.

On a wall between two lace adorned windows hangs a shadow box carefully preserving Papaw Huff's coat that he wore when he was a baby a few years after the turn of the 20th century. There are more, you know; more shadow boxes with memories you can touch. One holds Mamaw Huff's old beige Sunday gloves along with a photo. That photo was made by Mama one week before Mamaw's passing. And still another shadow box holds dearly my daddy's old tin plate that he ate out of as a little one. Details such as these don't seem like much until you have them right before your eyes.

Mama may not be a little girl anymore, but she has never outgrown her dolls. Throughout the house you will see a slew of porcelain dolls with the sweetest faces. In the pink room, sitting in a small chair under a window rests a doll given to Mama by Mamaw several years before she passed away. And under Mama's year round Christmas tree drenched in Victorian pink ornaments lies a beautiful doll made by Aunt Katie in 1993.

Close by, held in a doll's hand, is a pillow hand made by Aunt Hilda and given to Mama for Christmas in 2009. The pillow was made out of material that belonged to Mamaw. Aunt Hilda called this a "memory pillow" and had stitched a flap on the outside that acted as an envelope and held a special message. The card inside that make-shift envelope was not signed by Hilda; but rather it read, "Love from Heaven, Mom." Did I mention that sentimentality in its purest form runs in my family?

There is so much more to see here! A well preserved kitchen chair that belonged to my great grandma and grandpa Proctor, who died when I was a toddler, sits in the hallway. Gently hugging that chair is Mamaw Huff's sewing basket. Inside is her last cross stitch, unfinished and just how she left it. It would have read, "Home, Sweet Home." Extra thread and scissors are nestled inside along with a note written in pencil by Mama: "Mom gave to me in 1996. Don't know when she started the cross stitch. But I will leave it the way she gave it to me." Are you smiling yet?

There are a few more items such as a bench built by the pastor who married my mama and daddy over fifty years ago; a desk crafted by my very own daddy when he was in high school; and a vintage

"Singer" sewing machine that Daddy bought for Mama when we lived in Greensboro. He paid $10 for it. The price alone tells you how old that piece of history is.

Without a doubt, one of the most remarkable memories Mama has on display here survived the Civil War. It is a Bible that belonged to her great, great grandfather, Shadric Bell. The cover is extremely fragile and the pages very worn and yellowed but well read. It touches my heart to see proof in front of me that God has been a part of my family for generations.

So what if I told you there is a forty year old sandwich bag also on display in this museum? Don't worry; you won't find my first sandwich that I took to school held captive here. What you will see is something far more precious and significant. At least it is to me.

On a scrap piece of paper, written by Mama in pencil is the caption "3-8-72, 6 years old." Secured by a green rubber band are a gazillion strands of my hair. My first haircut is more than a memory; it's right in front of me, even after forty years. And had it not been for my mama, that wouldn't be the case.

You see, God gives all of us special gifts. Mama's museum is truly a testament to that fact. The amount of history living within those walls and how it's displayed is timeless and precious. And while I can express a memory with words, I don't possess a fraction of the sentimentality that radiates from my mama. She has a unique ability to exhibit this special trait in ways that touch the heart while allowing you to lay your hands on the memory. To me, no one does it better.

The other day, Mama told me she had moved that "wad" of hair of mine to a new location. Hey, I said she was uber sentimental, not eloquent of speech. But that's okay. Sometimes words just aren't needed.

Feathers

Their flight swirls against the sky like streamers catching the air currents, poetic yet purposeful. Formally known as "Gulls" but lovingly referred to as "seagulls", I call them my friends. And for a reason that I have yet to discover, I feel a connection to them. Anytime I hear their piercing laugh or witness their graceful travel, I long to join them in their life on the beach.

Visually, they are distinctively simple dressed in gray or white. Their bleached color palette seems custom made for the weathered colors of the coast.

I once heard someone describe seagulls as "rats with wings" because of their scavenger nature. I feel this is a harsh description of one of God's coastal creations who's movement over the land and water is as necessary as the ocean itself. Like any other form of wildlife, they must hunt for food. A seagull is simply a survivor. Still, they tend to be highly social; social with seagulls while guarded around humans.

Whether I am sitting in the midst of a flock of them or underneath the shade of their wings as they fly over me on a sunny day, I am drawn to their presence.

I love to snatch a few slices of bread, grab my camera and secure a spot by water's edge, waiting patiently for the first seagull to find me. They will, you know. First one and then a few more. Before I know it, I am surrounded by these beautiful feathers.

They see me as a chance for a morsel of food, a snack. But what they don't realize is that I am just trying to immerse myself in their charm. Some are more trusting than others, making it easy to pick my favorite for this huddle. As I look around though, I notice one or two who just aren't quite quick enough to grab a bite, so I make a special effort to toss them an extra morsel or two.

I snap photos unconsciously, trying to capture all the life and beauty that is fluttering about me and unaware of my obsession. But the last crumb of bread has been tossed and they wait a bit longer, hoping for more edible treasures.

These seagulls are not as patient as I am. One by one, and sometimes all at once, they begin a new search for their next meal and fly away from me. I sigh and stand again, brushing the sand from my body.

As I retreat from my sandy haven and head back towards the house, I look over my shoulder one last time to see these beauties going about their business. Some have found a new human on the beach who is happy to share their food. Others are just standing there, as they often do. What are they thinking about when they just stand there looking out to the ocean for what seems like hours? I shake my head at the random thought and continue on my way.

But a single white feather lying on the sand catches my eye. I smile. Maybe they've got me figured out after all.

Musica Intrumentalis

Growing up, only three genres of music existed in our home: Christian, country and light or "elevator music." I'd like to think the latter was a distant precursor to modern day "Musak".

But despite my limited exposure to the outside musical world as a kid, my melodic maturity would find me eventually. Though I'm happy that it did, I can't help but be thankful for the journey leading me there. I feel like I've lived during the most eclectic era of music evolution. Some, I'm sure, would disagree. But humor me for a few moments while I reminisce and hum some history . . .

We all know what music *is*, technically; but what it *is* to each of us is sure to vary. To some, music is a beautiful vessel for praise and worship while it exists as a release for angst and hurt for others. Music can be a tender lullaby or a sentimental love song; sometimes it's that silly commercial jingle that you can't get out of your head and at other times, it's a treasured bookmark taking you back to a specific time in your life.

It's allure can be its unique lyrics penned by a true songwriter, the beautiful voice of the one delivering the melody or the amazing talent of the musician behind the instruments. Sometimes it's all three. It can tell a story, soothe you or inspire you. And the list most certainly goes on. Most often overlooked is that sometimes, music just needs to be fun, free of an agenda. Clearly, music is a chameleon. And with such potential for influence, there's no mistaking its subtle power.

But let's toss aside the hypothetical magnifying glass for a bit and have a little fun. While I have a respect and appreciation for many genres of music as well as the time they defined, I will always have a soft spot in my boom box for the eighties. Sugary sweet pop princesses and perfectly choreographed boy bands with rich harmonies and wholesome good looks were the lighter side to what saturated the air waves at the time: hair bands! Big sound, big hair and monster ballads.

With my musical maturity came a need to have a variety of genres in my ears, a sound for all seasons, if you will.

Christian music has been intertwined with my life for as long as I can remember. And I still enjoy my Southern Gospel music. It keeps me grounded and focused on what's most important in this life. What I feel inside my heart and soul when I listen to Southern gospel or contemporary Christian music is sincere and genuine and is not capable of arising out of any other genre of music. Christian music will always be part of my life.

My digital jukebox includes a variety of songs from many decades as well as other genres. And I have totally embraced instrumental tunes as well. Regardless of what it's called or when it emerged, if it sounds good in my ears, it works for me.

During my lifetime, trends in music have come and gone and some have even come back again. The whole cyclical nature no doubt due in part to the visual element added with the inception of the television plus our need to revisit a good thing. And believe it or not, there was life before MTV and American Idol. And it was called *The Lawrence Welk Show, American Bandstand, Hee Haw, Soul Train and Friday Night Videos.*

Before iTunes and file sharing removed the tactile element from music, there were 8-track tapes, cassettes and the classic album. As foreign as those components may seem to today's youth, they were an integral part in the evolution of music. Whereas music seems to live in the ether these days, there was a time when it was much more tangible—and fun. Interesting though when new music is released, it's still referred to as an "album." Point made.

Everyone knows there is a dark side to the music business—if you're focus is on the artist rather than the music. But occasionally, there is a feel-good success story worth mentioning.

Take Chris Daughtry, for instance. In 2005, he was employed by Crown Honda of Greensboro, N.C. By 2006, he was the fourth place finisher on season five of *American Idol* and on his way to an impressive career fronting his own very successful band, Daughtry.

And then there are some success stories that are a little less conventional. Journey, one of the greatest stadium bands of the '80s, discovered their newest lead singer via YouTube. And, they found him all the way in the Philippines. Talk about an overnight success story!

Another successful group back in the day, Def Leppard, faced a unique challenge as their drummer was in a horrific auto accident. While he survived the crash, the doctors were not able to save his badly mangled left arm. With a passion for his craft and for the music, he manufactured a way to continue to play drums with that one remaining arm. That was in 1984. He was and still is the only drummer that band has ever had.

Though I didn't join the concert circuit until my early twenties, I believe I've seen my share of live shows. And I will never forget my first. A girlfriend and I went to Raleigh to see Richard Marx, a classic eighties artist. He had the hair, the good looks and a voice that could make a girl melt. His sound was light and unique yet rich. He was a gifted songwriter who penned such memorable hits as "Endless Summer Nights" and "I'll Be Waiting"—classic chick songs. But there is one song in particular that will always cause a smile to light up my face.

A few years ago, some twenty years after his run on the top of the charts, I came across one of his videos on You Tube as I was researching ideas for a media project. About ten seconds into the video "Hold Onto the Nights", I unexpectedly saw a familiar face: mine! Yep, without knowing it, I made my video debut at the tender age of twenty-one.

I remember the show clearly. The first few familiar chords of the song began as Richard and his piano, along with a cloud of smoke, appeared from below the stage. I was impressed with the entrance and I'm sure my eyes were as wide as they could get. Dave Koz was his saxophonist at the time and Jon Walmsley, aka Jason from *The Waltons*, was in his band as well. I still have the program book from that show.

Through the years I've seen some amazing shows and made some special memories as well. There was a a period of time almost nine years ago where I got engrossed in one particular artist from Raleigh who jump started his career from a little show called *American Idol*.

Now, you have to understand; as a teenager, I didn't experience some of the silliness that most girls did in those days. I didn't buy up all the teen magazines and have posters splattered all over my wall; I didn't go "ga-ga" over teen heartthrobs and gush about them with a group of girlfriends. Yes, I'd have to say that I finally made up for that omission. Better late than never, right?

For about three and a half years I went to a ridiculous amount of concerts all over the country. When I would arrive at each show, I was guaranteed to run into at least twenty gals I had met from shows in other states. We would hug and babble at a high pitch like we had known each other forever. It was like a weird reunion of some sort. I say weird because some of the ladies I still keep in touch with from that, um, era-well, we speak of that time in our lives as a "secret society." Yes, the sheer volume and magnitude of those events would render you speechless for a few seconds, wondering if we had truly lost our minds.

We planned and hosted pre-concert parties that sometimes had over 600 guests in attendance from all over the country and usually a few from beyond. We threw CD release parties that lasted until midnight and was known to sleep outside overnight for book signings and parades.

The ticket frenzy that ensued courtesy of Ticketmaster on the morning of concert tickets going on sale was not for the faint of heart. I have many memories of sitting at my computer with a girlfriend at hubby's computer in the other room as we yelled back and forth to each other, "How about this seat? No, we can do better-keep searching."

And it was not uncommon to have a friend on speaker phone on my cell as we frantically searched for the best seat in the house, which usually eluded us and went to someone with more money in their pockets and less brains in their heads. But I digress.

Meeting ladies from other countries like New Zealand and China was way cool; travelling all over the country just to see a show was exciting; the anticipation of a show, the chatter on the message boards and the ridiculous amount of photos and videos to enjoy after the event had come and gone was a treat. And most of all, the concert itself never disappointed. You see, it's all about the music. And despite the accessibility of a CD or the production going into a CD to give it the most perfect sound, live music matters. Because the energy it generates cannot be duplicated in a studio.

But I would have to say the most treasured part of that craziness, um, "Secret Society" for me was the new friendships I made. The girls even threw me my first surprise birthday party when I turned thirty eight. Aside from nearly giving me a heart attack as they screamed "surprise" as I walked into my friend's home, they short sheeted the bed I slept in that night and thought that sprinkling a ton of birthday confetti between those sheets added a nice touch.

It's funny; I was in that very same home recently with a few of those ladies for a bridal shower and I must say a smile crept on our faces as we reminisced about "those" days. Facebook has kept me in touch with several of these ladies. And I have one special friend who I get together with a few times a year and whom I talk to frequently.

You see, music brings people together.

Like I said before, music is a chameleon. It's diverse and it's multi-faceted. Music most definitely softens the rough edges of life while enhancing the high points. Would a dramatic scene in a movie be the same without a musical score behind it? Would a tender moment on your favorite TV show touch your heart the same without sweet sounds in the background? Would you still laugh out loud during a comedy if there were no quirky, lighthearted tunes accompanying the visual? What would everyday life be without music? I hope we never find out.

From singing in the shower or in your car to singing for millions, every artist and musician on every level has their own story behind the music. But whether their career is never realized or simply local, is one of worldwide longevity or they've been crowned a "one hit wonder, the star of the show will always be the music they've made.

Touched

The silence was broken by the ringing of my office phone. On the other end of the line I found a familiar voice.

It was Doug. He was about seven years my senior and I had known him for many years. We went to the same Christian school and attended the same church. He had even been my youth pastor at Andrews Memorial for a time. But now, he was a potential client.

Doug had suffered through and survived colon cancer, but now found himself facing cancer yet again. He had been diagnosed with a tumor on his sacrum. Apparently cells not killed by the treatment received during his first bout with cancer had remained behind with an agenda.

Now, he was reaching out to me for help.

He was in a tremendous amount of pain due to the tumor pressing on the nerves in his spine. And I could hear it in his voice. He was hurting. He was hoping that I could help. At the time, I was a newly licensed massage and bodywork therapist. I have no idea if he had ever received a massage before that day; had he chosen me or had God led him to me?

I hung up the phone and awaited his arrival. My career was in its infancy and I was a bit unsure of what I was about to do. This was not only someone suffering active cancer, but someone I knew; someone I respected and thought a lot of. But somehow I knew that seeing Doug and offering him some relief for his pain was what I needed to do no matter what.

I'll never forget his arrival to my office. I opened the door to find that he could barely stand, using the doorframe to support his weakened body. Doug had always been athletic. He was an incredible soccer player during high school and was otherwise strong, lean and healthy. The cancer was challenging his body. But he wasn't giving in.

I helped him into the treatment room and still to this day, remember him literally crawling onto the massage table. It broke my heart.

I can't say that I was prepared for this at all. My training had taught me that massage, as good a tool as it was for relieving suffering, still had to be administered with extreme care and caution when dealing with someone diagnosed with cancer.

Doug knew me. And I know he trusted me. Better yet, I know the godly man he was and his complete trust was in the Lord. I believe that made all the difference-for both of us.

In this room he was able to relax while I gently applied the lightest touch, the lightest pressure to his legs. If you've ever experienced back pain, you know the toll it can take on your legs as they try to support a body whose center of gravity has been compromised in the worst way.

The session wasn't long, but it was long enough. When he emerged from the treatment room and ready to leave, I was amazed how he was now standing completely upright and with a fresh, almost pain free look on his face.

He thanked me and left my office. That was the only time I was privileged enough to work with him. His health deteriorated and eventually, the cancer won this battle. But cancer did not win the war.

Before Doug passed away, I felt moved to ask to visit him at his home. And he agreed. I can't say why I felt compelled to visit him in the last months of his earthly journey. But I followed my heart. I bought some therapeutic pillows I had come across because I knew how much pain he was in. I knew these pillows might help to take the edge off. As always, he was grateful.

Like my visit with my high school teacher, Mr. B. who was battling cancer, I remember only one statement that Doug made during this visit. Doug was a Christian and he loved the Lord. But he was also human. He loved his wife and boys and he wasn't ready to leave them behind. His honesty in sharing this with me amidst such a difficult time in his life stuck with me.

So what, might you ask, is the point of me sharing this story with you? I can't say that I really know. Of my eight years as a massage therapist, that one appointment with Doug was clearly the highlight. To help someone on that level in a most painful and challenging time in their life was worth everything that went into becoming a therapist in the first place. And though this moment came very early in my career, it was never topped. And I can live with that.

As for my brief visit with Doug before he lost his battle with cancer, I can't explain it. This is a story where the plot isn't revealed and there really isn't a conclusion. It's up to the reader to pull some meaning from it.

He was so young and had so much potential ahead of him. With two young boys and a wife he had loved since high school, Doug was 42 years old when he went to be with the Lord. Why would God take away such a godly man who lived his life for the Lord first and for his family second?

For me, the answer to that wondering came during the funeral. I looked around at the masses of friends and family that had come to pay their respects. There were so many tears and so much hurt. This is what I saw on the surface. And I realized that sometimes the Lord can accomplish more for His glory in the death of one so dedicated than He can in the life of one that's not.

For a brief time, I was in a profession where I could use the power of touch to help heal and to comfort. But through this brief yet poignant experience with Doug, I also realized that the power of touch was a stronger gift when administered and felt by the heart and soul.

The Traveler

I was eleven when we took our first family vacation. At least, it was the first one that I recall. When I asked Daddy how we came to start planning these trips, I believe his words were "We decided we wanted to go, so we went." Well, you can't argue with that logic, now can you?

Back in those days, vacations consisted of a lot of Holiday Inns, McDonalds and Stuckey's. A family of four could eat at "Mickey Dee's" for under $8 and that same family could rest their heads on a nice fluffy pillow for about $50 a night. There was no internet, no digital cameras, and the speed limit was a pokey 55mph, at best. Cell phones with an app for everything didn't exist and our GPS was a folding map that begged lots of strategic planning.

Lacking a lot of today's modern conveniences, we toured this beautiful land of ours from sea to shining sea in station wagons and vans of the not so mini persuasion. And still, we had fun doing it . . . as a family.

Our quest to see the country started in 1977 with our first road trip taking us up north to the New England states. Mamaw Huff actually was up for the adventure and joined us on this maiden voyage. With only a week to work with, we still managed to hit twelve states along the way. Now, it is my belief that at the time, someone forgot to put Rhode Island on those maps because somehow we missed that little track of land. Despite that omission, the trip was a success and we were ready for more! A tradition was born.

That tradition would continue for eight more years with the end of an era screeching to a halt in 1985. As out of the blue as those trips began, they disappeared with the sunset. I got married that year and didn't share in the last family excursion. Looking back now, I should have skipped the marriage and gone on vacation with my family instead. The memories would certainly have been sweeter. Go west, young Sonja.

After a couple of years of squeezing in so much sightseeing and mileage into one week, we extended our summer road trips to three weeks and headed west each time, never venturing north again.

Over the years in a period of a few short months, collectively, we had visited 46 of the 48 continental states (multiple times), save Michigan and that darned Rhode Island.

Of the 58 National Parks, we visited at least sixteen that I can recall, and probably drove through even more that I don't have record of, including state parks. Of the 155 national forests, we might have ventured through a third of them. We travelled tens of thousands of miles by vehicle, never once using flight as our mode of transportation. We wanted to see it all up close and personal.

And that we did!

When you try to recollect events from your life that happened so long ago, it can be a bit humorous what actually comes to mind first.

In 1981, we were zipping through the Midwest when Mama inadvertently swallowed a piece of hard candy prompting a quick stop on the side of the road by a panicked Daddy. His version of the Heimlich maneuver was ineffective. However, my mama's decision to consume multiple cans of soda with blinding speed seemed to do the trick. My brother even noted the time of this emergency stop in his vacation log: "11:44a.m. on Wednesday, July 8, 1981. The incident took about 12 minutes." Now, what relevance that event had to the course of history, I do not know. Yet, it is documented forever.

I, too, had my brush with death in an event involving hard candy; it was butterscotch, I believe. However, my episode didn't warrant an impromptu Heimlich by any family member nor did it even rate an emergency stop or log in the vacation annals. When exclaiming that I was choking, my cry for help was met by a response from my dear mother that I will never forget: "If you were choking, you wouldn't be able to talk." And that was that. Needless to say, the candy eventually dislodged and I lived to tell about it.

During those years of travel, there were two rituals that were sure to take place. First, Mama would always take a snapshot of any and every sign marking our passage through a state or park; and second, Daddy and my brother would succeed to take their many photos of the beautiful scenery only after rolling all over the ground and contorting into any twister position to do so. Because there was depth and foreground to consider, blah, blah, blah. Meanwhile, Mama and I would execute our right to "point and shoot" and get the same photo taken before the moment was gone. Even now, we still laugh about these things. They were certainly part of the charm of our travels.

More charm from our travels came from our contact with wildlife. And I'm talking REAL wildlife. During our first visit to Arizona, we decided to hike down to Indian Gardens, about 4.5 miles below the rim of the Grand Canyon. The steep and winding trajectory lent to an amusing descent. As my speed would pickup, I would find myself strategically dodging mule poop and giggling with every hop, skip and jump.

There was one memorable point where the path had somewhat leveled off and we were approached by a mule train. Those who were more adventurous than us (or lazy, depending on how you looked at it) opted for a mule ride down into the canyon rather than the more challenging obstacle course that we had set out on via foot. We had been instructed to be very quiet as the mules with their precious cargo passed, as to not spook them into a fatal plunge down the side of the canyon.

I found this especially challenging as one flatulent mule melodically passed his gas with each step on the gravelly path. I did my best to restrain the giggles but I knew I had been found out when the tour guide nonchalantly stated, "I see you laughing."

One year while scooting through the wide open spaces in Wyoming, our progress was interrupted by a herd of cattle that had decided to do a little jaywalking. I'm not talking one or two future burgers; we humans were definitely in the minority, but ultimately not in any danger. As a young teenager I found this temporary obstruction totally cool. How many folks from suburban North Carolina find themselves trapped in their middle class Chevrolet station wagon sitting in the middle of a cattle drive in Wyoming? "Don't mind us," I imagined they would have said could they talk, "we'll be out of your way shortly. Much obliged."

The first and last days of these longer trips were always the most challenging and the dullest. They usually consisted of twelve to fourteen hours on the road. While Daddy drove and my brother navigated (and logged every detail in a notebook), Mama and I had our own stringent ritual to carry out in the back of the van: eat, sleep and rest stops.

Beyond the humorous yet totally necessary aspects of these travels was the reason for hitting the road in the first place: witnessing first hand God's incredible handiwork. And there was much to take in . . .

The Great American Road Trip (Brown Style)

ROCKY MOUNTAIN HIGH

I have often said that if I ever had to live in a state not bordering the ocean, I would choose Colorado. For me, it's aura is unsurpassed. So spacious and so untouched in many ways. Several of my fondest memories from our trips out west took place in this beautiful state.

The Flying W Ranch is an actual working mountain cattle ranch located in the foothills of Colorado Springs, Colorado. Each time we visited we enjoyed a Chuckwagon Supper followed by a great western show.

The meal was typical of what might have been served to the cowboys back in the day. The friendly staff rounded up a chuck wagon steak, baked potato, apple sauce, a roll, lemonade or coffee and spice cake. All of this was served in tin plates and tin cups to 1400 hungry guests in the span of half an hour. Impressive, delicious and always a highlight of our trips.

Close by was the Garden of the Gods, a park with over 1300 acres of unique red sandstone rock formations and numerous well maintained trails for exploration on foot. We even found a few unmaintained trails of our own.

In contrast, we couldn't miss a visit to Mesa Verde National Park. Mesa Verde is Spanish for "green table." And it certainly was! But nestled deep within were over 600 cliff dwellings and over 4000 known archaeological sites now protected by the park.

I vividly remember our trek to the Cliff Palace, one of the better known cliff dwellings, which required us to climb a 32-foot ladder (not your Lowes Home Improvement variety) in order to reach our destination. My brother and I might have found this to be exciting at the time but I'm not so sure my mama felt the same enthusiasm. Nevertheless, not wanting to be left behind, she somehow mustered up the courage to overcome the challenge and climb her Everest.

I can still remember my descent into one of the basement areas of the ruins, known as a "kiva", looking up at the small amount of light making its way into this hole that people once called home. At that moment, I was integrated with history I couldn't even fathom.

While in Colorado we also visited the United States Air Force Academy which was an attractive piece of architecture and definitely evoked a sense of pride since my daddy had once served in the Air Force.

THE GRAND STAIRCASE

No, I'm not referring to the staircase on the Titanic, but rather more than six thousand vertical feet of alternating cliffs, slopes and terraces of sedimentary rock layers stretching from the North Rim of the Grand Canyon to southern Utah, including Bryce Canyon and Zion Canyon. This is where "grand" was born, in my opinion, as it preserves more Earth history than any other place on earth.

We were fortunate enough to visit the Grand Canyon more than once, taking in the ambiance of the North Rim on one trip and the massive art canvas that is the South Rim on another. Both rims may be part of the Grand Canyon, but they are polar opposites in most ways.

The South Rim probably receives 90% of the parks visitors and is more accessible from larger cities in Arizona making it easier to enjoy as a day trip. It has all of the amenities you could hope for such as lodging, dining, groceries and souvenir shopping. It has the most views of the canyon but also the larger crowds of tourists. You have to make your own peace and quiet here.

In contrast, the North Rim takes a lot more effort to reach and the views are fewer as well as the amenities and the crowds. If it's tranquility you're in search of, you will probably find it here.

For myself, as a teenager at the time, I wasn't in search of much. But what I found at each rim, as different as they were, was the same: awesome beauty.

I recall the North Rim making me feel a bit smothered in terms of the absence of space and vastness around me which easily defined the South Rim. It was a less developed area at the time and so your exploring options were limited. However, Bright Angel Point was easily the most memorable highlight of our visit to the rim less travelled.

We took an evening tour to Bright Angel Point, a mere four tenths of a mile to its lookout. We were given specific instructions by the tour guide which included holding hands like a line of kindergartners, if you will. I distinctly remember the howl coming from the depths of the canyon. The sound was full yet hollow and very haunting. And the moonlight provided very little spotlight for the experience. The next day proved why that was a good thing.

Visiting this same path in the daylight was a very different story as the path projected you out into the belly of the canyon with little room for missteps on either side of you. Seeing in the day what I only heard at night literally took my breath away.

The South Rim was a totally different experience. Much more developed and much more crowded, I often felt like I had been set down in the middle of another country as the languages that could be heard were anything but English. But beauty is the same in any language and I didn't mind sharing it with others who felt the same. The views at the South Rim were positively stunning. The sheer vastness of the canyon, the amazing colors that changed with the position of the sun, the intricacies of what I was in front of—I was in awe. You cannot stand in front of this spectacle and not know in your heart and soul that God is responsible. You just can't.

But there were other canyons to lose yourself in. Bryce and Zion, both in Utah, were spectacular in a very different way. My experience with Zion was more like window shopping, but what I saw from the dusty windows of our van made an impression. And Bryce is not really a canyon as much as it is an amphitheatre of sandstone with hundreds of pink and orange pinnacles, or "hoodoos", shooting upwards in an amazing display of detail and rugged originality. I easily remember our moderate hike to the bottom of Bryce Canyon. This particular trail curved in such a way that, from a distance, the streams of people walking back and forth in their descent resembled an army of ants, focused on their destination with every twist and turn.

Once to the bottom, I didn't feel dwarfed or intimidated at all by the walls that towered over me. Rather, I felt protected and cradled. It really is a shame that this work of natural art receives far fewer visitors than nearby Zion or Grand Canyon, largely due to its remote location. But in my opinion, totally worth the trip off the beaten dirt path.

SUPERVOLCANO

If you have ever visited Yellowstone National Park, you fumble around for a place to start when describing it to others. Let me start by saying that I can't believe my own daddy sat us on top of this massive caldera for a little family R&R. He admits that he sort of knew that Yellowstone was sitting in the middle of this large crater (atop a volcano, mind you) but he also admits he really didn't know enough about it to understand what this meant. Let's just say that knowing what I know now about the geothermal wonderland that is Yellowstone, I'm just glad I got that visit in when I did. As they say, ignorance is bliss.

Bliss is also the incredible experience of visiting Yellowstone National Park. Our stay came prior to the fires of the late eighties that reportedly changed the surrounding landscape quite a bit. Old Faithful was without a doubt the star of the show. I remember seeing an eruption schedule posted at the visitor center at the park and wondering how that was even possible to predict. Folks would sit on the benches that lined the safe outer limits of the geyser and the rest of us would stand by eagerly anticipating show time which came several times a day and on time.

And with a park spanning over 2,000,000 acres that contained over 10,000 thermal features and more than 300 geysers; over 290 waterfalls, over 1,100 species of native plants, more than 200 species of exotic plants and over 400 species of thermophiles; 7 species of ungulates (bison, moose, elk, pronghorn), 2 species of bear and 67 other mammals; 322 species of birds, 16 species of fish and of course the gray wolf—well, there was just plenty to see.

There's no way a photo can replicate what you're seeing and provide you with a "wish you were here" postcard experience. You can't hear the hissing of the steam all around you in a photo. And a photo can't capture the perpetual bubbly pulses that makes this unusual place a living, breathing, formidable threat to our planet. Even a video can't do justice to this place. To respect all that it is, one must take the risk to simply be there in person taking in the rich colors, the constant movement, the sounds of nature in constant transformation and the unusual smells of such a natural wonder.

I was a young girl when I last unknowingly toured that super volcano so many years ago. Would I ever go back as an adult so I could appreciate the experience more and on a different level, while taking my digital camera and hi-def video camera along for the ride? Maybe I watch a little too much Discovery Channel because I honestly don't know . . .

THE BEST OF THE REST

It's hard to highlight eight years of trips that covered thousands of miles and enough McDonald's French fries that could probably wrap around the world a few times. We saw some amazing sites along the way.

And I would be remiss if I didn't share a few more places with you that would certainly be worth your time should you decide to take your own great American road trip and see how the west was fun!

Anyone who knows me knows how much I love the coast! Well, an important element of the coast is sand. I love it's texture, I love the feel of it; something about those tiny grains of wonder just puts me at peace. So you can imagine how a visit to White Sands, New Mexico might send me over the edge.

I have never seen so much brilliant, sugary white sand in my entire life. This natural wonder is abundant in wave-like dunes of cool, gypsum sand that have engulfed 275 square miles of desert. The photo ops are like no other!

But if a lot of sand doesn't put a twinkle in your eye, how about a gigantic hole in the ground? Then you might want to swing by (near) Winslow, Arizona to catch a gander at the best preserved meteorite impact site on earth. Apparently, a wayward piece of asteroid crash landed a really long time ago at a cruising speed of 26,000 miles per hour creating quite the dent in mother earth. It's pretty impressive and definitely not something you see every day.

If rugged yet majestic mountains, pristine lakes, lush meadows and a healthy splash of extraordinary wildlife are more your speed, you cannot miss visiting the Grand Teton National Park in Wyoming or Glacier National Park in Montana. Here you will find rich history, miles of trails, wilderness and solitude . . . and more photo ops than you could ever hope for.

Our trip to Jackson Hole, a very popular destination within the Tetons in Wyoming, was at least thirty years ago. I may not be able to write pages about my experiences there, but I know in my heart and deep in my soul it was an incredible place to be. That memory alone speaks volumes.

And the list goes on . . .

SECOND CHANCES

As a teenager, I hadn't matured nearly enough to value the time spent with my family while on these trips nor had I matured enough to appreciate what I was seeing and experiencing. That's just part of life, I suppose.

When I sat down to organize my thoughts for this story, I found that the logical place to begin would be to sift through old vacation logs. I know, who does that? Fortunately for me, we did back then and I'm thankful that my brother preserved these logs all these years.

Going through them, it was almost as if I were there again, but without the visual. And since scenery was a big part of the story, I turned to the one medium that didn't exist when we began this journey: the Internet. And I have done quite a bit of surfing to enhance these memories that have collected a bit of dust over the years.

And as I have awakened these memories from decades of sleep and bound them between the covers of my life, I find that I cling to them now with a special urgency.

Of course we took some photos, and they are stored...somewhere. The greatest volume of our snapshots are actually on slides which have not been opened or viewed for far too many years. With the writing of this story, a lot is about to change.

Again, with modern technology making it possible, I will be transforming all of those forgotten slides into digital images that I can put together to tell this story all over again. And we will make new memories as we sit down as a family to relive the experience with a new appreciation.

As good as all this sounds to me, I am still dreaming of a bit more. I want a second chance to experience these amazing places for the first time again. Inside, I'm still that awkward teenager who giggled at the flatulent mule in the Grand Canyon; but even deeper inside, I know that I am finally at a place in my life now where I can truly appreciate what's in front of me. My eyes may not be so perfect anymore. But I don't have to put on my glasses to see with fresh eyes; it takes vision. I have that now, and a digital camera.

Now as my daddy would say, "Let's head 'em up and move 'em out."

Family Ties

I would be remiss if I did not share a few words about my family. I'm talking about my extended family—grandparents, cousins, aunts, uncles. A way of life that I have been accustomed to since birth, I am learning, is unfamiliar to so many people these days. And there are various reasons why this is so.

Neither one of my parents (or their brothers and sisters, for that matter) ventured too far from home once they became adults. I know that these days, with so many young people heading off to college, there is distance between them and their family that sometimes is never recovered.

But back in "those days", that wasn't the norm for country folk growing up in the foothills of North Carolina. And for those who did make it to college, like my daddy, most came back "home." There's no doubt a college education is important. But to me, a close knit family is of more long term value.

There are also many broken homes these days. And whatever the circumstances may be behind these situations, often the result is family ties coming terribly undone.

In the case of my husband, who faced a bit of culture shock when he married into my family, family traditions were a bit foreign to him. His dad was in the military which forced them to be constantly uprooted and on the move; and his mom was from Canada which presented a different challenge. These facts of life created a near impossibility for family functions to be a part of his life.

I am blessed with solid family structure on both my mama and daddy's side of the family. And though we are not perfect by any means, over the years we have maintained a core stability that has become a dying breed in today's world.

Growing up, it was pretty much standard that we would hit the road each Saturday heading to the hills to either Mamaw and Papaw Brown's or Mamaw and Papaw Huff's. Some Saturdays, I would see all of my aunts and uncles and cousins on one side of the family, and on others I would see a few. Either way, they all were a part of my life, for which I am thankful.

As I grew into an adult and was finding my own life, I would miss a family function here and there. And there are some days now when I think back on those times wishing I had made different choices. But by God's grace, you live and learn.

One by one, as my grandparents passed away, each of our families—The Brown's and The Huff's—found ourselves at a crossroads. Would we still have family get-togethers or would we become one of the statistics of traditional families who have faded into a thing of the past?

With a bit of alteration, we still have our Christmas gatherings each year. And though we don't hit the road each Saturday headed to my grandparents to spend the day with family, each side of the family has formed new traditions of summertime cookouts and fall "stews".

Last weekend, we headed to Statesville to Lakewood Park to enjoy an afternoon of good food and fellowship, a new summer tradition for the Huff family. And just last night, we enjoyed the 17th annual Memorial Day Cookout for the Brown family at Uncle Wayne's home in Greensboro. The Lord blessed us with beautiful weather so we could be outside and enjoy hotdogs, yummy desserts and plenty of entertainment like nail biting games of horseshoes.

To some, these events may sound less than exciting and a bit hum-drum. To this kid who has been surrounded by family events all her life, it's magic. Though I have lost the physical presence of all four of my grandparents, I am still blessed to see and spend time with my cousins, aunts and uncles on a regular basis.

I know without a doubt how blessed I am. And though as a young lady in her twenties I occasionally took all of this for granted, I have learned as still a young lady in her forties that family ties as rich as ours is rare and a true treasure.

And as I sat in a lawn chair last night watching the flurry of activity around me, hearing those familiar voices, and seeing little cousins who now had children of their own, I couldn't help but smile.

In a New York Minute

"Today is the day I have my first Anatomy and Physiology test and it's going to be a tough one. I think I can get in a little more studying at work in between patients or while on the phone with insurance companies. Gosh, I'm tired of studying. I just need some rest."

These were the thoughts that were occupying my mind as I made my way to work on Tuesday morning, September 11, 2001. I had already devoured my coffee so I settled in at my desk ready to tackle the annoying pile of paperwork that lay before me.

I work at a physical therapy clinic. Shannon, one of my co-workers, had been in the back where the patients are treated. Sometime after 8:30 a.m. she hurried up the hall saying, "You missed it. A plane just flew into the World Trade Center."

Not knowing at the time that this was a deliberate crash, I unsuspectingly replied, "Ooh, let me go see." I was not prepared for what I was about to witness. I was familiar with the New York skyline via pictures, but had never really given much attention to the World Trade Center. I barely recall the first bombing there in 1993.

My first contact of the tragedy was seeing repeatedly the second plane spearing World Trade Center #2. I was confused about what was going on. Shaken employees and patients alike who had been watching the broadcast from the beginning were talking unbelievingly of a terrorist attack. "A terrorist attack in New York? Hijackers? I don't understand what has just happened," I thought.

Being at work, I couldn't plant myself in front of the television the way I normally would in a situation such as this. So I dazedly walked back to my desk. I was of no use. My concentration was gone, so I hurried back to the TV. Shaking my head in disbelief, I called my mama and husband to inform them of the events. They too, responded in shock and confusion.

Feelings that I had never experienced before imprisoned my body as reports of an attack on the Pentagon came across the CNN broadcast. My body, heart and soul felt paralyzed at that very moment. *Red Dawn, Executive Decision, and Independence Day,* all very well known terrorist-type movies, prophetically flashed through my mind. How ironic and disturbing, I thought. Life was now imitating art.

I believe the first of surreal of moments, with plenty to follow in the days ahead, came as I sat in front of the television along with a room full of motionless co-workers and patients. Together we had witnessed the World Trade Center #1 crumbling to the ground.

Appropriately, I was kneeling on the floor as I watched in horror. Not only was a magnificent American structure plummeting to the ground like it was made of sticks, but it was also innocently taking with it the lives and dreams of thousands of people in a cloud of hellish smoke and fire. I cried quietly. The loss of life and the thought of what the people in the ill-fated buildings and planes had to endure in the final moments of their lives was more than I could comprehend.

I replay these sights and sounds in my mind, amidst the constant coverage of the terrorist attack that I refuse to be separated from. September 11, 2001, is a tragic yet defining and pivotal moment in American history and in my life. I can't put into words how it has changed me; I only know that it has.

Forever Buddy

Lightning in a bottle. That is how I would describe Buddy.

Buddy was our precious little boy kitty that we adopted in the attempt to fill a void left by Cougar, our first boy, who we had to put down. If you're a pet owner, you will know what I mean when I say this: when you lose a pet, you are not just losing an animal; you're losing a family member. And you just can't replace them because you loved them for all the things that made them unique and who they were as an individual. Cougar was my first indoor pet and at times, my best friend. You never forget that. But in my loss, I just knew I wanted another cat and I was determined he would be a black, male cat just like Cougar. In my mind, I thought an "identical" visual replacement might ease the pain.

With the unexpected addition of two new kittens instead of one, the bonding process was in full swing in our home. And actually, having two siblings was a bit endearing. At three months old they were inseparable. And I found it quite easy to carry them both around at the same time, one in each arm. Let's face it; I was eating it up. Not a "real" mom myself, this was the closest I would ever be and it felt good. Life in the DeChene home was entertaining, to say the least, though I'm pretty sure Rumi was not laughing.

Physically, it was fairly easy to tell the two little fur balls apart. Sage (formerly known as Kiwi) was the "runt" of the two. She had a stubbier tail and shorter legs. Her fur was a bit fuzzier, more disheveled and the hair on her ears came to a cute, little point. She was black with a couple of white markings that seemed to be random; and there was a little bit of brown fur mixed in with the black around her nose and mouth, almost as if she had gotten into some chocolate and was still innocently wearing the evidence.

Buddy, on the other hand, strutted an obvious difference visually. Even at a young age, he was noticeably larger than Sage. His build was sturdy and lean. His fur was a beautiful, shiny black with brown strands mixed throughout. I often compared him to the build and looks of a thoroughbred horse. He was just stunning.

Unlike Sage, he had long, strong legs and a strikingly long tale. At six months old, he was a very lean nine pounds. I often thought he would grow up to be a giant cat . . . and I was eagerly looking forward to observing the transformation. He also always had this look on his face of total surprise and anticipation. Just as Cougar had earned the nickname "Buddy", Buddy had lovingly earned the nickname "Bug-eyed Buddy."

As I said, he was lightning in a bottle. He was quick. He was strong. He was ambitious. And he was the boy I had hoped for. He would stand at my feet looking up at me; and all I had to do was clap my two hands together as an invitation and he would stand on his hind legs and reach for me with his front two paws. It was more than adorable. I would pick him up and bring him to me as you would a baby. And with his hind legs dangling, he held on to me tightly with his front legs. He was definitely a mama's boy.

It was a Sunday morning. And like always, once we woke up, we would call to the "kids". But something was wrong. Buddy was not moving like lightning, but more like a bulb flickering its last bits of light. He appeared at our door and it was as if someone had stolen the life out of him. It didn't take us long to realize Buddy had a problem. He seemed to be struggling to breathe. His posture was slouched like an old man bent over by age, yet he was less than a year old.

After a bit of observation, we decided we needed to take him to the Alamance Animal Emergency Hospital. Thinking it was something routine that the vet could fix, I decided I would take Buddy to the vet myself. As Buddy lay in the back seat struggling to breathe, I nervously waved to my husband at the door as we pulled away. There were no goodbyes; only, "be back soon."

After a wait that seemed to last forever while filling out forms for assistance to cover the medicals costs, a diagnosis was finally given. Buddy had a diaphragmatic hernia. And whether it was congenital or acquired, we didn't know. As active as Buddy was, we had never witnessed him having any sort of trauma to his body. When we went to bed Saturday night, he was Buddy. When we got up Sunday morning, he was anything but. All I knew was that he was hurting, and I wanted him to feel better again so I could take him back home where he belonged. Surgery was our only option.

The vet had stabilized Buddy and I wanted to see him. I walked in only to see his long, lean frame stretched out on a cold table with tape wrapped around his mid-section. This tape was acting as support for his stomach and diaphragm, which also helped him to breathe without as much struggle. He also had a breathing mask near his face to supply additional oxygen.

I couldn't believe what I was seeing. My little Buddy, so strong and indestructible was lying helpless on this table and the light in his usually bugged-eyes was dim and hopeless. I stroked him gently and talked to him, with little reaction in his eyes. He was scared and he was hurting; of that I was sure. And seeing this hurt me. The vet told me they would stabilize him and prep him for surgery to correct the hernia. There was nothing more I could do here, so I kissed his little head and walked out the door.

Not knowing how long a wait there might be, I was encouraged to head home for the evening. Once home, I rejoined hubby along with Sage and Rumi. We sat down in front of the television to eat some fast food I had picked up on the way home. We might have been a few bites into the meal when the phone rang. It was Dr. Beagle.

As I stood at the kitchen listening to her words on the other end of the phone, you could have knocked me over with a single breath. My exclamation of an incredulous "No!" prompted David to approach me with concern smothering his face. Dead. Buddy is dead. We were not prepared to hear this. This couldn't be happening. But it was. And I was powerless to make the reality anything else.

Before they could get him stabilized, Buddy had gone into cardiac arrest and they lost him. We . . . had lost him. We had lost another treasure within the span of a year. And this hurt as much but different. It was a promising life cut too short. Some would say, he was just a cat. To us, he was more. And now, there was a void in our home, once again.

David and I drove to the animal hospital. There were decisions to be made. And though we had already spent money that we didn't have on Buddy's medical bills, David was adamant about Buddy's resting place. We would have him cremated and bring him home with us, just like we had done for Cougar. We wanted our family to stay together. But before we left the hospital that evening, I wanted to go in to see Buddy. David couldn't do it. And I respected his decision. But I had to see my little boy one last time.

And there he lay, still and lifeless. So much love and potential stifled way too soon. What could I do but tell him I loved him, stroke his beautiful fur one last time, and kiss him goodbye.

God saw fit to create animals of all kinds. I believe they all have a purpose in life. If you've never had a pet in your home, you will never understand the bond that exists between a human and their animal of choice. For David and me, it went far beyond a "pet". And to lose what we considered to be a member of the family was just painful. It hurt. And it still hurts now knowing all the wonderful years we missed out on because of his untimely death.

But even in his few short months with us, he touched us more than you could have imagined. He truly softened the transition of life without Cougar. He made us smile, he made us laugh and there was no doubt that he loved us.

You might say that it's an endless cycle if you try to replace one pet with another, and so on. It could be. But what I learned from this is that you can't fill the void of someone lost with anything but the good memories made while that someone was with you. There was only one Cougar; there was only one Buddy.

But can a cat rescued from the side of a road really have an effect on a person after just a few short months? When I called the vet in Mebane that we adopted Buddy and Sage from and told them of his death, the sobs by the tech on the other end of the phone told me all I needed to know.

The Almost Tornado

It was the summer of 1998 and I had already moved into what would soon be "our" apartment upon the conclusion of our October nuptials. It was a new structure; three stories high perched on a hill directly behind the Wal-Mart in Burlington. David and his computer (his second love) were back at his parent's house in Graham, a mere 15 minutes away.

The skies were starting to look a little threatening. But that was nothing new; it was a summer evening in North Carolina. Dark clouds and a distant rumble are pretty standard stuff.

I remember sitting on my bed, watching TV as nightfall had set in. The picture on the television had started getting a little disrupted by static. Occasional popping noises from the TV distracted me enough to get up and walk to the window to take a peek outside. It was too dark at this point to see very much in the way of clouds, but the howling and effects of the increasing winds caused me a bit of concern.

As I turned away from the window and back towards the TV to check the weather reports, the faint solid white line near the bottom of the screen flipped a panic switch inside of me. I had heard about this, but never witnessed it . . . until now. Saw it in a movie once. I have no idea whether this was an actual, fact based tornado prediction or not. What I do know is that it was real enough to me that the pit of my stomach felt as if a bomb had just went off.

From that point on, things started happening quickly. The rain began, the winds picked up and I had a bad feeling about everything that was going on around me. And that feeling was not just because I was alone, but also because I really felt it deep in my soul. With a strong sense of urgency, I called my then fiancé and told him about the decline in the weather conditions and begged him to join me at the apartment . . . . and soon! He knew I was afraid of storms, especially at night, but I don't think either one of us expected what actually came.

Within minutes, I was pacing that apartment from room to room. It wasn't long before looking out the window was not even an option. The rain sounded like a gang of people had aimed their garden hoses directly at my window. The wind howled, whistled and had a deep roar to it that I had never heard before.

My heart sank.

This was it. A tornado was coming. What other answer could there be for what I was experiencing? The windows were rattling and the building was vibrating from the force of the chaotic gusts outside. Inside, I was fumbling around for a plan. I didn't have one. Where was David and what was taking him so long?

Cougar, my beloved cat, was there with me but he was not capable of giving me adequate comfort. And for the next few minutes, I even forgot to protect him. I couldn't even tell you where he was. All I know is, I had never been that scared before and I knew it was justified fear.

Unfortunately, I didn't handle the situation well at all. The conditions outside were so ominous and I knew I had to take cover. I was convinced that at any moment, the monster that was raging outside would soon invade my home.

My best judgment led me to the small space off of the kitchen where Cougar's food and water bowl lived. Oh yes, and the water heater. A water heater! This was an explosion waiting for the right conditions. And I'm pretty sure low barometric pressure and a direct hit from a tornado could have done it. What was I thinking? Let's be honest, I wasn't. And during my irrational response to my situation, I tried to hide under a rug that measured two feet by three feet. Cougar couldn't even have fit safely under that pathetic excuse for a safe haven, much less me. What happened to getting in the tub and covering my head with blankets and pillows? I couldn't tell you.

What I can tell you is that I have never felt fear like that before. It was a feeling of impending doom and I felt helpless and void of brains. As I lay crumbled up in that room I do remember wondering what it was going to be like when the tornado tore off the roof to my home and I was at its mercy.

The transition to safety was a blur. It would seem that the storm's apparent sudden departure and David's long awaited knock at the door were simultaneous. I felt so much at that moment; relief that he was there, shock at what had just almost happened and guilt; guilt because I let down Cougar, the littlest member of my family, when he needed me most.

And just like that, conditions had improved enough that folks were starting to emerge to survey the damage. I later heard stories of neighbors taking cover at the edge of the hill that our apartment complex sat on top of. I also learned that what we experienced was not a tornado but rather a straight-line wind. But trust me; it didn't feel anything of the sort.

While the brunt of the storm was fast and furious, it felt more like time had stood still. I can't help but think about those who have actually survived a real tornado and I can't even begin to understand how they got through it. I would like to think that if I ever faced a real tornado that I would make more sensible decisions and handle myself better than I did that evening. Let's just say, I sure hope I never have to find out.

Comforting Breezes

A hot bath first thing in the morning when my eyes are still half closed; it's like a warm blanket that's waterproof.

A Saturday afternoon matinee of a much anticipated movie is only complete with overpriced popcorn, candy and a soda. Just sit back and get lost in the cinematic journey. It's as if time has stood still until you walk outside after it's over. I feel like I have been gone for so long. It's good to get lost sometimes.

Sitting on the deck at my in-laws home surrounded by nature's beauty and soothing sounds on a summer evening. We enjoy a delicious meal from the grill and plenty of laughs and great conversation about life and such. But the best part is just being together as family. These moments are precious.

Don't ya just love to be sitting back flipping channels on your TV only to come across one of your favorite movies? It's like an unexpected surprise. I get giddy. That is, until your husband reminds you that you have that movie on Blu-ray and can watch it anytime. Clearly, he has missed the point.

To walk outside during an evening snowfall is to know what peace and quiet truly sounds like.

The entrancing rhythm of a light rain intertwined with a harmless rumble of distant thunder. A comfy chair on a covered porch loves days like this.

Sunrise

I'm on vacation and there is no alarm clock, yet I awake. Habit, I guess. Is there a way I can turn off my internal alarm clock? Maybe I could hit the temporary snooze button, if just for a few days.

The bed is warm and I'm wrapped up in my own little cocoon. My head plops to the left to see the love of my life peacefully soaring through dreamland. The room is less than pitch black and the breeze from the ceiling fan tickles my face like a feather. I smile a lazy smile knowing God has seen fit to grace with me with another day. I can hear the mesmerizing rhythm of the tide tapping the shore and it coerces my eyelids into meeting once again. Wake up, sleepy head or you'll miss one of the most amazing spectacles of God's creation. I promise, it will be worth the sacrifice.

Reluctantly, I arise from my nest and wipe the good night's sleep from my eyes. With a small bit of natural light to guide me, I fumble around the room quietly, trying to unearth some clothes to put on. Peeking through the blinds on my window, I see the destination that awaits me.

I open the door and as the sea air greets me, I inhale and step my feet onto the damp, wooden deck. The random grains of sand on the timber planks stimulate my feet and it seems as if they wake up before I do. As a yawn of epic proportions escapes my sleepy self, I continue down the boardwalk that leads me to my sandy paradise. It's as if I am being pulled by an invisible force.

My feet hit the silky, cool sand and a smile that comes from deep within takes control. With camera in hand and my eyes fixed on the eastern skies, I walk clumsily across the sand, finding the best seat in the house. I look around to see who is joining me for this event. Down the beach, to the west, I observe an early risin' fisherman grounded and ready for a big catch. A lone seagull, my favorite inhabitant of the beach, gracefully skims the shoreline searching for breakfast. I follow his flight which leads me back to the east.

As I sit with quiet anticipation, I am suddenly aware of all my senses, each one being caressed unapologetically by the vast appeal of the edge of creation; the aroma of the sea air, the entrancing hum of the crashing waves, the coolness of the elements brushing across my skin from head to toe . . . so much stimulation that I need a moment to process it all; a few moments of reflection; silent lucidity.

As the first burst of color appears on the horizon, I'm brought back to the present, to the moment of why I am sitting in the sand at 7 o'clock in the morning. Every morning brings a blank canvas, waiting for the rising sun to paint a new work of art; the yellows, the reds, the blues . . . each color vibrant and rich.

As the sun continues its morning ritual, there's a metamorphosis taking place before my very eyes. And I am entranced. For those few moments, it's as if time stands still and I am in peaceful solitude. No worries, no thoughts; nothing to do but breathe and take it in. And then, as if God has snapped His fingers in front of my face, I am aware that my camera, still in my grasp, is with me for a reason. I begin snapping photographs, a memento of this occasion.

After what seems like hours has passed, the beach is suddenly alive with the voices of families and beachcombers. Life goes on.

If you allow yourself to look beyond what your eyes see and invite your heart and soul to join you, you are suddenly overcome by the awesome power and majesty of our Lord. He didn't just play the role of builder when He created our earthly home. He also perfected the responsibility of landscaper and artist as well. He orchestrated visual music that drenches us in beauty every moment of every day and draws us to Him and His priceless work of art—creation. We need only open our eyes. A sunrise is our first glimpse of the day and of His glory and a reminder that God has blessed us with a new day. To sleep through it every single day of your life is to miss a golden opportunity.

My life may be filled with routine that prevents me from taking advantage of this gift. But if at no other time than my moments spent by the sea each year, I'm aware of the unfolding tapestry that is a sunrise.

160

God, America and Me

Seven years ago, in 2004, I made a trip up to Washington, D.C. with a few friends to attend the Capitol Fourth Celebration. While our sole purpose of the trip was to see a favorite artist of ours perform on this nationally televised event, I came away with memories that far exceeded my expectations.

This trip was full of a lot of firsts for me. It was really my first visit to D.C. with any amount of sightseeing involved. And I had never witnessed a homeless person balled up on the side of the street before. While I was a bit unnerved by the site, I was also sympathetic and wondered what had happened in this person's life to bring him to this point. I caught a glimpse of one of these folks using the side mirror of my vehicle one morning to groom their hair. Maybe they hadn't lost everything . . .

I also experienced my first adventure on a subway, the Metro. While it was a bit exciting at first, that feeling quickly disappeared as I soon felt more like a sardine in an over packed can than a passenger. I didn't like it and I wanted off. But luckily I had a friend close by who was as uncomfortable as I was. And when I caught her eye, we couldn't help but laugh as we noticed that her head was directly under the armpit of another rider holding on for dear life. For that reason, I think it would be safe to say my friend wanted off that subway more than I did.

Just three years post 9/11, the security for this event and the rehearsal the day before, was sobering. There were policemen everywhere paired with impressive motorcycles. These guys were huge. Not your typical mall cop variety with an empty holster. And as intimidating as they appeared, they still managed to be pleasant to the masses of people in town for the celebration. Their presence reminded me of the times we were living in now. I wasn't in my small, seemingly safe hometown anymore. I was in our nation's capitol, a city that terrorists had violated not so long ago. But somehow, I still felt safe.

The show itself, televised live on PBS, was a treat. The weather, however, left a lot to be desired. But the storms were just another ingredient in this unsuspecting learning lesson that the weekend turned out to be. The weather broke in time for the show and the magnificent fireworks display and as I sat wringing out my socks for the umpteenth time, I recall pausing to turn around to look behind me almost in disbelief. I was sitting on the steps of our capitol building. Though I was hundreds of feet away from the artist I had travelled to see, I knew without a doubt, that I had the best seat in the house; or rather, on the West Lawn.

As much fun as I was having with my friends, the highlight of the trip for me was yet to come.

The next day, after we had dried out and rested up, we were ready to hit the streets again with some sightseeing before heading back home. The Washington Monument was tall, the Reflecting Pool was pristine, and I expected the Lincoln Memorial to be nothing more than a big stone reproduction of our 16th president and a great photo op.

But as I walked up the steps of that memorial and drew closer to the white Georgia marble replica of a man I had only read about in a history book, something unexpected happened. It was as if history had come alive before my very eyes. It was real. What I had been taught, what I had read about all those years ago, what I had only seen in pictures—it existed. And there I stood, dwarfed by its overwhelming presence. I was overcome with emotion. And that caught me by surprise. As a kid, I had never been a fan of history. But as an adult, life deals you a reality check and you are abruptly reminded of important treasures you have innocently taken for granted as a child and even young adult. As the tears welled up in my eyes, I was suddenly more than aware of so many things.

As our tour progressed, we found ourselves at Arlington National Cemetery. The site of white tombstones in formation as far as the eye could see was both breathtaking and alarming. But you had to see below the surface to "get it". And I did. Those tombstones represented brave men and women who served our country, fought for our freedom and for me. And though I thought there were far too many of those memorials before me, I was both humbled and grateful.

And to the citizen who ignorantly displays the anti-war bumper stickers on their car, I challenge you to visit this place, read the *real* history books (not *Revisionist History)* and understand that freedom was not obtained by a chat over afternoon coffee. I encourage you to read the U.S. Constitution, the Bill of Rights, and the Declaration of Independence. Reacquaint yourself with the original America because the America we live in today is both altered and tainted.

Countless men and women have chosen to serve our country and fight for our freedom, a fight that always comes at a high price. Some have paid the ultimate price, losing their life so that our country could continue to be free. And though most who serve have come home alive, they still have given their life for our country. A veteran should be revered as a national treasure, treated with respect. A veteran, though human and capable of making mistakes, should never be homeless in a country they vowed to serve and protect.

Once again, I would find my emotions being stirred as we came across the Tomb of the Unknown Soldier just minutes before the changing of the guard. We had no idea about our timing, but I believe that was because it was God's timing. He wasn't through with my history lesson just yet.

I don't believe I have ever witnessed anything so undeniably powerful or inspiring in my entire life. Even now as I try to share the experience with you, I struggle to find the words. The Tomb of the Unknowns has been perpetually guarded since July 2, 1937 by the U.S. Army. Perpetually! That means continuously, unending, uninterrupted, and permanent.

As I watched the ceremony unfold before me, I was touched and speechless. The tears revisited and I was again reminded of just what it means to be an American: honor, commitment, and pride. I know the values that America was founded on and *that* origin is what I am proudest of. I still believe in those values and what our founding fathers intended this country to be, to stand for. Those principles will always represent the American I want to be and the America I know our country can be again.

That weekend in Washington was a pivotal trip for me. And it wasn't until I sat down to write this book seven years later that I allowed myself proper reflection to know just why. Again, it's all about God's timing, not mine. And I believe that trip to Washington was just a part of a series of events and epiphanies coming together to give me a better understanding of the bond between God, America and me.

I believe I grew up in days much safer, more wholesome and happier than we're living in now. For that, I am so thankful. And it's easy for me to become nostalgic when I think about the America that used to be. For kids and adults alike, the past offers a glimpse into an America that was truly good.

Growing up, my family didn't have cable TV and on a good night we could get four stations instead of three. That was a treat. There were full service gas stations which meant the attendant would pump the gas for you as well as clean your windshield (for free). Going out to dinner with my parents meant McDonalds and we were excited about it. There were no safety caps on consumer items because no one had yet tried to poison a perfect stranger. Kids were safe at school and folks were safe in their own homes. Principals at school still had the authority to paddle children. And as a matter of fact, so did parents.

Summers included a week at my grandparent's farm with my brother where we rode tractors, rode our bikes and played outside with the animals until dark. We didn't have iPads, but rather, an imagination instead. A family could survive on one income assuring that children weren't left home alone after school. The only cigarettes you had to worry about a kid consuming were the candy kind. We listened to albums at home rather than owning our own MP3 players. We had curfews that didn't involve a call or text from mom or dad on our cell phone. Heck, there were no cell phones. We knew the rules and that was it.

Sunday was for going to church; not for waiting for 1pm to arrive so you could buy alcohol or mow your lawn because you were too lazy or too busy to do it on Saturday. You could see the American flag flying proudly in every neighborhood. Folks still placed their hand over their heart when the National Anthem played and "In God We Trust" meant so much more than a debate about a phrase on our money.

People respected God, our Flag and each other. Patriotism, Christianity, morals and morale were pillars of our society then versus the endangered species they all seem to be today.

I am a Bible-believing, born-again Christian. I am an American. I am a conservative. I am far from perfect and truly a work in progress. I don't understand everything going on around me, but I have beliefs and opinions which I stand firmly by. And contrary to the misconception of others, that does not classify me as close minded.

I believe our inalienable rights come from God, not from government. But I also believe we should pray for our leaders, whether we voted them in or not. And I believe our founding fathers had a vision for this country that included God as the foundation. For many years, He was. And I believe that is why our country quickly evolved into a great country, sought after by many.

It has been both alleged and disputed that Alexis de Tocqueville, a Frenchman who came to America in 1879 to observe our country, made this statement upon conclusion of his findings: "I sought for the greatness and genius of America in her commodious harbors and her ample rivers—and it was not there . . . in her fertile fields and boundless forests and it was not there . . . in her rich mines and her vast world commerce—and it was not there . . . in her democratic Congress and her matchless Constitution—and it was not there. Not until I went into the churches of America and heard her pulpits flame with righteousness did I understand the secret of her genius and power. America is great because she is good, and if America ever ceases to be good, she will cease to be great."

To me, the mouth that these words came from does not mean as much as the meaning of this statement. And as my pastor said in the pulpit not so long ago "The truth is the truth no matter how we *feel* about it."

And the truth comes from the Bible. Psalm 11:3 says "If the foundations be destroyed, what can the righteous do?" America used to be called "The Melting Pot." There were people from everywhere all around the world, who had different cultures and different customs. But when they came to America, they blended in, as one nation. And as I was researching the origin of this phrase, I came across what I thought to be a more accurate description.

We (the U.S.) are now more akin to a "Salad Bowl." A melting pot implies that those coming here not only adopt our way of living but contribute to our society as well, and become as one, sort of like fondue. But in a salad bowl, even though the ingredients are contained in one place, you can still look at each piece and distinguish it from another. Each has its own flavor and texture and composition. There is very little about it that is unified.

Translated, folks are coming from all over and bringing their cultures with them and trying to live them out here. You've heard of "China Town" right? That's just one example. Moving to this country does not mean forgetting where you came from or not being proud or familiar with your own native culture. It means blending in and adopting *this* culture. It means learning our language, not expecting our citizens to learn yours. Making America your new home means to love this country, to support its Constitution, to obey its laws, to respect its flag, and to defend it against **all** enemies. It means becoming a legal citizen. It does not mean getting what you can from this land without reciprocation.

I believe Kennedy said it best in his presidential inaugural speech in 1961, "And so, my fellow Americans: ask not what your country can do for you—ask what you can do for your country. My fellow citizens of the world: ask not what America will do for you, but what together we can do for the freedom of man."

At the end of the day, you made the choice to leave your country and to make your home here. And due to loose borders, politics and "political correctness", a term I have grown to loathe, America, I'm afraid, has developed an identity crisis.

I, for one, enjoy meeting folks from different countries and cultures. I enjoy having them here and learning from them. I believe everyone has the right to enjoy freedom and pursue happiness in this life. But I also believe that with that pursuit and the decisions you make in that journey comes responsibility and accountability. This not only applies to those seeking out a home in our great country, but to those blessed enough to be born here. "But to whom much is given, much is to be required."

Psalm 33:12 says "Blessed is the nation whose God is the Lord." "God bless America" seems to be a recurring phrase that we have heard from various presidents and elected officials over the years.

It's almost an unofficial motto for our country. And as good as those words sound, people need to wake up and realize that God *has* blessed America, for a very long time.

But how can you expect God to continue to bless our country when we continue to evict him from our country and stray so far from the foundations this nation thrived on in the beginning? We have taken prayer out of our schools, we've legalized murder (abortion) and we are gradually chipping away at the traditional family structure by endorsing gay marriage. And these are just a few examples.

There is simply so much wrong with our society that you can't help but wonder what's left that is good. Proverbs 14:34 says "Righteousness exalteth a nation; but sin is a reproach to any people." God has blessed America, but God cannot bless sin, He can only judge it! It's all pretty simple really. You take God out of our homes, our schools, our society, and you are left with nothing.

But I believe there is hope. You see, I am also an optimist. The Bible says in II Chronicles 7:14 "If my people who are called by My name will humble themselves and pray and seek My face and turn from their wicked ways, then I will hear from heaven, and will forgive their sins and heal their land."

It starts with me. And it starts with you. And as Christians, it's our responsibility to go out and preach the gospel; to live by example. It's time that we live on our knees, not in submission or defeat but in prayer grounded by faith. And while I am an optimist, I'm also well aware of where we are really headed. Because the Bible tells us so. But it is possible to keep it real while keeping it positive. After all, as Christians, I believe we have the most to live for.

I can only speak for myself. I love my Lord. And I love my country. I love America for what it is at the core and not what it has become. It is being a child of God and my faith in God that allow me to preserve these feelings. It is because of God that this country was a chosen nation. And it is because of God that I was blessed to be born here. How dare I ever take those blessings for granted!

You know, I don't often speak out loud about politics. But I'm making an exception to give you the full story here. So with a little bit of frivolity and stepping off the path for the moment, I can share that if it were possible, my political dream team would be Ronald Reagan and Sarah Palin. I smile to think how good it would be to live in that reality.

But, it is what it is. And in my childlike reflection, I still see my country as a Mayberry sort of place; safe, simple, respected and God-fearing with lots of promise. And I am thankful to have grown up and lived in that America, if only for a time.

The Mailbox

Every once in a while, something unassuming comes along, gets your attention and places an unexpected smile on your heart.

In May of 2011, my husband and I took a much deserved long weekend to Ocean Isle Beach, NC. On a whim, we decided to make our first visit to Sunset Beach which was only three miles away. Stopping at every surf shop and gift store as is customary for me while at any beach, I kept seeing books and memorabilia about an old, weathered mailbox nestled in the dunes on Sunset Beach. And it wasn't just any mailbox; this one had a name: "Kindred Spirit."

The name alone peaked my curiosity and with a gentle nudge that came from within, I asked the attendant at the store to tell me about this mailbox. And he did. I left wanting to know more of the story so once back in our hotel room, I came across a single video on YouTube that a gentleman had posted after his visit to this mailbox. The music serenaded the images he captured and I knew that I wanted to visit this post office by the sea someday soon.

Soon came in September, 2011, while on our family vacation to Oak Island. And I was beyond excited about discovering the best kept secret on Sunset Beach for myself.

But getting there would be half the fun. David and I had recently purchased bicycles with the intent of someday being able to do a lot of riding on the beach. Giving up our mountain bikes and pavement for whimsical beach cruisers and sand was an easy choice.

I'll admit that I had envisioned this adventure including a beautiful sunny morning with a vibrant blue sky and the cheery sounds of seagulls welcoming me to my destination. But sometimes those visions don't make it past your imagination. The reality, at least on this day, was simply muted and overcast.

But I wasn't going to let that detail dull my excitement. So we unloaded the bikes, grabbed our cameras and followed the long boardwalk to the last beach access on Sunset. We had initially planned on walking but after David injured his knee on the first night of our vacation, he decided the only way he could make this journey was via the bicycle. And to be honest, it was a blessing in disguise. I was so excited to see others on the beach with their bikes! And quickly realized, yet again, how there is a silver lining to even the smallest of gray clouds, if you open your eyes and allow yourself to see it.

The ride on the beach was ultra smooth, pleasant and simply refreshing. As we made our way towards our destination, we weaved in and out around thousands of sand dollar pieces, stopping occasionally to pick up one still intact. The distance to the mailbox was less than two miles, one way, and on our wheels, it seems we were there in no time. As we approached, I could see an American Flag waving proudly in the background and I was giddy with excitement. I knew we were almost there.

I'm sure to any onlookers that happened to be close by, the scene was comical. I sped up to the clearing where the mailbox was, jumped off and parked my cruiser carelessly against the towering dunes. Grabbing my camera, I lunged up the hill that had been carved by Sunset's most recent unwanted visitor, Hurricane Irene. The area really didn't look much like the video I had seen on YouTube. I actually learned later that the mailbox had been moved recently because the hit by the storm exposed its post and it was no longer secure.

You know, looking back, I realize now I did not savor the moment like I should have. But in all fairness to me, I was attacked by an invisible swarm of "no-see-ums". And, I was anxious to capture the image I hoped would be the cover of my book. In no time, I quickly covered all the angles that I wanted while David had retreated back to his bike, closer to the water where those little suckers seemed to be absent from.

At this point, you're probably wondering, "So what is the big deal about this mailbox?" I guess that is something you just have to decide for yourself. Yes, it is a little odd to see a mailbox perched on a dune with no house in site. And though the unsuspecting location is definitely part of its charm, its greatest mystique actually lies within.

Open the door to the mailbox and you will see the heart and soul of the Kindred Spirit—the journals tucked safely and thoughtfully inside.

The story of how the Kindred Spirit mailbox came to be differs depending on who you ask. One thing that most locals agree on, however, is Frank Nesmith's contribution as he helped to plant the first Kindred Spirit mailbox in 1981. And for thirty years, folks have travelled from all over with different agendas to experience this gift by the sea. Photographers and artists have made the journey to capture the essence of this mysterious mailbox while nature lovers and beachcombers have strolled the spacious beach to sit for a spell and get lost in the thoughts penned on the pages of those notebooks.

The pages are filled with stories of new love, lost love, tragedy and triumph . . . so I've heard.

You see, on my first visit, I chose not to open the notebooks and read the very personal thoughts of the many that had passed by. For me, the moment to do so just wasn't meant to be during this visit. And I know I will go back and be ready to absorb the essence of what's really inside of the Kindred Spirit. And who knows; I might even be ready to share a thought or two of my own.

As we were peddling our way back towards reality, I had a chance meeting with an older gentleman who had been visiting Sunset Beach for over 40 years. He told us how Sunset Beach and Bird Island (where the Kindred Spirit resides) used to be separated by Madd Inlet. He went on to reminisce how he would carry his kids on his shoulders to get across to Bird Island and how he had to be very careful because sometimes the current was so strong. I think his eyes actually lit up a bit as he shared the memories with us.

I suppose Mother Nature knew that Kindred Spirit had untapped potential and in 1997, an unnamed storm filled in the inlet making the path to visit this special place a surer and safer journey. For that force of nature, I am thankful.

You see, life is filled with unexpected and unique treasures. I consider Kindred Spirit to be one of those little gems. And as brief and uneventful as my first encounter with the mailbox was, I believe there's something more there for me waiting to be discovered. And I really can't wait until the birth of a new spring paves the way for me, my beach cruiser and a clear mind so I can soak in the experience like the sun that is sure to greet me the next time around.

If you want to see this story come to life, please visit the link below to view the video that I referred to in this story. Maybe someday soon you'll find your barefoot self making the same journey.

http://www.youtube.com/watch?v=B065d4URFfg

Papaw's are People, Too

Up until now, the process of understanding what family means to me has been a subtle one. One of my most recent realizations has been that grandparents are real people, too. Whether you call him grandpa, grandfather, or in my case, Papaw, I'm sure your grandpa is as unique to you as mine is to me.

I remember as a young girl looking up at Papaw's six-foot frame thinking he was the tallest man I had ever seen. His hands were like a giant's and his skin was tough like a worn piece of leather. And when we had a family gathering, which was quite often, he would make his quiet entrance wearing his faded, green shop clothes. He had a very distinctive walk; time and hard work was starting to bend him forward and his knees were starting to wear down. Papaw had been in business for himself for as long as I could remember, operating a tire recapping shop. I remember visiting it only once though.

Unfortunately for me, I don't have a lot of recollections of special moments with Papaw. I'm sure it's not because they didn't exist, but because my memory is selective for a reason. However, I do remember going to see my grandparents every Saturday. And for the greater part of the day, Papaw would be at the shop. Like clockwork though, he would find his way to the head of the table for lunch where Mamaw would have homemade corn bread and hot pinto beans waiting for him. Full, rejuvenated and wearing that very special grin, back to work he would go.

How he loved to work. More than anything, I believe, he loved to work with his hands. When he wasn't at the tire shop, he would be quietly tucked away in his wood shop at home. Through the years, Papaw built all five of his children grandfather clocks, mantle clocks, and other wooden treasures. I remember as I got older hoping he would make something special for me someday.

I guess I would describe Papaw as a proud, hardworking man with a well preserved adoration for his family. He loved us all. He loved us all equally and unconditionally. I smile when I recall that he always adored my long hair. He never wanted to hear that I was going to cut it. I believe it reminded him of the long hair Mamaw once had and oh, how he loved her!

Well, as life goes, I was growing into an adult and suddenly I had a life of my own. The family trips that had been my standard weekend for over 20 years were now lost in my own plans. I started paying more attention to myself and less to my family. I regret that now. It was as if one day I woke up and my grandparents were old. Where had the time gone? What had I done?

Thanksgiving of 2000 found my once larger than life papaw in a wheel chair, hard of hearing and engulfed with arthritic pain. As I sat by his side, watching an old black and white western show, I felt something in my hair and turned to see my papaw's hand grazing my hair and smiling. He always loved my long hair!

As we approached Christmas, I had an overwhelming feeling that one of my grandparents wouldn't be around much longer. Two days after Christmas, Papaw was admitted to the hospital with pneumonia and was released a little over a week later. Just days after that, we received a frantic call from family that he had been rushed to the emergency room and it didn't look good.

I took Mama to the hospital, which was out of town, planning to return home that same day after seeing Papaw. After all, he was going to be okay, right? I would not leave Papaw or the hospital for the next ten days and nights.

Papaw's previously diagnosed pneumonia was overshadowed now by the newly discovered lung disease he had developed due to years of breathing in tire dust and working as a mechanic.

Our family, all 43 of us at the time, was stunned and devastated at the news and the prognosis. We would be losing him soon. "This isn't how it is supposed to be," I thought. "Aren't grandparents supposed to live forever?"

I saw a lot in those ten days and nights that I spent with Papaw in the ICU; from the fear in his eyes when he couldn't breathe to the humor he displayed when he flipped his breathing mask off his face when our backs were turned. And of course, there was the love in his eyes the last time he reached his massive, weathered hand to my cheek and with a twinkle in his baby blue eyes flashed his famous grin. I realized for the first time in my life that he was more than a papaw, but a real person with real emotions and fears and so much more. For that, I loved him even more.

Among all the emotions that beat us all down those ten days, I will never forget the defining moment for me. Standing by his bedside, along with my cousin, Trena, I believe I saw into my papaw's soul.

Eyes open, but staring blankly at nothing, he began reaching for invisible things on the bed. Invisible to us, that is. We were afraid he would uncover himself as he had done before, so we made our hands available for him. I don't know if it was because of all the medication he had endured or if Papaw was revisiting better days, but the most amazing thing started to happen. First, he firmly grasped my hand and began to twist and turn my fingers as if he were shaping them. He would carefully put mine aside and then take Trena's hands and work with them for a bit. At times he would embrace both our hands and try to make them fit together. It was a very meticulous process.

After observing all of this in several minutes of magical silence, we asked Papaw what he was building. His clear, nonchalant reply of "Oh, I'm just messin'," was so sincere and so Papaw. It brought tears and smiles to our child-like faces. I guess you could say my wish that Papaw would make me something someday was coming true.

On his deathbed, Papaw was once again doing what he had done and loved for so many years: building with his hands. More significant than any tangible gift Papaw had ever crafted with his hands, he had built a legacy. This is the special gift he had made for me. He was so much more than just a papaw to a wonderful and loving family who would soon be grieving his loss.

I was with Papaw when he took his last breath, along with my cousin who had shared that defining moment with me. We held his hands and sobbed uncontrollably as he quietly entered into heaven where he'd see Jesus for the first time and once again stand tall and larger than life. As heartbroken as I was to lose him, I felt he gave me the most amazing gift by allowing me to get to know him more as a real person and not just a papaw.

We all say, "If I had it to do all over again . . ." knowing it isn't possible. It is possible, however, to take what is right before you and make something of it. I felt that Papaw's passing allowed me the joy of getting to know him and myself, better than I ever had before.

The Strange in the Familiar: Hi, my name is . . .

Well hello there, my friend! You remember me, don't you? I just feel like lately, you might have forgotten about me. So much is going on in your life right now, I know. But I came a long way to meet you. If you've got a minute, let's get reacquainted, okay?

I've been around for a long, long time. You weren't around when I first came to visit, so I understand how you might not be able to appreciate my journey. Yes, you've read stories about me and there are still more stories that will be written, I'm sure. I do love to travel, so it is hard to say just where I call "home". I guess you could say that home is anywhere that I am welcome.

It's not always been an easy road that I've traveled. When I first got started on my journey, I wasn't sure I would reach my destination. But fortunately, a long time ago, there were those who saw my potential and fought to keep me around. As time passed, there were even more who invited me to visit. But to this day, people still disagree about where I should go next and how I should get there. They even argue about what I should pack in my suitcase. I haven't been everywhere . . . yet. But I'm looking forward to the journey.

You should know that I'm not cheap; I am actually quite pricey. But as they say, you get what you pay for, right? And I admit, I am high maintenance. You just can't invite me to visit and then ignore me. If you want me to hang around, I need to know that you appreciate and respect me. Is that too much to ask?

You know, quite a few people know me and there are still those that are eager to meet me. Am I being arrogant? I don't think so. I just realize my worth and am proud of it.

Yes, I am quite popular, but that hasn't always been the case. Even now, not everyone likes me. I sense there are actually some who may hate me. I don't understand; and I don't think they understand what I am really about. They even hate some of my closest friends because of me! I believe if they would just give me a chance, they would feel differently. Maybe it is just not meant for everyone to welcome me with open arms.

I have to admit that there are even times I feel betrayed by some of those that I thought loved me the most. So many times they just take me for granted. I guess they assume I will always be here no matter what. I suppose they expect it! After all, I have been around a long time. But I need love and respect, too. I have needs! I need to know that I am wanted here.

There are even those I've known along the way who have actually given their life for me! Can you believe that? My fondest memories are of them. They believed in me so much that they were willing to make the ultimate sacrifice to keep me around!

There have even been those who believed in me so much that they wanted to share me with people they didn't even know. But then there are those who stand by apathetically as if their hands were tied behind their backs and refuse to lend a hand to help me out when I need it most. Haven't I taught them anything? That breaks my heart!

I have to be careful about my "fair-weather" friends. I have a lot of those. They think I don't notice, but I do. Some of them forget about me when all that touches their life is going fine, but when the going gets a little rough, they'll hide behind what I stand for as an excuse to stay passive and detached. They think this will keep me around.

There are others who use me to hurt some of my closest friends by spreading rumors and prejudiced information, and the like, via the television and newspapers. I never thought it would come to this.

I don't have an exclusive relationship with just one group of people. I have many friends from all walks of life, and still more friends to meet. Why just today, I met some people that I have wanted to meet for a very long time. And you know, right about now, I'm willing to bet that they know my value more than a lot of you who have known me all your lives. You might know them-they're the Iraqi's.

Remember me now? *My name is freedom.*

Note: This story was written on April 9, 2003, the day that Saddam Hussein's statue, which stood in downtown Baghdad, was brought down by the Iraqi people.

Highlights

Yeah, I'm a girl and I love sports. I'm an easy going spectator and proud to call myself an athlete.

I played sports all through high school. And then played competitive amateur volleyball until my early thirties. To this day, you could pit me against a pre-teen in a friendly game of ping pong at a Christmas party and I would have no mercy on that kid. I guess you could say I'm a bit competitive.

Sports has always been a part of my life. Aside from kick ball in the backyard with my brother, some of my earliest memories of sports came during the seventies while watching Carolina basketball, of course. Dean Smith was coach, Phil Ford was "the" player, and "the Four Corners" defined college hoops back then. No one told me who to pull for. It just came naturally.

But I'm more than Carolina basketball. For as long as I can remember I have enthusiastically enjoyed a Sunday afternoon of nothing but the NFL. As a matter of fact, the Super Bowl and I are the same age. So in addition to enjoying one of sport's greatest events on or about my birthday each year, I am sure to never forget my real age.

As a kid, I remember never hesitating to join in a lame game of football with the family when we would visit my grandparents on Thanksgiving Day. And when the JC Penney's "Wishbook" would come out each year before Christmas, I would flip straight to the sports pages to see what NFL apparel I could find. Of course it was always something in blue and silver to support my Dallas Cowboys. And for a reason that is a mystery to me, I began collecting NFL trading cards. Yes, I had baby dolls and Barbie's, but the cards were pretty cool, too.

And I cannot talk about sports without talking about the Olympics. As early as six years old, I remember names like Mark Spitz and Olga Korbut. In the 1976 Olympics, I recall soaking in the grace of Nadia Comaneci and the speed and endurance of Bruce Jenner.

But the greatest Olympics memory of all just might be the greatest sports moment of all time: The U.S. hockey team (a group of college kids) defeated the Soviet Union (a band of seasoned professionals) during the 1980 Olympics. Through the gift of You Tube, I get to relive that moment. It wasn't just one for the sports pages, but the pages of American History as well. Yes, it was that big.

The goose bumps are quick to return to my body as even they haven't forgotten after all this time. It's been over 30 years since we heard Al Michaels exclaim "Do you believe in miracles . . . YES!!!" And as our team celebrated on the ice, the stunned Russians could do nothing but watch. Wouldn't you just love to know what was going through their minds at that very moment?

The American pride that filled that arena was seismic. What a gift to be an athlete and take your talent global to compete for your country. And what a privilege to witness that miracle on ice. I may have only been fourteen at the time, but I knew the magnitude of that moment.

I have been in the Dean Dome, "Blue Heaven", to experience a sweet Carolina victory. I have sat in a frenzied crowd at an NCAA National Championship; there's a reason why they call it "March Madness." I have survived below freezing temperatures to see Emmitt Smith and the Cowboys play the Redskins at RFK. I have even walked the streets of Atlanta to be a tiny part of the thrill of the 1996 Summer Olympics.

Sitting in the stands or sitting on the sofa glued to your TV; which brand of fan are you?

If live is your vibe, you might indulge in some healthy tailgating, a dab of face painting or ill advised ceremonial dress. The pitch of your scream would surely get lost amongst the wail of the rabid fans surrounding you. Now if the sofa and big screen is your motif, you've got room to move, no bathroom line, endless eats and a man-clap that would do any mama proud. Plus, if the game starts going south, the mute button seems to dull the pain. Trust me, it's a tried and true technique.

Growing up, ABC's Wide World of Sports dominated television sports coverage. Hosted by legendary announcer Jim McKay, who could forget the show's opening spiel: "Spanning the globe to bring you the constant variety of sports; the thrill of victory, the agony of defeat <insert the 1970 infamous grainy footage of the young Yugoslavian skier who tumbled down the slope in a terrible crash just before liftoff> . . . the human drama of athletic competition." That was then . . .

ESPN is now.

And for over 30 years, ESPN has been broadcasting sports 24/7. Who knew? So you can imagine how their sports anytime-all the time approach has stimulated some healthy competition amongst the other networks. Sports shows have even spilled over into other cable giants such as HBO and Showtime with great success. Maybe it's their stellar coverage, flashy intros or vast array of enigmatic announcers. It could be their comical commercials using real athletes and their sense of humor that somehow reminds us to not take it all so serious.

No matter what it is, fans are never at a loss for their latest fix of sports news or highlights. And when I channel flip and can't find anything to watch, I can always rely on ESPN to keep me entertained no matter what.

Now, I may love sports, but I don't believe all sports are created equal. I believe there are athletes and then there are those individuals with particular skills. So you won't ever see me hunkering down for a mind numbing bowling match or a golf game where the announcers are continuously using their inside voices to commentate; nor will you see me sitting in front of my TV watching cars speeding in a circle for what seems like an eternity. My interests lie solely in college basketball, the NFL and of course, the Olympics.

I love a healthy dose of Chris "Boomer" Berman's eclectic commentary. A punchy "He could . . . . go . . . all . . . the . . . way" still makes me smile. He tells the story and thoroughly entertains me at the same time.

I'm certainly all for retired athletes and coaches becoming a part of the sports casting family. It adds a certain authenticity to the coverage, not to mention you get to see these guys as "real people". Their personalities off the court and off the field can sometimes surprise you. I think that aspect alone has done a lot to enhance the sports world.

So what is it exactly about sports that captivates us so? Well, I guess that answer depends on the person. I believe each sport has its own personality making it appeal to different folks. But all sports, whether team or individual, ultimately involve the same long list of ingredients. There's commitment and passion, insurmountable odds and triumph, controversy and adversity, satisfaction and of course, raw talent. The list goes on and on.

Would the game have the same rush without a rivalry, the hype or the anticipation? Would the competition play out the same if you never faced a Peyton Manning, an Apollo Ohno or a Michael Jordan?

I'm not blind or naive; I know there is an ugly side to sports. But I'd like to believe the good outweighs the bad. Sports is a profession for some and an emotional and physical outlet for many more. That's a fairly simple description. But if you feel the need to minimize "the game" or what being an athlete really means—if you think sports is simply a game—then you simply don't get it.

Sports is real human drama and it flexes the gamut of human emotions for both the athlete and the fan. Sports documentaries such as ESPN's "E:60" or a simple highlight reel set to music succeed in peeling back the layers, taking us beyond the physical and exposing the heart of the athlete and their craft. Expect heartbreak, expect joy, expect the unexpected . . . expect it all!

There are so many incredible sports moments throughout history that inspire us and enrich our everyday lives on some level. There is always something to be learned from the public display of another's personal journey. And often, it's what's going on beyond the camera's eye that touches us even more.

Every year as one career begins, another ends. Some players are looking to recapture the magic from championships lost; some coaches are seeking to chase away demons left over from unfulfilled careers. Older athletes are hoping the clock doesn't run out on their career while rookies are chasing away the nerves. There are those who have left their mark by a long, legendary career. And others whose dreams have been dashed in an instant by a crushing injury.

No matter the sport, being called a "Champion" is a word that will never leave you. For others it's a title that will never be obtained. But the dream to get there and to get there with integrity is what it's all about.

At the end of the day, sports is no different than anything else. There's got to be balance. Whether it's March Madness or the NFL Playoffs, be a fan, not a fanatic and enjoy sports for all the good stuff it has to offer. Sports isn't life, it's just another amazing part of it.

Moments in Mortality

I imagine that most children, unless presented with it at an early age, do not think a lot about death. The thought of my grandparents dying some day, one by one, never crossed my mind until it happened the first time. All four of my grandparents were still living into my twenties. For this, I was thankful. And we didn't call them grandma and grandpa or grandmother and grandfather; we lovingly called them "Mamaw and Papaw". This is my reflection on the unique aspects of each of their deaths . . .

1995. Mamaw Brown was my daddy's mama and the youngest of the four grandparents. At 78, she was a petite, godly woman who loved her family, flowers and apparently chocolate. I recall the last time I saw her before she went into a coma was on Thanksgiving Day, 1994. She had been bedridden for several years after having several mini strokes and fighting osteoporosis. As I walked into her room to visit that day, I was met by a little woman lying in her bed licking the wrapper of a Butterfinger, saying with purpose "I've been working on this for two weeks." Even now I chuckle and I don't think I will ever get that vision out of my head. A line from a favorite movie of mine says "It takes time to extract joy from life." And at that moment, Mamaw Brown was taking the time to extract a lot of joy from that chocolate bar.

I was not present for the unique moment surrounding Mamaw's death on February 20, 1995, but my mama and daddy and many other family members were. And they could only speak of its beauty. As the family stood holding hands encircling Mamaw, they knew the moment was near as her breathing turned into a rattle. As she was passing from this life into eternity, they witnessed the biggest smile dancing across her face as she drew her last breath. As Christians, we knew that at that moment, she was seeing our Lord and Savior Jesus Christ for the first time and the joy of that moment was something those present were able to share. Mama said that the rest of the hospital probably wondered what was going on, because instead of sobs and tears of grief, there were tears of joy and a celebration as Jesus embraced our precious Mamaw and said "Welcome home, my child."

2000. *Papaw* *Brown* was my daddy's daddy. I remember him as sort of a serious, stern type who always wore bibbed overalls and occasionally let a smile make its way out. He made his living as a farmer. After Mamaw passed away and he got a little older, that tough persona gave way to the kid in him that had been just waiting for an opportunity to make an appearance. And it did. One thing he loved to do that he couldn't do while Mamaw was alive was nail his favorite Polaroid's to the wall. He loved to snap those Polaroid's.

Though his whole entrance into the hospital seemed a bit odd to me, apparently he had a few things wrong with him that none of the family was aware of. And the culmination of these maladies would be the last straw for a lonely, old farmer. His stay in the hospital would not be a long one. I recall visiting him once. The wear and tear of a life lived through the depression had softened and now he seemed so care-free but vulnerable. Yet, he smiled. And he made us laugh; a bit ironic. And a man who had once been surrounded by loving family now lay in his tiny, dark hospital room, alone with his Polaroid camera. I think maybe this is what he wanted. After the last relative left the evening of January 30, 2000, at 86, Papaw shut his eyes forever.

2001. *Papaw* *Huff* was my mama's daddy. Self employed, he was a hard worker and always walked tall with a home-grown presence. I had a soft spot in my heart for him. There was a sweetness that surrounded Papaw which always complimented the magical twinkle that seemed to be in his eyes when he would look at me. I'll never forget how much he liked my long hair. Sometimes, even now, I think that is why I don't want to cut my hair. I don't want to lose that memory . . .

Just before Christmas of 2000, hubby and I bought our first digital camera. I remember wanting one with the ability to capture video, because our grandparents were getting older and we just might want to capture some moments in case something were to happen to one of them. Falling victim to pneumonia and lung disease just after Christmas, I found myself sitting in a quiet, lowly lit hospital room along with my aunt and cousin in late January of 2001. Just a few hours prior, every family member, more than 40 of us, had been by his bedside to say our goodbyes. Though he wasn't conscience, my heart tells me he knew we were there. It was late that night, and Mamaw whispered her goodbyes to Papaw. They had been married for over 66 years. She told him that she loved him. She told him it was okay to go. She told him that the girls (my mama and her two sisters) would take care of her. And she quietly walked out of the room.

With continually declining vital signs and various hospital aids unable to hide the inevitable outcome from their faces, we knew it was almost time to say our final goodbyes to Papaw, too. The scene was surreal. There was a sense of controlled panic as the life slowly seeped from Papaw's 87 year old body. We gathered by his bedside; Aunt Hilda and Cousin Trena on his right side, and myself on his left. As we held his hands, his breathing quietly began to diminish. Yet it was one of the loudest sounds I have ever heard. Even our sobs seemed to be muffled in the presence of our sweet Papaw leaving this world. It's an experience you just can't put into words. Every action, every word, and every thought in the few moments just before, during and just after his last breath flowed seamlessly; I believe everything was as it should have been.

And as I held Papaw's hand in the early morning hours of January 20, 2001, I knew that was the closest I had ever been to heaven.

2006. *Mamaw Huff* was one of the strongest women I've ever known but always a lady. She loved her family dearly, and she grieved so much after Papaw's death five years earlier that we really weren't sure if she would pull through. But she did. With eyesight failing and hearing slowly slipping away as well, Mamaw became dependant on her three daughters to care for her. Even in her nineties, she was still stronger than most. She never went on a shopping trip with my mama or my aunts where she couldn't keep up. She wouldn't allow it. But at age 96 she had lost so much, both physically and emotionally. And she was tired.

For over five years, since the death of Papaw, Mama and her two sisters had been taking care of Mamaw one week at a time, between their three residences. Living out of a suitcase week after week, year after year was taking its toll on a woman who once travelled in a covered wagon. Home wasn't home anymore.

But still she forged on.

She had said more than once that she would like to live to be 100. And I really thought she would make it. But towards the end of Mama's week with Mamaw in August of 2006, she began to feel ill. Mamaw had experienced rough spells before, but this seemed to be different. Aunt Hilda came in on Sunday to take over as Mama headed home, the usual Sunday routine. But on the following day, Mama received a call from her sister that she had taken Mamaw to the hospital.

Mamaw's kidneys were shutting down and we all knew what that meant. So much so that we called a family meeting with Mamaw's doctor to discuss our options. Again, it was surreal. It's not a situation I had ever imagined I would be a part of, yet, it was very real. There I sat with aunts, uncles, cousins and my parents in a sterile conference room in the hospital . . . . and we are discussing the best way to let Mamaw go. Of course, Mamaw just wanted to go home. And that's what we wanted for her, too. So we brought her home and hospice was put in place, though their involvement would be minimal. Mama and her sisters still took care of Mamaw, right up until the very end. It was hard to see my mamaw in a totally dependent state, but such is life.

We would end up having a few quiet moments together and I told her that I loved her. In her familiar tone that didn't reflect a life in its sunset, she sweetly replied "I love you, too." Those were my goodbyes, and I let her go. In retrospect, I believe I enjoyed my moments with her those last few years more than any other because she had learned to laugh more. Like Papaw Brown, her edges were softer now. And on the evening of August 19, 2006 less than a week after falling ill, with her children by her bedside, she was finally being reunited with Papaw in heaven. She didn't quite make it to a hundred years old, but that's okay, because now she had a new body that would last an eternity.

August 10, *2010:* *Dedicated to the memory of my four sweet grandparents that God blessed me with. I look forward to seeing you again, one sweet day, in Heaven. I love you all, still.* ♡

all Hearts Come Home for Christmas

INTRODUCTION

As I sit at home wrapped in my soft blanket on an icy December night, with Christmas just a week away, my thoughts lovingly drift to memories of Christmas' past. Tumbling the marshmallows around in my mug of hot cocoa, I struggle with penning my thoughts about Christmas so that these moments in time no longer exist just in my memory, but on paper for the entire world to ponder. As so often is the case, the Lord works in mysterious ways and I needn't look far for the answer. As I cradle the warm mug in my cold hands, I notice two simple words on this chosen vessel that tell me what I need to do next: "Let go."

When I reminisce about Christmas' past, I become very nostalgic. I'm taken back to a kinder, simpler time when a Norman Rockwell illustration or the beautiful lyrics of "What A Wonderful World" easily described life at the time. I can still hear the opening notes to "A Charlie Brown Christmas", a classic holiday special. Rudolph, the Grinch and other seasonal characters owned the television, if only for a short time. Of course, I was always partial to "Frosty the Snowman" because every time he melted, my heart melted, too. But none made the eyes of children and adults alike twinkle quite like Santa himself.

The sparkling lights and vibrant colors of red, green and gold always seemed to make the world burst with joy and anticipation of things to come. The smell of fresh baked cakes, pies and candies made your mouth water and your tummy sing with glee. And the music—the classic Christmas songs made the season come alive with warmth and history and substance. They were written and recorded in a time where families spent Christmas' together at home with a fire crackling in the fireplace and the fresh smell of a real Christmas tree filling the air.

But Christmas would not be Christmas without the celebration of the birth of our Lord and Savior, Jesus Christ. Life was truly as perfect and as peaceful then as an untouched snowfall on Christmas morning.

PART 1: DAS GESCHENK (THE GIFT)

As a kid, my family would receive a Christmas gift every year from an old friend of my daddy's. While he was in the Air Force, Daddy was stationed in Germany and spent Christmas with a family in Essen one year. From that point on, all through the years, Daddy stayed in touch with this family that had embraced this American serviceman. And though Mama, my brother and I never met him, we affectionately called him "Uncle Willy". We saw photos of him and his family and where he lived. So getting a package wrapped in heavy brown paper and string from a far away land during the holidays was always very exciting for us. In the package, there was always a little something for each one of us, wrapped in German newspaper. I remember receiving beautiful German baby dolls, some of which I still have. But the treat inside that always caused the most commotion was the yummy German chocolates. I mean really, only the Germans would put liquor in candy, right?

We stopped receiving packages from Uncle Willy some time ago. And Daddy thinks he died in 2005. I never met him, and he never knew this, but Uncle Willy has a permanent place among my fondest Christmas memories. And I savor those memories anytime I hear a classic Christmas carol like "Here We Come A Caroling" or "Drummer Boy" because I think of Uncle Willy, Germany, nutcrackers, soldiers and snow and it just fits into my mental snow globe.

Mama and Daddy received a Christmas card from Willy's son just yesterday. And as I sat here writing this portion of my story, I wondered for a brief moment if Germany had Facebook. You didn't see that one coming did you? Even so, I took a shot at searching for Uncle Willy's son's name on Facebook and came up with one match. No photo, just a name. And on a whim, I sent him a message asking him if his father was Willy Brosch, never expecting a reply.

I got up this morning to get ready for work and was blown away to see a reply to this message in my mailbox. "Frohe Weihnachten und ein glückliches neues Jahr wünschen Euch Wilfried und Lieselotte Brosch. Ich bin der Sohn von Willy Brosch aus Essen (1921-2005)." Translation: "Merry Christmas and Happy New Year from Wilfried and Lieselotte Brosch. I am the son of Willy Brosch from Essen (born 1921, died 2005)." The smile started in my heart and leapt onto my face where it's been all day. It's funny how using a little modern technology along with a "what if" mentality can breathe new life into an old memory . . .

Note: From time to time I check Wilfred's Facebook wall for activity. His only friends are me, my daddy and brother and the only activity on his wall are our messages from Christmas 2010 along with a simple "like" from Wilfred on one of our posts. I have since been "friended" by Martin, grandson of Uncle Willy. The Lord works in mysterious ways . . . .

PART 2: TRADITIONS

Merriam-Webster defines tradition as "an inherited, established, or customary pattern of thought, action, or behavior (as a religious practice or a social custom); the handing down of information, beliefs, and customs by word of mouth or by example from one generation to another without written instruction." As far as I'm concerned, a picture of my family Christmas might as well accompany these words.

And up until a few years ago, for me, the Christmas season had always had two distinct parts to it: Christmas Eve and Christmas day.

As a child, I remember the anticipation of the long drive to Mamaw and Papaw Huff's on Christmas Eve. They lived in the beautiful foothills of North Carolina. I would get to see all of my cousins, aunts and uncles, and of course, my sweet mamaw and papaw. And every year my mouth was in danger of drowning. It would instantly water as all the homemade southern dishes would parade in the door, right passed my nose only to find a place on the dinner table. And within this family tradition laid another one: the fact that my younger cousin, Trena, and I always positioned ourselves at the head of the line, ready to lead the troops into battle as soon as prayers were said. I don't think anyone ever challenged us on that one. It's just how it was.

Though there was always a tree with all the trimmings, every year it seemed to disappear behind the mounds of colorfully wrapped gifts. But once us kids (and some adults) dove in and did our thing, it was no longer the tree that was hard to find, but us kids who had been buried under tons of wrapping paper. Paper balls flew through the air like missiles and my daddy always seemed to be the one adorned with ribbon flowing from his follicley challenged head. There was always something remarkably comforting about sitting in the floor camouflaged by gift wrap and soaking in the smiles and laughter of a close knit family. That in itself was a gift. And the memory of it still is.

In my early days, most Christmas Eve gatherings would be at Mamaw and Papaw's house. In 1979, we had our Christmas gathering out in the big, red barn built by Papaw Huff and Uncle Ken. But over the years, the location would change occasionally from my aunt and uncle's homes to church fellowship halls. It would appear we had finally outgrown even the largest home in our family.

One year in the seventies, our entire family (30 or more of us at the time) piled into a church bus decorated with colorful, blinking lights and headed up to the mountains to see the Christmas decorations. Even then, I remember thinking how blessed I was. I mean, forget now, but even back then, who did that?

No matter the weather, no matter where we were, the night was never over until the hugs were passed around. And as much as I loved the food and the presents, I loved the hugs the most because it reminded me of how much I was loved.

I can't tell you much about my relationship with Santa Claus. I don't remember having any discussions about him and whether he was real or not; but what I do remember is listening to the radio during the long drive home from Mamaw's every Christmas Eve. The Christmas music was nice but my ears always perked up a little more when that Santa Claus report would hit the airwaves. And as his location was given, I would be looking up into the sky with wide eyes to see if I could see him and his sleigh making its way through the stars. This memory alone proves to me that at one time, I believed.

Christmas Day was but a continuation of Christmas Eve—just different relatives. Of course, we would gather around our own tree first. I was always up early and letting anyone else get any more sleep once I was up was not an option. Mama would have all of the Christmas lights on with traditional Christmas music playing merrily and we would all take our places around the tree. Even tradition found its way to where we sat on the floor: me right next to the tree, my brother to my left, Mama across from me managing the other side of the tree and Daddy next to her.

Once our festivities had concluded, we would pile in the car with more homemade dishes, more presents and hit the road for the long trip back up that same country road to Mamaw and Papaw Brown's.

I still remember the ride as if it were yesterday. Because every year, until I outgrew it of course, I would have my mesh Christmas stocking, full of candy and toys, hanging in the car at my window. The frost of the window provided such a nice backdrop for something I couldn't get into until after we had lunch. Nonetheless, it still makes me smile.

At Mamaw and Papaw's it was like country déjà vu. More food than you could shake a stick at, mounds of gifts that morphed into a deluge of paper, laughs, hugs and who could forget . . . . the gag gifts. Yes, even on Christmas Day, humor found its way into the celebration. I don't know how or when or who started the tradition, but oversized granny panties made as many appearances on Christmas Day as Santa Claus. Remember, laughter is a gift, too and it never goes out of style.

PART 3: CELEBRATE ME HOME

The story never changes. Sometimes, there is just a "P.S".

With the passing of my first grandparent in 1995 to the passing of my last grandparent in 2006, I have witnessed the subtle changes in our family Christmas get-togethers. And you don't realize what an anchor your grandparents are during the Christmas season until they are not there. After all, for this kid, that's where the tradition was born. But it continues on through my dear mama, daddy, brother and husband.

Christmas Day at Mamaw and Papaw Browns has now become a Christmas gathering at one of the "kids" homes on a Saturday in December. All seven children, including my daddy, are still living so each year our celebration is at a different home but with that same ol' "down home" feel. We don't draw names anymore like we used to, but my aunts still make a homemade treat wrapped up and in ribbons to go under the tree for all the nieces and nephews. There's plenty of food and still as many camera flashes today as in Christmas' past. Hugs are still plentiful and we are finding how easy it is to squeeze so many people into a home when it's built with love.

Christmas Eve at Mamaw and Papaw Huffs is still on Christmas Eve, though the location changes from year to year. But this year, 2010, doors were closing as we were trying to decide where to hold our Huff Family Christmas. Who needs an open door when you've got a window that's cracked open just enough?

My daddy came up with the idea to hold Christmas at Mamaw and Papaw's old home. And Uncle Ken, whose house sits on the same property next door, has worked a lot of thankless hours remodeling those old walls, inside and out. It's been rented out to a family here and there. And not as fate would have it, but as the Lord would have it, it was vacant last year and begging for the laughter and love again of a family who had made so many memories there.

Gone were Mamaw's multitudes of flowers that once adorned the outside of the home built in 1962. But we all know that it's what's on the inside that counts. Here's where that "P.S." comes in . . .

Christmas lights and decorations, floor heaters, tables and chairs were the nudge those old walls needed to come alive again for a Christmas present reminiscent of Christmas' past. It was as if we had gone back in time. One by one, family walked through the doors on Christmas Eve just like we had so many times before. Different but the same. Sure, the years had caught up with some of us, while others were still cruising youth; but we still knew how to laugh and love because it's all about what's on the inside. And though the cornerstone of our family, Mamaw and Papaw, were not physically with us, their legacy of love and tradition flowed through that house that night just the same.

For me, Christmas Eve 2010 was more profound than I think I can even grasp right now. Life goes on and times change. We grow up, and we grow old. We lose loved ones and sometimes we even lose touch with what really matters in this world. It's our choice how we deal with the subtle changes in life. Tradition is never lost, just redirected. And in a family like ours you realize the truth in the saying "All Hearts Come Home For Christmas."

Buddy and Sage were inseparable for their few short months together

Buddy, my precious boy

Great American road trip, Brown style (minus the style)

Me, hanging out with a few of my friends

Papaw Brown's last Polaroid taken from his hospital bed

Uncle Willy; I only wish we had met

The Kindred Spirit Mailbox

Love Story, Part One:
"Hey, I Was Using That"

I have never been the sort of girl to believe in fairytales. That is, until I found myself in the middle of one. No, it wasn't your "glass slipper" variety, but it was my fairytale and everything this girl had ever dreamed of . . .

In 1997, I was working in a local gym and had started going to school to become a licensed therapeutic massage and bodywork therapist. My life seemed to be at a crossroads. Divorced in my early twenties, I was now in my early thirties and had pretty much given up on love. Who needed it? To be honest, I think I had decided it didn't exist. Not for me, anyway.

Like many, I had been through more than my share of lies, rejections and unhappy endings. Looking back, I had also made some pretty poor choices on my own which aided in my suffering; but hindsight, as they say, is 20/20. My cat, Cougar (R.I.P), had witnessed too many of my tears and meltdowns, but I was so glad he was always there for me.

Spending Saturday nights at my house eating take-out and watching TV with my mama and daddy had become the norm, and I enjoyed it. In my mind, I had decided I didn't need a man in my life and that I was going to be happy all on my own.

Yep, that's when it happened. He came into my life and blew that thought process to megabytes.

Now, I believe his first words to me were "Hey, I was using that." He was a member of the gym I worked at and I guess it was his way of either flirting or just being nice. No matter the reason, he had me at the first giggle. And that short but sweet conversation was pretty much a practice run for the full Monty that would show up soon.

As a student and future massage therapist, I wanted to start building my clientele before I was totally out on my own. So, I made some business cards trying to drum up interest for my practice sessions, which were a requirement. I had worked at the gym for a few years, so most everyone knew who I was. I pinned a card to the bulletin board at the gym hoping for the best.

Days, maybe weeks later, I was at a Barnes and Noble in Greensboro with Mama. And yes, as a matter of fact, it WAS on a Saturday night. I had left my pager in the car so I missed "the" page. I didn't recognize the number, but since I had posted my card on the board at the gym, I was sure I had a future client calling.

I don't really remember how the conversation started . . . or went . . . or ended. I believe he introduced himself and when I didn't seem to know who he was (regardless of first and last names), he reminded me how he had picked on me at the gym recently, regarding a piece of equipment. Ah, yes. I remembered. Cute guy. Seems nice enough. Sense of humor. He wanted to ask ME out. Unfortunately, I was going to be in a weekend seminar at my school and, well, I figured he thought I was dodging him and pretty much decided I wouldn't hear from him again.

But I did.

A couple of weeks later, I got another page. This time, I recognized the number. And he was calling back to ask me out again. Hmmm! Maybe . . .

I worked at the gym most Sundays and had to open the doors at 1:00PM. And so I had gotten into the habit of leaving church a little early and heading to Golden Corral for lunch. I remember one particular Sunday when I was eating, alone, when he walked up to say "Hello". I managed to squeak out some sort of greeting as I sheepishly tried to camouflage the towering stack of chocolate chip cookies sitting on my plate. Being a trainer at the gym, I had a reputation to protect and though I was hoping he wouldn't notice, he did. "Don't tell anyone at the gym", I pleaded. We shared a short but friendly conversation as well as a chuckle about the leaning tower of yum before we went our separate ways. Little did either one of us know how many more laughs (or cookies) were in our future . . .

Back to "the" page . . . . So, he wanted to meet for lunch on a Sunday afternoon at—you guessed it—Golden Corral. I am thinking he was playing the odds that I would like this suggestion since I frequented it most Sundays and had a bit of a crush on the dessert bar.

We were to meet there. And as is often the case, I was early. It was Sunday, October 24th, 1997 and it was raining. He was wearing blue jeans, mountain boots, a green mock turtleneck and a green jacket with a little duck on the chest. I know I was dressed but those details are not for me to remember. All I know is that I wasn't nervous, at all, and I waited with anticipation for him to meet me inside.

To this day, I often kid him about the fact he didn't pay for my lunch that day. Truth is, one of the cashiers (from the Middle East I think) who barely spoke English, liked to buy me lunch on Sunday's. I think he had a bit of a crush, or felt sorry for me, and Sonja was not one to turn down a free meal. Poor thing didn't realize that THIS lunch was so very different from any other Sunday.

I'll spare you the details and hit the highpoints. There was a stack of chocolate chip cookies involved as well as lots of talking. Time flew and before we knew it, our lunch had turned into something more. "So", he finally said after almost three hours, "Would you like to go out sometime?" And without skipping a beat, I leaned forward and replied "When?" Thinking quickly, he exclaimed, "How about tonight?"

Now first of all, most would think this thing we were doing was a date. Heck, I thought it was a date. But David has made it clear that had the cashier at the register not paid for my meal, it would have been a date. Therefore, this was something else. We'll just go with that since things worked out so well. Second of all, my response might surprise you; it certainly caught my future husband off guard, but in a pleasant way . . .

"I can't tonight" I blurted. "The World Series is on but you're welcome to come over and watch it with me if you'd like!" I'm not even sure how or why that particular response came out of my mouth so quickly, but it did. Maybe my resolve in living the rest of my life alone needed to be toned down a bit when faced with the possibility of a "real" date. Nevertheless, it set the stage for things to come. My future hubby was stoked because he had found himself a woman who loved sports!

When he showed up at my door that evening, he came bearing gifts, which is always a good thing when one is trying to impress. Flowers? Chocolates? Nooooo . . . . chips and salsa in one hand and a computer generated Cleveland Indians flag in the other. I was most certainly impressed.

Now, I can't even tell you who won the game that night; didn't really care. Because I knew that this whole day had been the start of something really special. I just knew it. And the rest, as they say, is history.

Love Story, Part Two: The Proposal

October 24, 1997 will be a date etched in my heart forever. That was the day my new life began.

I am sure at the close of our first date, there was the standard departing words of "I'll call you." Of course I wanted him to, but I can't really say that I thought he would. Remember, I had pretty much dismissed a future with any guy. And I had most certainly developed trust issues with the mightier sex. For me, seeing would be believing and even that would be a tough sale to this girl.

The following Monday, I ran into David at the gym and he asked me if I wanted to go to Applebee's for a bite after we finished our workouts. This was a totally unexpected surprise but an easy "yes" for me.

This would end up being a very revealing impromptu date as the conversation centered on topics usually discussed when contemplating a future. I guess we were both at the point in our lives where we didn't want to just have fun with someone anymore; we wanted a future. We were old enough and had been through enough to know that time was now. And apparently deep down, we suspected we had finally found that someone to build a future with.

Beyond those first two dates, the timeline begins to blur. And I feel that is because we were meant to be together. Just today, my boss said David and I were like peanut butter and jelly. We just go together. So when I think back trying to recollect the natural progression of things, I can't. It just seems as if we have been together forever. And that's a good thing.

I do remember a couple of pivotal points early on that played a huge part in the direction our relationship was headed.

The last few relationships I had before meeting David had really taken a toll on me emotionally. I had been lied to so many times and developed some serious trust issues. My new way of dealing with this was a defense mechanism called sarcasm. I took it to the extreme and poor David got the brunt of it. But I was determined that he, along with any other guy that might come into my life, would not use my heart as a rug or a punching bag anymore. And while it helped me to feel in control and invincible in matters of the heart, unbeknownst to me, my new found stance was repelling this wonderful man that God had sent me.

Unbeknownst, that is, until he had tolerated enough and handed me a yellow card letting me know I was in violation. He wanted to be with me, but not like this. The amount of sarcasm and defensiveness was too much for anyone to have to endure and he told me so. "If this is the way you are," he said, "then this is not going to work." I knew in my heart, that this person David was referring to wasn't really me. And I wanted this to work. Reality hit and that force field I was hiding behind began to crumble. The change, David said, was almost instant.

But don't think that with this adjustment I threw up a white flag and dismissed all of my fears and concerns. On the contrary; if I was going to open my heart to him and invite the cultivation of trust, he was going to have to meet me more than halfway.

While dropping the tough girl facade was a step in the right direction, it wasn't enough. See, my backup plan was to keep my options open. This, I thought, would also keep my heart out of harm's way. I could date David and maybe go out with this other guy that I had been interested in for some time. After all, I had done it before. Why should this time be any different? An ultimatum (though not presented that way-but hey, if it looks and tastes like a jelly bean, it probably is a jelly bean) gave me that final jolt I needed. And it entered my atmosphere at warp speed. If I was going to go out with this guy, then David wanted the same freedom. I didn't have to ponder that one long. Sharing David with anyone else was not an option. And just like that, I never dated another guy (other than him) again.

The sky cleared and it seemed to be written in the stars that we were destined to be together. One month into our relationship, I think we both "knew." We took lots of road trips visiting family in South Carolina and found that we always had plenty to talk about. I had never enjoyed talking to someone that much in my life. Riding in a (Ford) Explorer, ironically, is where we really got to know each other well.

A little over two months after our first date, the gentle whirlwind romance that we had been enjoying suddenly took a serious turn. On December 31, 1997, David and I were in Greensboro, NC enjoying a fabulous New Year's Eve party with his parents. As we sat at our table in the middle of an extravagant room full of scrumptious food, festive music, and folks ready to ring in a new year, the moment had finally arrived. Enjoying a stolen moment alone, David held my hand and began twirling the ring that donned the ring finger on my left hand. We looked at each other with grins that were both genuine yet in sync as he said with a loving determination, "I think we need to talk about this a little bit."

And so we did. "Three, two, one . . . Happy New Year!" And it already was!

Our wedding date was chosen, the location was secured, and the ring . . . well, the story of the ring is a beautiful yet personal one that I wish I could share. But a woman's heart is a deep ocean of secrets. Yes, I stole that line from Titanic. But isn't it so true?

So February rolled around and so did my birthday. I was so excited to share my first birthday with the man I loved. I just knew it would be a birthday like none other. David and I had planned to meet at my house before heading to Lake McIntosh to check out the venue for our wedding. I was so ecstatic about doing this until I found out the park closed at 4:30pm that day. By the time David arrived at my home to whisk me away, our opportunity to get a preview slowly faded into the grey winter sky.

So a change of plans was in order. And I waited patiently while David ran out to his truck to . . . well, to be honest, at the time I really didn't know why he ran out to his truck so suddenly.

But I didn't have to wonder for long. As I stood between the sofa and the coffee table watching him run back in, he made a deliberate beeline straight to me. With zero hesitation, he raised a quivering arm with fingers tightly gripping a small velvet box. And the words "Will you marry me?" spoken with a slight tremble flowed from his heart passed his lips like a little boy asking his best girl for their first dance.

Though his plan to propose at the very place where we would be exchanging our vows was well thought out and romantic . . . there was something so endearing and completely perfect about how that question ended up being asked that day. Like everything in our relationship to that point, it was as it should be. I didn't doubt that for a second.

And of course, *I said yes!*

The months of planning the wedding along with all the expected and unexpected stress that comes with such an important time in one's life was worth every ounce of energy it took to get to that moment. The moment where you knew everything had come together the way it was meant to be. That you were marrying your best friend, that everything you had ever dreamed of was right in front of you. And most importantly, that it was of and because of God. Of that, I am sure.

You see, back in those first few weeks when I made the decision to put my heart out there, to invite trust, I knew David would have to meet me more than halfway. And he did. And like me, his time also came when he realized there were some things he had to let go of as well. We both brought unwanted baggage into this new life. Not little duffle bags, but the supersized pieces of luggage. It took great effort to unpack those emotional and symbolic suitcases. But we did. And we did it together.

On October 17, 1998, I accepted God's gift to me with thankfulness and married my best friend. I may not have been wearing a glass slipper that day, but I most certainly felt like I was the most beautiful girl in the world. After all, my prince told me so. And that was all that mattered.

And at the end of the day, when asked what was next, it was very easy for us to reply as one "We're going to Disneyworld!"

Love Story, Part Three: The Time of Our Lives

It was the clearest, bluest sky I think I have ever seen. We woke up early with the sort of excitement you would expect from a couple of kids on Christmas morning. The air was cool and crisp, but that was just a typical October morning in North Carolina. Giggly and all smiles, we packed our truck and were on our way.

In 2008, David and I celebrated our 10th wedding anniversary. Up to that point, the only vacations we had taken were with our family to Oak Island each September and our honeymoon back in 1998 at Disneyworld. We had never really had the funds to take a trip and I think we had just gotten really comfortable with not even trying. But this year would be different.

We decided pretty easily, actually, that this anniversary deserved a special celebration. It had been a decade, after all, of marital bliss. So we started entertaining the idea of a real trip. Being the dreamer that I am, plus a bit of a control freak, David was more than happy to let the wheels of my imagination start spinning until I came up with some ideas that were financially doable and would provide us with a memorable vacation.

With October being peak foliage season, plus the fact that we're both beach bums always making a bee line to the coast, we opted to head to the mountains for this little get-a-way.

I started researching and Googling; basically, I was releasing my inner travel agent. And before you know it, this little retreat had taken on a life of its own. And that life was conceived straight from a 1980's blockbuster movie.

But not before we pulled up and rang the doorbell of the largest home in America. Our first stop on that far from ordinary Wednesday would be a visit to the Biltmore House in Asheville, NC. We had never visited this historic home so we were quite excited at what we would see. Inside, the home was massive and displayed much history. The colors were a bit muted and lifeless for my taste which made me feel a tad ho-hum. As impressive and elegant as the architecture was, we quickly decided one visit inside was enough for us.

But outside was a completely different vibe. With fall flowers in bloom, the beautiful colors were enhanced by the flawless blue sky. Clearly we were drawn outdoors to the fresh mountain air and bright pallet. The beauty seemed to encourage our adrenalin to surge.

By late afternoon we said "so long" to the Vanderbilt's humble abode and eagerly hit the road headed for our next destination where we would be spending our next two evenings. I had heard of this town but my research had turned up very little to impress me outside of one minor detail. You've heard of a little movie from the eighties called "Dirty Dancing", right?

As it turns out, this movie had two key visually memorable shooting locations. And I don't think you will find anyone who disagrees. One location is situated in the mountains of North Carolina and the other a bit north in the mountains of Virginia. With both states claiming bragging rights of "where Dirty Dancing was filmed", I was intrigued. Being one who was a fan and had seen this film a number of times over the years, I felt it my right to supply some input in this little tug-of-war. And in order to do this, I simply had to see it for myself. I mean, **we** had to see it. It was, after all, **our** anniversary. I'll just go ahead and put this out there now—I did get a little carried away with encouraging the theme of this trip.

Sitting in the heart of Hickory Nut Gorge, the barely populated town of Lake Lure is a true gem. I think David and I fell in love with the area as soon as we laid eyes on it. It was simple and so North Carolina. We nabbed ourselves a cozy little cabin called "Magnolia" at "The Arbor", a privately owned property of cabin getaways just around the corner from the lake. With fresh baked goods, a warm blanket and genuine southern hospitality greeting us upon our arrival, it felt like home. It was indeed, a hidden treasure.

Our dinner that evening couldn't have been more perfect. We dined outdoors at the only restaurant that sits on the banks overlooking the lake. With the sky still as blue as it was when we set out on our journey early that morning and the late afternoon sun reflecting off of the still waters of the lake, an unsuspecting paradise had found us.

With such an incredible start to the trip, it was hard to believe we still had more than three days of bliss ahead of us. But we did.

While at Lake Lure, we visited Chimney Rock Park for some light hiking and breath taking photo ops from way up above. We explored Chimney Rock Village which spanned several hundred yards along the main street through town. We visited the shops and purchased a couple of unique gifts such as locally made jewelry. We enjoyed a relaxed lunch at the Riverwatch Deli and Grill on the banks of the Broad River and indulged in some homemade sweets courtesy of a local gift shop. Tasty food and rugged scenery made for a great combination.

Loving the outdoors the way we do, we decided to explore the river a little closer. We noticed it seemed fairly low as a number of boulders and rocks of all sizes were positioned in the river so accessible to curious folks such as ourselves. With David leading the way, we started making our steps from rock to rock until we found ourselves in the middle of the flow. The sound of the current making its way around the geography was so soothing and mesmerizing. Nestled between the towering mountains and the abundance of trees, enjoying the scenery from this vantage point made us feel cradled by nature.

Of course, the main attraction at this stop was Lake Lure itself. And what better way to experience it than to take a guided tour of it on a pontoon boat. I was so unaware of its history. *National Geographic* knew what it was talking about when they declared Lake Lure one of the most beautiful man-made lakes in the world. The natural beauty was stunning as well as the unique million dollar homes that graced the perimeter.

But what got me completely giddy and star struck was coasting into the cove where the famous "dip" scene from the movie *Dirty Dancing* was filmed. In addition, the guide pointed out the cascading steps where "Baby" not only carried a watermelon, but practiced her dance routine in a scene serenaded by the classic tune "Wipeout." Twenty years had passed since these moments were captured on film and the steps were no longer a lively white but rather weathered and falling apart. Still, if you were a fan of the movie, you knew what you were seeing and it was beyond cool as you suddenly felt a part of the original experience.

With Friday morning greeting us, it was time to reluctantly depart this wonderful place and move on to our final destination. We would take with us so many beautiful memories of our time at Lake Lure with the resolve to come back again someday. And after two days of gorgeous skies and warm weather, we woke up to an overcast canopy pillowed by a heavy fog. There was a nip in the air that caused us to be suspicious of what lied ahead for us in Virginia. But we were up for the mystery. With a four hour drive staring us in the face, we could hardly wait to reach destination #2 of this themed journey.

Arriving at Mountain Lake Resort in Pembroke, Virginia, the mystery was about to unfold. Our entrance paralleled a memorable scene from the movie as the fog and drizzle camouflaged our approach to the famous stone hotel. I honestly couldn't believe we were here. But we were. We settled into our cozy cabin and tried to sneak a peek at the beautiful lake which made several appearances in the movie. Evening was about to fall and the fog was just too thick to catch a good look, so we decided it could wait until morning.

It was October 17th, 2008 and time to officially celebrate our 10th wedding anniversary. So we dressed for dinner and made our way up to the hotel where all meals were served in resort style. As we walked into the lobby, the impressive stone fireplace caught our attention first and would later serve as the location for our celebratory photo with a crackling fire as a backdrop. Photos from the set of *Dirty Dancing* lined the hallway with a young Patrick Swayze and Jennifer Gray smiling at us from behind the glass.

As wonderful as this trip had been already, the magic would continue as we were seated for dinner. As we waited for our food to arrive, David and I quickly realized we were sitting on the porch (now enclosed) where "Baby" and her family had breakfast, a scene from the movie.

It was a perfect end to yet another perfect day. But the next morning would reveal a startling discovery.

As we walked out the door the next morning, ready to head to the hotel for what was sure to be a decadent breakfast, there was definitely something missing. Water. There wasn't any. Mountain Lake had drained. We later learned that this had happened perhaps only three other times in the last 6000 years. Disappointed and a bit stunned, the reality of such an event increased the mystery meter. We were handed a little piece of history.

After breakfast, we bundled up and set out to explore the lake and the rest of the property, looking for familiar scenes from the movie. We found several, but one of the most recognizable focal points would have to be the gazebo. Once again, giddiness took over as I pranced around this weathered wooden structure in all my silliness, still not believing I was here. This was where the guests gathered in the evenings for a slow dance or two and this was where Baby had the teary eyed heart to heart with her dad. And as David and I paused for a moment and focused our gaze outward, the scene was something to behold. Overgrown grass and inches of moist yet hardened mud owned this space. The glistening water and tranquil existence that was captured in the movie were nowhere to be found.

But like the other guests who were here and so intrigued by this anomaly, we took advantage of this rare occurrence and set out on foot to explore the lake bed. Honestly, that is something few living people could say they have experienced. Throughout the day in talking to staff and other guests, we learned that there was more than one guess as to why and how the lake had emptied. And we also learned during this time of barrenness, actual remains of a gentleman from the 1930's had been discovered by a guest. We had never seen anything like this before, and though an empty lake is not what we expected to see, what we did witness personalized this whole experience that much more.

We captured many beautiful images of the grounds and the striking stone hotel which was so prominent in the movie. We learned that the actual final dance scene was not filmed in this hotel dining room as we had believed. This fact was obvious once we took the time to look around and really take in what we were seeing. Even "Baby's corner" was a manufactured prop but that didn't stop me from getting a photo taken there that looked pretty authentic. Our whole experience here had enlightened us a bit about the world of movies and TV. Things are not always as they appear.

But, I do know one setting that was totally authentic and real.

As I was gushing to one of the wait staff in between meals about being a fan of the movie (like they hadn't heard that one before), she graciously and enthusiastically asked me if I would like to visit the kitchen where one of the scenes had been filmed. If you know the movie, you will remember when Baby and Neal (the boss's grandson) had gone to the kitchen for a late night snack. While he had his head buried in the fridge, Baby heard sobbing and noticed Penny (the dancer) crumbled up on the floor against the wall weeping uncontrollably. Throwing all my dignity to the wind, I sat in that very same spot and acted out my best "Penny" and David humored me by snapping my photo. I left that kitchen feeling as if I had won the lottery. This was definitely the coolest trip ever.

It was Sunday morning and the fog had finally lifted. Feeling like we were at a camp for grownups, we made our way to the dining room one last time to enjoy yet another scrumptious meal. We nabbed a first class seat by the large window with a view of the property, including beautiful Mountain Lake. How fitting. This trip really had been perfect. And we couldn't believe it was coming to a close. Once again, the sky was as blue as it had been on Wednesday morning when we first left home. And it almost seemed as if the vibrant colors saturating the landscape around us applauded as we walked the grounds one last time.

Over the last four days, we had seen a lot of beauty, learned a lot of history, and had enjoyed turning every moment spent together into a lasting memory. The lake that once was, the gazebo that had seen a lot of special moments over the years and the stone hotel full of its charm and history and really, a celebrity in its own right—these, along with Lake Lure and its charm, had been a part of movie history. And now, they were a part of ours.

And as cliché as it sounds, it couldn't be more true; we really had the time of our lives!

To be continued ♡

In Sage's World

I can't help but suffer a little guilt for not choosing her first; for having my heart so set on a ghost that I dismissed her need for a home and to be loved for all of her unique qualities.

In the three short months that we had Buddy before his death, he pretty much overshadowed his sister, Sage. He was everything that she wasn't. For a kitten, his looks were exceptional. He was smart, he was fast. It was clear he was going to grow up to be an above average feline. And there was no doubt he was the center of my attention. Sage was simply a tag-a-long. And looking back, I believe that even with all of her challenges, if nothing else, she sensed this from me.

Life without Buddy shifted my focus to Sage. But Sage had already become a daddy's girl. She wanted little to do with me and I took that very personal. So, there was no bonding between Sage and myself in the beginning. This, like so much else about that little marvel, would come with time.

In the early days, Sage did not meow. And eventually when she started experimenting with sounds, there was very little that resembled a typical feline vocal. But over time, she has developed a healthy voice although it sounds more like a sudden outburst of a squeeze toy than anything else. And there are some times when the tone eerily sounds like sadness personified. It weeps. It pleads, almost.

You've seen greeting cards, perhaps, and comical drawings where a cat's eye's are bugged with that "scared-y cat" expression? Sage is the poster child for that look. And if you see her, don't be alarmed. She does have that expression on her face 99% of the time. This is the only characteristic that she and Buddy shared from the gene pool. I guess you could say she has Buddy's eyes . . .

There are other physical attributes that are simply Sage. She has shorter legs than the average kitty that aren't in proportion with the rest of her body. They're stocky and she tends to hold her left paw up off the ground when sitting around. We believe this is due to an infection in her paws after she was declawed. She is freakishly strong. When we would try to discipline her after she misbehaved, to hold her by the scruff of the neck was next to impossible.

She also has a bit of a stumpy tail. And that tail typically resembles the shape of a question mark. Her fur is an underwhelming black that most days looks like she just rolled out of bed; disheveled, even. And the fur on her ears comes to a devilish little point. This is one way we were able to distinguish Sage and Buddy when we first brought them home.

Sometimes we will catch her staring at nothing. I'm not sure where she is in that moment but it's obvious there's some sort of a disconnect occurring for a few seconds. And a sure fire way to pull her out of that is to rattle a plastic bag. She hates that. More accurately, she is terrified by it. While Rumi, our calico, loves to explore the inside of a plastic bag, Sage sees it as a threat and usually distances herself from it.

However, I must say that as of recent, we see Sage progressing in that she is beginning to conquer her fears, one by one. And one of those conquests seems to be that plastic bag. Just this morning, we heard the familiar rattle of a plastic bag and when we looked expecting to see Rumi, we saw Sage sitting defiantly on her nemesis while clumsily swatting it with her stocky paws, peeking her head inside occasionally. She looked up at us with a look of pride and accomplishment. Every day, she surprises us.

Loud noises and quick movements also draw a retreat out of Sage. With surround sound, it's almost a given that an action movie with all of its special sound effects will drive Sage to the far, quieter corners of the house, while Rumi lies on the man chair taking it all in stride. The recoil isn't immediate. It's almost as if her feline CPU is extremely outdated and is taking longer than it should to process the information. It's like telling a joke, and laughing at the punch line five minutes later. That is so Sage.

Over the years, we have learned that Sage needs familiarity. With people, she isn't comfortable with you until you have been in the house a number of times and she deems you not a threat. I was no exception as I, too, had to earn her trust. But even now, if you approach her too quickly or in a way that she is not sure of, she will literally back up. I can almost hear the shrill "beep, beep, beep" as she retreats. So, if you come by to visit but never see a hint of her, you can probably find her taking shelter in the closet behind David's clothes.

One of the most endearing characteristics of this walking question mark is one bred from familiarity. Sage and I share this special ritual. I will say in my best parentese, "Do you want me to rub your belly?" And after repeating that atypical question to my furry child numerous times, what happens next is always the same.

After breaking her empty stare, the neurons start firing again and she slowly looks around with purpose before tumbling down on her back, with legs in the air, exposing her belly. As I move towards her, she cutely cocks her head sideways as if to get a better look at my approach. For a cat that seems to have so many issues, the fact that she freely exposes her vulnerability to me, for most, would be something of a wonder. But in Sage's world, it's simply just a day in the life.

What comes next is a gentle belly rubbing. Her fur is beyond soft, so plush. And she seems to be at total ease. Our belief is that the trauma from being spayed as a young kitten scarred her far worse than what we could see on the outside. And with no regard for the norm, her means of overcoming the pain is to smother it with positive attention. In cat terms, it just feels good.

There is a bit of a clumsy side to Sage. Who am I kidding; it's more than a bit. But that, we have determined, is just part of her charm. Upstairs is David's "man-room" and it consists of a half wall overlooking the stairs. This happens to be a favorite lounging spot for Rumi; and apparently a deathtrap for Sage.

One night, David was working on his computer. Sage and Rumi were playing; rather, Sage was playing and Rumi was being annoyed. Rumi decided she had had enough and made a mad dash around the wall headed down the steps. Now in theory, the shortest distance between two points is a straight line. For recognizing that reality, I give kudos to Sage. But in this case, the fact that the straight line included Sage leaping over the half wall to catch her sister lost her some cool points.

Out of the corner of his eye, my husband saw the take off followed by the thud and quick plop of a cat with now 8 lives, hitting the hardwood floor below. As he rushed around the corner to check on her, Sage was dazed but unharmed. She managed to leave a few hairs stuck to the wall on her rapid descent. Rumi got away and I am sure had a good laugh about the whole thing.

There was another night when Sage was resting on top of that same wall. David was working on his computer (do you sense a trend here) and again, out of the corner of his eye, noticed Sage disappearing . . . again. Except this time, she wasn't in a foot race with her sister. She had fallen into such a deep sleep, that her body just oozed over the side. Once again, the cold, hardwood steps below broke her fall. Fortunately, that was all that was broken that day. I don't think I have noticed her on that wall since.

On more than one occasion, I have referred to Sage as a "special kitty". When she's nervous, she sticks out her tongue for a quick lick and gulps as she retrieves it. When she's excited to see us, her tail will quiver like a rattlesnake. And sometimes she will even fall into such a deep sleep that you can't wake her up and then suddenly, she snaps out of it. I have often wondered if she, indeed, might be mentally challenged. But due to the lack of findings in my research, I have given up the quest to put a label on her. She is what she is.

Sage is special. And I love her. It's been an interesting journey to see her grow and develop from a discarded kitten on the side of the road into a one of kind family member that I can't imagine our lives without. All of her unique behaviors that raise an eyebrow or have caused us to scratch our heads over the years are the very qualities that have endeared her to us. It hasn't been easy. But looking at the whole picture, we've seen her struggle to overcome her own demons. Her progress isn't absent, just a little slower than most.

She's six plus years old now and in some ways, still every bit the kitten we brought home by mistake. And even that bonding we detoured back in the beginning has found a place with Sage and me. When I sit in the man chair at night watching TV with hubby and hear an almost human sigh, I don't even have to look because I know she's there. I reach my hand behind me to feel her warm furry belly haloing my head. I don't even mind that back paw of hers jabbing me in the back of the shoulder.

Or, if I wake up during the night and squirm a bit, I know the weight I feel at my feet is her, resting comfortably. She's finally found her place at home. And that purr that needed love, that needed acceptance, that needed a home so desperately, never gave up on me. For a cat that once wouldn't even let me think about picking her up, she now enjoys being a bit of a lap cat, on her terms, of course. And as far as I'm concerned, I'm the lucky one getting to live in Sage's world.

Against Blue Skies

Two young ladies in a high rise building just blocks from the World Trade Center are capturing the images of the burning North Tower on video. They can hardly believe what they are seeing as bodies begin to fall one after the other to escape the flames. The blood curling screams begin. The camera jars momentarily and refocuses on a new ball of fire exploding from another building. They have just witnessed with their own eyes a second plane flying purposely into the South Tower. Their reaction pierces your soul. They are overcome by fear and sobs because immediately they know that what has just happened is no accident. It's terrorism.

It is one thing to see the footage that the media provides to you along with their professional commentary, perfect camera angles, polished delivery and composure. It is very much a different story to witness the sights and sounds from those living the horror at ground zero that had the presence of mind to pick up a video camera and show us what we could have only imagined otherwise.

Today is September 11, 2011. It's 8:46a.m. It is a beautiful, sunny morning, much like that unforgettable day. I am sitting in the safety of my own home in rural America with my husband before heading to church. We're watching a special presentation on the History Channel: *102 Minutes That Changed America.* There will be a lot of these shows on today covering various aspects of 9/11, a day that has its place in our history.

Ten years have passed since that horrible day. And as I watch these programs now, I find that my emotions are still just beneath the surface. No, I wasn't there, but like you, like everyone, I was affected by what took place. And in the midst of so much tragedy and loss, I have come to realize a unique opportunity exists to see, to learn, and to extract moments that cause me to pause and ponder. And be moved.

The sights and sounds were surreal.

From the impact of the first plane into the North Tower, office papers and such drifted through the air like confetti at a ticket tape parade. Something you would normally find lying neatly on a desk or filed safely away in a cabinet was now floating in the air with its value eradicated in an instant. Each piece that once held some sort of importance now reduced to litter under the feet of those fleeing the scene in panic.

Smoldering plane parts along with random pieces of wood, metal and glass from the towers hundreds of feet above rained down on the ambushed citizens below in a scene worse than any Hollywood movie could depict. And there were jumpers. People like you and me who had just gone to work that day as they would any other day. Now, they were hanging out of these infernos, trying to escape the flames, trying to get just one gulp of fresh air, praying for some sort of miracle; a miracle that would not come. If they were above the point of impact and lived through it, their fate was sealed. And they had a choice to make. All the while, the world was watching.

As the towers eventually fell, a wave of pulverized cement and other debris pushed violently through the streets of lower Manhattan like a pyroclastic cloud. Some were able to escape its grip, most did not.

As one eye witness was trying to distance himself from the raging rubble, his video camera continued to record and you could hear someone behind him scream, "Don't look back."

And as the toxic dust began to settle, the vibrant blue sky over the city had mutated into a lifeless gray with the landscape resembling that of a nuclear winter. Reaching out from the darkness was the eerie chirping of distress alarms of fallen fireman and "Musak" still playing in the streets as if this was just another ordinary day.

On that day there were victims, heroes, decision makers and every day citizens like you and me; real people with real lives and real families. And each face told a story. Such is a time when words aren't needed and are simply inadequate. Folks in the streets with hands over their mouths looking on in complete disbelief; fireman showing no fear as they tackled their biggest challenge ever; our president sitting in front of a class full of children as the news of a second crash is whispered into his ear; *these* are the faces of 9/11 that I will not forget.

I am certain that there was not one person who woke up that day expecting to turn into a hero or to die one either. But I am thankful for the passengers of Flight 93 who looked death in the eye and said "Not without a fight." Because in doing so, they saved countless lives and our country from another blow that might have taken us down.

There is no real time video to document the events that took place on Flight 93; we can't see the resolve in the faces of those passengers. We can only imagine the scene because of the details that have been pieced together from phone calls to loved ones. Chilling, to say the least, but brings pride to the forefront that these people not only fought to live, but were the first line of defense for our country in doing so. It wasn't just a display of human spirit, but also the American Spirit. "Let's roll!"

It has been ten years. And, history never stops.

When a tragedy such as this occurs, one so inhumane and unthinkable resulting in such inconceivable devastation, the process of recovery is incredibly complex yet catapulted in place in an instant. There must be some sort of balance and when so much death is involved, to achieve that balance seems humanly impossible. And while true justice seems to be out of our reach, the simplest gestures are not.

Symbolism, as pointless and transparent as it can be at times, ended up being an unlikely source for a fraction of that balance.

It began with "Tribute in Light", a temporary installation of 88 searchlights placed next to the barren World Trade Center site that formed two columns of light reaching from the earth to the heavens. Whether you have witnessed this tribute in person or have only seen it in photos, what you really receive from this display depends on what eyes you are seeing through. I see a glowing reminder of what once was and was not lost but rather taken from us. I see unwavering resilience of a people not willing to forget while finding a way to move on. Truly a beautiful and moving tribute whose light accomplishes more than filling a tremendous void left by the absence of the Twin Towers. It has been an annual tradition on the anniversary since it first lit up the Manhattan skyline in 2002.

An even more stunning and permanent tribute was unveiled during a dedication ceremony on September 11, 2011. The National September 11 Memorial & Museum is impressive yet simplistic. It's a look that has softened the face of the lower Manhattan geography with the green trees and soothing waterfalls in the midst of a high tech industrial setting. It stands out in character as much as the World Trade Center stood tall.

With the names of every victim from the 1993 and 2001 attacks of the World Trade Center, the memorial makes a statement of its own; how the site of such utter devastation can be transformed into something so serene and so beautiful. A memorial that has literally risen from the ashes to honor the lives lost and to show the world, once again, that though we move on, we do not forget.

But the most improbable symbol from this whole ordeal that depicts healing better than these other man-made attempts, for me, is the "Survivor Tree." A pear tree from ground zero found beneath the rubble of the fallen towers was retrieved and taken to another location to be nursed back to health.

Eight feet tall when it was taken down by the attacks, it now stands about 30 feet high and lives in the September 11 Memorial Plaza. It is a true example of moving on and living with the scars of life as one half of the tree appears normal and healthy while the other half of it cannot hide its absence of branches lost during the tragedy. God bless the hands and hearts who truly saw the worth of this one little tree and sought to save it.

We all have our own memories of 9/11, whether we were there or watched the events unfold on TV. And we all have had, and in some ways still have our own way of dealing with it all; the shock, the fear, the rage, the grief, the speculations, the uncertainties and the changes. And as isolated as we feel at a time like that, we are by no means the first to walk that path, nor will we be the last.

So why, you might ask, would I share yet another story about 9/11? Well, it's simple, really. First of all, I am sharing thoughts from my personal journey. And, I believe it's imperative that we do not ever forget what happened that day. There is still much we can learn. We must revisit what happened in order to maintain proper focus in a post-9/11 world. Forgetting only brings about complacency and that is a trait we can no longer afford. Remembering reminds us that life for anyone can change in an instant and that real evil exists, even in this once untouchable land of ours.

And we humans have an innate way of slipping back into old habits and thought processes once the immediate threat appears to be over. Today's top news story is replaced by tomorrows and so on. We profess today that we will not forget, yet tomorrow our actions paint a different story.

The magnitude of 9/11 wasn't enough to really render a permanent change in us as a nation. It was temporary, and that is the sad reality. And as optimistic as I tend to be, I know there are those individuals who will never "get it"; much like the gentleman at my place of work on 9/11 who made the comment (in reference to the television coverage of the attacks that morning), "I guess this is all that will be on TV today."

9/11 is an ocean of facts, emotions, opinions and the list goes on. And there's no other way for me to let these thoughts rest than to say thanks be to God, because He is still in control. Not the terrorists, definitely not Washington, and most certainly not me. In Him alone I put my faith and my hope. Amidst the most horrible of circumstances, that blue sky is still there. And it is because of His amazing grace that I can say it is well with my soul.

Nature's Breezes

The approaching storm is captivating. The sky looks angry. It darkens, it moves. The flashes of light are mesmerizing and the clap of the thunder challenges the beating of my heart. I rush from window to window for a better view. The wind takes command. I'm scared, yet intrigued. My adrenalin is out of control. I love its approach yet I fear is power and I miss it when it's gone . . .

After a long cold winter, my bare feet touch the new, soft, green grass for the first time . . . and it tickles. I feel a surge of fresh energy and I smile.

Pony tail grass . . . one of the most beautiful and peaceful gems of nature that I have ever encountered. They are the emerald green of spring. To the touch, soft as silk and when my fingers make contact with the blooms, it's as if I am strumming a harp. The sound they make as they sway to and fro from the breeze is not audible, but I do hear it in my soul. And as they blow in the breeze, each strand dances as graceful as a ballerina. It saddens me to see their beauty turn brown and hard at the end of their season; alas, they will be back again, with spring.

A soft, warm breeze and the sound of nature going about its business . . . so simple yet necessary to life itself. The chirp of a carefree bird, the buzz of a busy bee and the rustling of leaves as a gentle wind blows. Just stop and listen now and again. God's gifts are abundant.

Beautifully Broken

There are many things in life that once they break, become of little or no value to others; a glass, a toy, a promise. But there are some things that can be mended or accepted as they are and become even more valuable.

One of my favorite pastimes when I head to the coast is collecting seashells; or as I like to call it, "sea shelling". Though I had been to various beaches a few times in my life before, the obsession seemed to be born in the late eighties. Through the years, the passion has matured and evolved. And like anything meaningful in life, it has become a treasured part of my time at lands end.

Most beach goers walk along the shores of our beaches for many reasons other than noticing what lies beneath their feet. More times than not, the realization that one has passed over a forgotten treasure is the abrupt crackling sound that can be heard as they lift their foot for the next step. Some may look down to see what has been crushed, most continue on believing it was nothing.

In the early days of my collecting, it was all about finding the most shells and the largest shells, the perfect ones. Finding a conch shell half buried in the sand was like panning for gold and finding a huge nugget resting in your palm after the trash had been cleared away. Even in recent years, Mama and I would race to each other after a find to show off our treasures. You could easily observe us quietly strolling by the water only to see one of us break into a run down the beach because we thought we had spotted a large shell. More times than not, it ended up being a wad of seaweed or a mound of sea foam getting its last laugh.

But in the last few years there's been a noticeable shift in the dynamics of this favorite pastime of mine. Erosion, off shore drilling, storms, and such—all these factors, in my opinion, have played a part in what washes up on our shores and what does not. The days of finding beautiful conch shells with my own hands are all but gone for me. Sure, there is the occasional sand dollar or rare starfish after a hefty storm or hurricane, but those massive ocean jewels now seem to show up only on the shelves of gift shops at a pretty price.

For me, the journey is as meaningful as the destination. The real joy comes in walking the sand day after day in search of that shell I've never seen before. Finding it, and then washing the sand off of it in the ocean to closer examine its character and beauty.

The frustration of never finding "good" shells anymore (or not as often as I liked) seemed to detract from the joy I once felt when I would head out with plastic bag in hand and high hopes of great finds. I found myself picking up shell after shell and hardly giving them a second look before tossing them back into the very ocean that had handed me so many treasures for so many years. Mama and I would go out on these missions together only to come back complaining how the beach was so clean and the shells were all gone.

I don't know the exact moment that the proverbial light bulb flickered on for me, but I attribute a new tradition that Mama and I started a few years ago to the rebirth of our shelling joy and a pivotal moment in my shallow thinking.

Three years ago, Mama and I decided to try something new on our annual family beach trip. Well, I should be honest. It was her idea. "Let's come up with a craft project." "Okayyy . . . lame", I thought to myself, but okay. With an inward sigh, I agreed.

We collected a moderate amount of small and less than exciting seashells and with glue gun in hand, began to create our first tangible memory: two quite attractive seashell frames that would later proudly display our annual family photo from beautiful Oak Island.

Pardon my play on the musical words, but "a tradition is born." The experience was not only fresh and special, but something more. It was a silent turning point for me. Silent, because it was a realization that I had within my heart. But where would that epiphany take me next?

The following year, Tropical Storm Hanna nearly rained on our parade as she passed over Oak Island on the very morning of our departure for our family beach trip. With an "all clear" phone call from our realtor, we headed down to the coast with our usual uncontainable excitement and our shell project in tow for our 2nd year of this new tradition.

Once there, all the joy of those big finds that seemed to be a thing of the past resurfaced compliments of Mother Nature. We found conch shells and our first starfish. We were like children on Christmas morning! We were ecstatic! But that joy was fleeting. By day three of the trip, the shoreline once again was as clean as a fresh basket of laundry.

It wasn't until last year's trip that my eyes were really opened. The stress of life causes each of us to decompress in various ways. And as I took my walks on the beach alone, my gaze to the sand seemed to have more purpose than in years past. It was as if I were looking for something. What that was, I still don't know. But what I found was a new appreciation for what I had passed over for so many years.

Decorating my beloved and disappearing shores of Oak Island were endless pieces of broken seashells. But for some reason, I no longer saw them as broken, but as undiscovered treasures, each one as unique as each one of us; each one with a story to tell. What did they look like before life had chipped away at them? Where did they come from? What had their journey been like? How were they broken? How many times had they been picked up by eager hands only to be thrown back down because they weren't good enough?

Obviously, I would never know the answers to these questions. But what I did know was that these broken pieces of shells were a representation of me and you; folks who had been through the storms of life and seen its peaceful waters. Some had come through intact and others had been battered and broken by life's elements. Thought to be useless, they now lay there rejected. I like to believe all this was a subtle object lesson that God had been trying to share with me for years.

There is beauty in everyone and everything. For years, I had missed the big picture by focusing my attention on the apparent flawless shell, large and unbroken. But by bringing my gaze down to my feet as I walked along our seashores, I saw the truest beauty in the broken pieces of shell that decorated my path like breadcrumbs leading a lost traveler home.

Whether tucked away in a plastic container that I visit now and again or a colorful dish sitting in my home gently holding a prized collection of special shells, I will always treasure my collection of seashells. I'll continue to go shelling on our beautiful shores every chance I get. I don't look for the big seashells anymore. These days my attention is focused on the broken shells with the edges softened by the sands of time and colors faded from the journey. Individually, a broken shell may not represent beauty to most, but together with others just like it, can be a work of art.

So next time you decide to take a stroll on the beach, don't forget to look down and marvel at the worth of the beautiful broken shell.

I Dig It

It's 3am on a Saturday morning. The alarm goes off and as I wipe the sleep from my eyes, the excitement of what's ahead hits me like a splash of ice cold water in the face. My bag is already packed and ready to go. Grab a bath, throw on my clothes, flip flops and hat and I am out the door! I pick up my friend who is a little less of a morning person than I am, and we're off! Headed to the beach for the day with the top down on the mustang and tunes saturating the air around us . . . but it's not what you think!

❧

To this day, I still have no idea how I got involved in sports as a teenager. My brother didn't play, my parents weren't athletic, nor did they nudge me in that direction. Maybe I had some talent, some hidden competitiveness that needed to act out. Maybe there is a story behind it but I just don't remember. And maybe it just happened. Whatever the explanation is, I'm just glad that I hit the court.

In 8th grade I joined the JV basketball and volleyball teams and made the Varsity teams in 9th grade. I lettered in each sport all four years of high school but volleyball seemed to be "my" sport. As a sophomore in 1982, I even brought home a 2nd team all tournament trophy. As a self-proclaimed bit of an introvert, recognition like this was unimaginable and one of my proudest moments back then.

After high school, real life took center stage but it wasn't long before volleyball reentered my life. I played for several years in recreational leagues and with a travelling team in the USVBA in which we won our division three years in a row.

As stimulating, satisfying and exciting as the indoor volleyball experience was, it never delivered quite the same happiness as my years playing beach volleyball. Those years were, undoubtedly, one of the coolest periods in my life.

$$\mathcal{C}\mathcal{P}$$

Just a little FYI on beach volleyball for those who are unfamiliar with the game: beach volleyball is typically a game of two players on each team. You play on the beach (or a sand court if you are playing inland). You're barefoot and donned in beach attire. The rules are similar to indoor with slight variations and there are those additional sway factors of wind, sun and rain, to name a few.

I still remember my first beach volleyball tournament. It was in 1991 (I think) at Wrightsville Beach, North Carolina next to the Crystal Pier. I had travelled to the beach with a large group of volleyball players from our town that was playing in this tournament. I hadn't signed up to play, but rather was coming along with my boyfriend at the time who was playing. I had met Rick at the YMCA playing volleyball, go figure.

I recall being on the beach that Saturday taking in the whole experience and thinking to myself, "This is pretty cool. I could do this." Though I was a volleyball player, I had never taken my game outside.

My boyfriend talked me into playing the next day in the co-ed tournament. We partnered up, he gave me a quick tutorial and before you knew it, I (we) had captured a 3rd place finish in my first beach volleyball tournament ever. I'm sure he doesn't realize this, but that day he gave me something special. He strolled me into the delightful world of beach volleyball. Thank you, Rick, for being the unsuspecting medium that introduced me to a most excellent time in my life. From ages 25 to 32 I played beach volleyball tournaments in Myrtle Beach, Wrightsville Beach, Wilmington, Norfolk and Virginia Beach along with many other inland locations. I had three different partners during that time: Lisa, Lee, and Misty—and I have fond memories of them all.

But my fondest memories are with my first beach volleyball partner, Lisa. We won our first tournament in Norfolk, Virginia. I remember playing so late into the day that the beach had emptied.

Meaning, there was no one around cheering us on or there to celebrate our first victory with us.

Truth is, it didn't stifle our elation one bit. And, we won a pair of awesome volleyball shorts. I kept those blue volleyball shorts as long as I could until a few years ago. The elastic had dry-rotted so badly that when you touched the waistband, it nearly fell to pieces. There comes a time when there are some things you just have to let go of.

We also won the East Coast Volleyball Championships, Division B, in 1992. This tournament was held in Virginia Beach and was a big deal to us. This was the first time we managed to get our names into *Volleyball Magazine*. I have that magazine cover and tournament results page framed and on wall in our gym at home. Some things you never forget.

We played the majority of our tournaments at Myrtle Beach. We were a "division B" team but many times had to play "up" due to lack of entrants. What did this mean? It meant that we played most of our tournaments against gals who were far more talented (and taller) than we were. And while typically a loss where you were obliterated on the court in front of many passersby and friends would be a memory that you would want to bury, we had one of those losses that I still remember fondly.

In 1992, we suffered an 11-3 butt kicking (yes, we actually scored) from the eventual 1993 Women's Pro Beach Volleyball Rookie of the Year. Some things, you do forget—like the player's name. But who cares. We scored against a future pro player—three times! How cool was that that for two nobody recreational players like us?

The "big" tournament back in those days that came along every summer was the Jose Cuervo, beach volleyballs first major sponsor beginning in 1976. With stops all across the country, the Jose Cuervo tournament showcased both pro players and amateurs. Yes, it was sponsored by Tequila, but I thought nothing of it. As a matter of fact, I didn't even know what Jose Cuervo was at first. I was there to play volleyball, after all.

There was one year that I distinctly remember looking up and down the beach and counting about 40 nets lined up on the abundant sands of Myrtle. It was a beautiful site and all kinds of fun being a part of it. Competitive beach bums like myself would come from all over the East Coast to hit these tourneys. You had the opportunity to win some cool stuff if you were good enough to still be playing by the end of the day.

You could see some incredible amateur volleyball talent at these bigger stops. Richard Petty's nephew, Jody Petty, was a top notch amateur player back then. And when he wasn't doing his thing on the sand, you could find him modeling or in music videos (such as "Don't Turn Around" by Ace of Base in 1994).

And to top off the experience, my partner and I actually finished well, sometimes winning, during all of our Cuervo appearances.

But there was much more to my volleyball years than just playing. Even volleyball players need a diversion. And what would that be? Watching the REAL pros play . . . and meeting them, too!

I was never really the groupie/star struck type; never really thought about it much until I met my first Pro Beach Volleyball Player, Sinjin Smith. Never heard of him? You should Google him. He was inducted into the Volleyball Hall of Fame in 2003. He was one of the first players to recognize the marketability of pro beach volleyball and participated in the formation of the Association of Volleyball Professionals (AVP) in 1983.

He was one half of one of the winningest teams in pro beach volleyball history, Smith-Stoklos. With over 100 open wins in over a decade, the team help bring global attention and recognition to the sport. He was an amazing athlete and dubbed "King of the Beach."

He was tall, handsome, and humorous and well, I had several photos taken with him back in those days. I even managed a signed poster from him saying "I miss you." Obviously, he had a flirty sense of humor. And as a twenty-something single gal, I ate it up. It's framed, of course, and hangs in our home gym along with other sports memorabilia.

I went to my first beach volleyball camp in the early nineties held at Pompano Beach Florida. Daddy and Mama took me, and with a 55mph speed limit at the time, it was undoubtedly the longest drive ever. This was where I met Sinjin the first time. I attended two more at Tampa Bay and Clearwater Beach, Florida, with friends. My partner, Lisa, actually got to play a doubles game with Sinjin. Was I jealous? Of course, but just being there was beyond cool. Frenchie's Salt Water Café in Clearwater Beach, Florida would be where I ate my first Cajun alligator tail. Trust me—much tastier than it sounds, but I digress.

Believe me when I say, you have not watched volleyball until you've sat on a bleacher on the beach with 15,000 other folks watching these guys duke it out on the court. ESPN would be there covering this tournament so it was cool to see the cameras and what not around the venue. The beautiful ocean was behind you and the non-stop action in front of you with the sand beneath your feet and gorgeous weather hovering over you. I think the old saying goes "It doesn't get any better than this."

Over the years, I met a slew of pro players in addition to Sinjin: Randy Stoklos, Kent Steffes, Brian Lewis, Mike Dodd, Brent Frohoff, Jose Loiola, Eric Fonoimoana, Bruk Vandewegh and Mike Whitmarsh (R.I.P). These were the big names during my volleyball years.

But easily the most recognized name in volleyball inside or out is Karch Kiraly. And I was giddy when I met him. He's a volleyball legend and three-time Olympic Gold Medalist winning two medals indoor with the United States and a gold in beach volleyball at the Olympics in Atlanta in 1996. He was Incredible to watch and seemingly a class act. His performance was usually flawless as he knew the game better than anyone. Known for that neon pink hat, he played with strength and grace and more smarts about the game than you could ever dream of.

I attended maybe two or three of these Pro Beach Volleyball Jose Cuervo tournaments in Florida during my volleyball run. Loving the beach the way I do, it was near perfect to be on a Florida beach and taking in some stellar volleyball in the middle of an atmosphere that was totally electric.

Not to be a cliché abuser, but it has also been said that "all good things must come to an end." I often wonder what became of my first volleyball partner, Lisa, and what her life is like now. Though I've lived in the same small town all these years, I never run into any of the old volleyball gang. I don't keep up with pro beach volleyball like I used to, but occasionally when I catch a glimpse, like in the Olympics, the warm memories are as fresh as if they were made yesterday.

It saddens me to see the AVP struggle to stay afloat. While beach volleyball is still going strong in various venues across the country, the spectacle that was a nineties pro beach tour venue is seemingly a thing of the past. I hope it makes a comeback.

During this walk down memory lane, I Googled names from my former volleyball life and discovered that Jody Petty is now known as Jody Lee Petty and has turned in his volleyball (after eight years in the pros) for a guitar and microphone. He now fronts his own country rock band and has opened for such names as Rascal Flatts, Montgomery Gentry, Toby Keith and Sugarland. I didn't see that one coming.

I "retired" from playing the game competitively back in 1998 as partners were scarce and my knees were starting to unveil the ugly side of playing sports. Plus, I got married and became somewhat of an adult. That was only temporary. I'm back to being a kid again. But don't think for a second that I wouldn't do it all again. The bigger reality shock has been that the once bronze, fresh faced Sinjin Smith now dons grey hair and some weathered wrinkles around the eyes. But that volleyball spirit is still there. I believe it's something you can always sense and something you always have if you've ever been involved in the game.

I still own a beach volleyball that comes out of retirement each time I take a trip to the beach. Hubby and I will "pepper" and the adrenalin of those volleyball years bubbles to the surface once again. I may not move as quickly or poetically as I once did, but in my mind—I still do.

Thanks to the Internet, I am actually able to revisit segments of those "glory days." During the writing of this memory, via You Tube, I was able to enjoy a clip of the 1992 Jose Cuervo Tournament held in Clearwater Beach, Florida—I was there. And it still seems like yesterday.

Coming off the sand and hitting the less forgiving ground, I managed to play a lot of grass tournaments as well. I even snagged a "silver medal" at the North Carolina Olympic Festival in the late nineties as the curtain closed on my run as an amateur player.

Still, my greatest joy came from being on the beach. Nets set up, guys and gals showing up at 8am on a Saturday morning to register for a tourney with a biscuit in one hand while wiping the sleep from their eyes with the other. The blazing sun, the blistering sand and sometimes pushing heatstroke couldn't keep us away. If the water hose stretched far enough from the venue, they would try to hose off the hot sand. I recall on more than one occasion trying to dig my feet into the sand in between plays because I was developing blisters on the bottom of my toes.

The comradery partnered with the competiveness to provide an atmosphere like none other. The music and the announcer motivated us all for hours as we would weather the elements for a game we loved. And it wasn't just a game to me. It was an attitude; a lifestyle. Laid back yet competitive and something unique I was proud to be a part of. Haven't you heard? Old volleyball players never die; they just agree to sit under the umbrella for a bit and share the sand with others who see the beauty of the game. Once a beach volleyball player, always a beach volleyball player; even if it's just in your heart and memories. How I miss those days.

It's 6pm and the sun is still beating down on our tired, sunburned, achy bodies. It was a good day. The beach was awesome, as always, and the weather was perfect. We played well and we had fun. We've said "so long" to the other players and friends that shared the beach with us today. The car is loaded and we're ready to hit the road for the long drive home. The top is down and the wind blows off the stray pieces of sand that have stuck to our sun kissed faces from a day of competitive bliss. We hit our second wind as we sing loudly into the air all the way home.

Once home, I shower and collapse on the bed. My body may be exhausted but my spirit has been rejuvenated. I eat Chinese takeout while relaxing and watching TV until I drift off into a deep, hard earned sleep. I can hardly wait until next weekend so I can do all this again . . .

Footnote: On July 10, 2011, my husband and I took a day trip to Wrightsville Beach where I played my first beach volleyball tournament some 20 years ago. The area had commercialized and changed quite a bit during this time and there was little I recognized. But there was enough. I vividly remembered the road off of the causeway curving around to the part of the beach where we would park our cars for the day. I remembered the walk past the Oceanic Restaurant onto the beach where we played. I could almost hear the thump of the volleyball as it was making contact with player's arms and popping over the net.

almost.

I asked an older lady who was a cashier at the gift shop on Johnny Mercer's Pier if they still had volleyball tournaments on Wrightsville Beach. She commented that she had worked there four years and hadn't seen any sign of a volleyball tournament. That made me sad.

As we walked on the beach that day, we saw one lone volleyball net, standing firm but being ignored. The absence of volleyball on the beach, for me, was like summer without sun. It was as if life had moved on and left this very special sport to die alone. I told my husband I realized things had changed, as I know they do, but I was thankful that my memories were secure in my own past, if nowhere else.

On the Sixth Day

I came out of the convenient store with snacks in hand headed back to work. Out of the corner of my eye I saw a man and a dog. The gentleman was in his job uniform and he looked as if he may drive a truck making deliveries to various businesses. The dog was clearly a stray.

This good Samaritan was thoughtfully feeding this dog who appeared as if he had not eaten in days. Each morsel barely hit the ground before the best friend without a man had swooped it up. I literally stopped in my tracks by the display.

As touched as I was by the scene, reality set in as the dog scurried away after the contents of the bag disappeared. Where was he going and what would become of him?

For as long as I can remember, I have been around animals. From stray cats at home to farm animals at my grandparents to trips to the zoo; loving animals came natural to me.

Over time, that love has deepened into a grateful appreciation and respect and become a part of who I am. I understand better their place in this world. And more importantly, I get that they are so much more than pets or exhibits.

Animals were not an afterthought when God created the universe and everything in it. As a matter of fact, animals and wildlife were created on the same day as man. God tells us that not only did He create all animals, but also that they belong to Him. He cares for them and provides for them, just as He does for us.

In scripture, God himself is likened to a lion, a leopard and a bear. The Bible describes angels to have characteristics like animals such as a lion, a bull and an eagle. Jesus is portrayed as the "Lamb of God" and the "Lion of Judah"; the Holy Spirit is symbolized as a dove. With so many references to animals, how is it that the worth of each and every one of God's creatures is still in question? Jesus himself was born in a stable among animals rather than an inn among sinful men. For me, that is a beautiful reality with a deeper meaning.

Proverbs 12:10 says, "A righteous *man* regards the life of his animal, but the tender mercies of the wicked *are* cruel." I hate animal cruelty and I think it's deplorable. Every day, animals are neglected, tortured and killed. And why? Out of sheer meanness? Out of some need to be in control over something to make one's self feel superior? Whatever the reason, it's inexcusable and will be judged by our Lord someday.

Despite what some may think, animals are more than pets tied to a chain outdoors. They are more than a circus act or an exhibit for us to gawk at through glass. They are capable of unconditional love. Animals think, they have talents, they have emotions, and they feel pain, just as we do. "Why do they keep beating me? When will I eat again? Will I ever get out of this cage?" They are scarred by abuse as much as they thrive on love and attention, just like us. And every time I see one of those commercials for homeless animals, I feel their pain. If you can't look into the eyes of one of those scared, beaten down animals and see what I'm saying, you need to check your humanity at the door.

God delegated some of His authority to us in that He gave man dominion over animals. And this authority was meant to be demonstrated in a responsible and loving fashion the way God himself has dominion over us. But I am afraid that over all, we have failed Him.

I am not a PETA pusher. But I do applaud and admire the ASPCA and the Humane Society for their never ending fight to save animals of all kinds. Their efforts give countless animals a chance for the quality of life God intended them to experience in the first place. There are many organizations established worldwide as well as laws in place for the sole purpose of the preservation of wildlife.

I understand that not everyone is capable of loving an animal. After all, they can be loud, annoying, dangerous and filthy. But so can we. Touché'. Still, we are all capable of respect and the ability to coexist.

Given the chance, animals can achieve remarkable things. "Winter", the dolphin, is a great example. Found washed up on shore in Florida, her tail was injured badly after being tangled up in a fishing cage. Her tail was later amputated, yet she survived.

What makes this amazing is that a dolphin's tail is how they swim. But due to the loss, she began swimming by using her whole body in a different way. This was great at first, but she later developed issues in her spine which would eventually end up being life threatening. Through modern technology and the vision of those not willing to give up on this amazing animal, Winter received a prosthetic tail and now lives on. Not only is she a survivor, but an inspiration to many.

Animals are also loyal comrades to our police officers. They are the eyes for humans who have lost their site. They are precious therapy to abused women and children, to the sick and to the elderly. And on an everyday level, they are simply companions to many who just need to love and feel loved.

But whether domestic or wild, all creatures were created by God for a specific purpose. Animals are simply an amazing display of beauty, power, fun, loyalty and downright cuteness. And put to the test, they can overcome amazing odds and teach us humans a thing or two. They are all precious in the eyes of the Lord.

"And God saw everything that he had made, and, behold, it was very good. And the evening and the morning were the sixth day." Genesis 1:31

Beacon

I think it's safe to say that I'm a gal who loves tradition. And I have come to the conclusion (in my own mind) that traditions can be both a security blanket of sorts and a blow to the gut.

While the tradition is in place, it's something you look forward to, count down the days with ridiculous anticipation and you long for it all over again after the event has come and gone. It's familiar and comforting; who isn't drawn to that? It truly is like a security blanket in a world where so many things in life are unpredictable and out of your control.

This is a special tale about my sandy security blanket known as our family beach trip. This particular tradition has not yet kicked me in the gut. That only happens once the tradition fades away or is halted by unforeseen circumstances. I choose not to see that scenario as a possibility at this time as I hope we have many more of these coastal getaways in our future.

How this tradition came about is not an exciting blurb. Mama and Daddy had taken a few beach trips with my aunt and uncle during the summer and one day decided that our family-Daddy, Mama, my brother, my husband and I-should do the same. That's it. And the rest, as they say, is history.

In 2002 we planned our first week long getaway to Oak Island, NC, a 12-mile long island at the southeastern edge of the state facing Florida and the Bahamas. Since none of us were fans of crowds or scorching heat, we thought a trip in September celebrating the end of the summer and lower rental rates seemed like a better fit for us. And with a countdown app on my smart phone telling me there's "108 days left" until this year's trip, year number ten, you could say the

249

whole ritual fit as well as a glass slipper on Cinderella. It has truly been magical.

We're a simple folk, you see. We don't require a lot of bells and whistles to make us happy. Once we find something we like, we tend to stick with it. So after almost ten years, that is why we consider "Adventures in Paradise II" to be our oceanfront home away from home. With a downstairs and upstairs living area, covered porch with rocking chairs and a private access boardwalk to the beach, we couldn't have asked for more.

Over the years, we have made a lot of memories while on these trips, many of those captured in a photo or in a goofy video clip. And every once in a while I enjoy going through these little incriminating treasures to have a good laugh or to reflect on how the Lord has blessed our family with this time together, year after year.

And being a family of tradition, it only makes sense to have more traditions within the tradition. Basically, our whole trip every year is chock full of them. To start the week off every year, after we check-in at the house, scope it out for changes and get settled in, we all drive back to the mainland for supper at Pizza Hut. You'd be surprised how many laughs you can have over a simple personal pan pizza. And as it turns out, the dinner table happens to be a huge draw for pure silliness and laughter until you nearly squirt beverages from your nose; moments definitely worthy of a few frames of video, which my husband happened to capture one year. If you want to see grown adults doing the most childish things and having a ball doing it, bring the popcorn and we'll sit down for a laugh or two.

At the beginning of the week after our first supper together, Mama and Daddy hit the local Food Lion to stock up on items that didn't make the trip with us. For the next week, we will consume a lot of Fruit Loops, Pop Tarts, chips, Oreos, ice cream and sandwiches, to name a few. You can also throw in a bag of Twizzlers or M&M's and a couple of visits to Dairy Queen while you're at it. It's not a menu for the faint of heart and clearly not the time to be eating clean, mind you. But still, Mama manages to whip up some home cooked meals for us while we're vacationing. And of course, we will hit our favorite seafood restaurant, "Sand Fiddlers" at least once for some authentic seafood.

A big pastime for Mama and me is sea shelling. Now granted, Oak Island is not a hotbed for seashells like Florida, Hawaii or some other tropical location. But, when you're a North Carolina native who hasn't had the pleasure of shelling at beaches abroad, you learn to appreciate what you have in front of you for what it is. Seashells are like people. They come in all shapes, sizes, and colors. Some are flawless and desirable while others are boring and broken. But they all have their own beauty that lies in the journey of how they landed on our beach. And if you are able to see this, you've achieved something special.

In 2007, Mama and I added yet another tradition to our trip—a craft project; something we could do together and have as a keepsake from our trip. There have been four projects so far that have included a seashell frame, a seashell and sea glass frame, a seashell keepsake box and then—there was something else.

In 2009 we decided to get extra creative and attempted to style a mosaic on a glass container. We purchased our supplies before heading to the beach and we had the plan totally in place. And with great enthusiasm and high expectations, we began. With a white substance floating through the air, hot glue stringing from all ten fingers to any solid object in sight and belly laughs that could rival the best stand-up comedian routine, I guess you could say the outcome was a total debacle. I don't think we have ever laid our eyes on an uglier craft project in our entire lives until then. But the process was so much fun and gave us so much joy that each of our pieces are proudly displayed in full view in each our homes.

Outside of eating and sleeping, the itinerary during the day is pretty blank. Daddy will write for his books, work various brain puzzles and nap. My brother Jeff will walk and bike for endless miles. I will spend as many hours as I can under the umbrella with my toes digging in the sand, daydreaming and thinking with an occasional nap.

Mama and I will, of course, walk for what feels like miles picking up seashells and other sundry items. We especially enjoy early morning walks while the beach is still quiet and the only traffic is a seagull searching for its next meal. Hubby likes to catch up on his sleep first. Then once he's up and ready to go, enjoys his video games including getting us all involved in some friendly competition with some Wii Bowling. He and I will also take brisk walks on the beach while talking about this or that and we always reserve enough time and energy for some football and volleyball. Of course, there is always my photography and quality time with the seagulls, my coastal kindred spirits.

A retired tradition, I'm sad to say, are the days when David and my brother hit the ocean with their trusty little boogie boards. Though the seas are not angry in this part of the world, the waves got the best of my husband on two separate occasions when he was slammed to the sand injuring his shoulder. He had surgery on that shoulder in 2008 and the famous bright yellow "Legend" boogie board was permanently retired.

Another fond memory that I recall is in 2003 is when we were lucky enough to witness the hatching of sea turtles. At the time, we weren't aware that Oak Island was home to a Sea Turtle Sanctuary and that the local officials were very strict with the care of the sea turtle nests. It was the most exciting event to be out on the beach late at night with flashlights in hand witnessing such a spectacle. A handful of vacationers gathered quietly around these nests and waited patiently as the process began. The sand slowly erupted and about 120 sea turtles emerged. And with our lights showing the way, we actually aided in these little ones finding their way safely to the ocean. It was truly something I will never forget.

Over the years, weather has always been a factor in our end-of-summer beach trips. And how could it not with September being the height of hurricane season. And though we never were present for one of these babies, we still felt the effects when one loomed commandingly off the coast. Storms such as Gustav, Ivan, Ophelia and Igor made the waves dance and added a dramatic presence to the shoreline. The power of the ocean even when a storm was hundreds of miles away was both mesmerizing and frightening.

I recall only one trip that was really threatened by the approaching weather. In 2008, Tropical Storm Hanna made landfall near Oak Island in the early morning hours of September 6—just hours before we were to hit the road. We were all glued to the Weather Channel, a long time friend of ours, while loading up the vehicles in faith and praying for a miracle. The thought of not making this trip we had been looking forward to for so long was painful and as scary as the weather itself. Alas, a phone call to the realtor in Oak Island alleviated our fears and we were given the all clear to "come on down." We started our trip on schedule and with renewed appreciation for God's grace.

By the time we made it to Oak Island, the sun was shining brightly and the only signs that a tropical storm had visited recently was the standing water in the roads and an unusually high tide that ended up sticking around for days. Oh, and Mama and I had exceptional success in our sea shell expeditions, courtesy of Miss Hanna, of course. This was the first year we found starfish on the beach, along with half a dozen truck tires carrying some deep sea crab as passengers.

Other years, there was the occasional thunderstorm that rocked the house back and forth and jolted us all out of bed. I remember one such storm a few years ago that was so violent that it brought the entire family together in the main level living area. You know these things always happen in the middle of the night. And a storm on the coast is always more dramatic than one inland. Despite the vivid lightning, there is a vast darkness that envelopes you during a storm on the coast making the whole scene a bit eerier than usual. All facets of a storm are exaggerated and your senses are heightened.

And with this particular storm, the wind was so fierce that it was blowing rain in between the door and the door frame; it howled and whistled like a pack of wolves outside our doors. The waves crashing sounded more like a roaring lion. And the thunder pierced your ears with an echo that seemed to last forever.

And though this was just a regular thunderstorm, it commanded our attention and we were more than aware of its power. As always, Chief Meteorologist Jim Cantore kept us in the know and we managed to stay safe and catch a few more winks (with the blanket pulled up around our faces, of course) before the calm set in just in time for sunrise.

In ten years there have been both subtle and drastic changes to the coastline due to natural erosion and horrific storms. With the island facing south, it seems to take more of a beating than other beaches. And it's been hard to see the island shrink before our very eyes.

Last year I even noticed that the handrail on the stairs of our boardwalk that takes us down to the beach now sits level with the sand—that's three feet of sand higher than years ago, yet the beach seems to retreat more and more every year with the tide taking over the once abundant stretch of soft sand.

But life goes on—dunes are protected even more now. One man-made change that we witnessed occurred in 2006 as "North Carolinas Longest Pier", built in the 1950's, closed for good and began disassembly, board by board.

Things change. But some things don't. And it goes without saying that the natural beauty and laid back lifestyle of Oak Island are just two of the many reasons why we keep going back. Every day while at the beach, I make a point to sit under my umbrella, clear my mind of all the clutter and just look around me. God is good. Every night once the sun has set, I take a few minutes to wrap up in sleeves and sit on the rocking chair out on the covered porch and just listen. God is oh so good. Just to be still.

There is a particular element of the week that seems to encircle all the emotions, all the joy, all of the deep sentimentality of the trip—family photo time. On our last night at the beach house, just before sunset, we gather outside on the boardwalk to take snapshots and enjoy total unrestrained silliness. Usually this spectacle spills out onto the beach where we sometimes walk and talk together for a bit just enjoying the simplest pleasures in life.

To me, this is paradise. All that I love in this world is right here with me, right now. I try not to think about having to leave this place, but departure is inevitable. And with each year that passes, I can't help but wonder if God will grant us another trip together. Only He knows the answer. So, for now, I brush the hair out of my face and dust the sand off my feet and catch one last glimpse over my shoulder as I dream and plan for the next family trip to Oak Island.

Simpler Days

There's no doubt, times have changed. You really don't need to look far to be reminded of this. But one thing that never changes for me is the memories of simpler days.

I grew up in a traditional family and it's one of my greatest treasures. My daddy, mama, older brother and I were and are still very close. To some, it would have been considered a strict household; to me, it was exactly as it should be. Daddy worked hard to provide everything our family needed including sending my brother and me to a private school where we got quality education in a Christian environment. And we grew up in a time where Mama was able to stay home with us as opposed to leaving us with a sitter or after school care. If I heard that I was "sheltered" one time, I heard it a million. And I don't recall it ever bothering me. In fact, I think it made me feel extra special.

Growing up, I don't recall a lot of interaction with other kids outside of church and school. I mean, my brother and I didn't run in a pack like kids do these days; but rather, we were each other's best bud. I have fond memories of sitting in his room or my room just drawing and playing with whatever toys we had or made; we even came up with our own make believe islands complete with every business and necessity one could have in a community. I remember when I was searching for names for some of my make believe residents, this is when I discovered the strangest name in the phonebook: *Geo*. And boy, there were a lot of folks with that name. It wasn't until years later that I figured out this name was actually "George." Sorry. Some of us just catch on slower than others . . .

Night life in the Brown home was truly riveting. During the week, there might be a nail biting kickball game between my brother and me; or, if we were feeling particularly adventurous, there would be a challenging evening of lightning bug hunts. By dark, we would take it inside for the nightly watermelon weighing (during the summer) followed by a session of seed spitting and melon gorging until you were about to burst.

By the weekend, the action would really pick up. There weren't mall trips with girlfriends or group dates at an early age. Instead, Mama, my brother and I would hop into our stylish station wagon and after Mama proceeded to whip out a five dollar bill for each us, we would let loose inside our local K-mart, hitting the blue light specials first, of course.

It really is quite astonishing how far you could stretch five bucks back then. And even now, as a gal in her forties, I still get that same excitement when Mama gives me a piece of greenery to spend. It's one of those simple thrills in life that you never outgrow.

Saturdays ended up being even more out of control. The routine was to hit the road and travel to my grandparents . . . or as we called them, Mamaw and Papaw. A Saturday such as this could carry a lot of variety. A visit to the Huff's always began with me checking out Mamaw's freezer for frozen doughnuts. They were always delish! Then, the afternoon would be pretty leisurely.

When we weren't hanging out with my cousins and playing in our pretend band "The Zingers", my brother and I would sit in front of the floor model TV for hours watching wrestling! We especially liked watching wrestling at the Huff's because they got extra channels and it would come on one show after the other. This is when we would really polish up on our skills.

If we headed to the Brown's for the day, it would be a lot of outdoor activity including running through the chicken house (the stink was so thick in there that you would have to part the hairs in your nose just to get air in) and terrorizing the little chirps or playing outside and enjoying an afternoon on the farm.

I loved to sit on Papaw's lap and blow out his match after he would light his cigarette. I still have one of those old wooden chairs he would sit in.

Compared to the rest of the week, Saturday evenings were pretty laid back. Of the three stations we picked up on our little black and white TV, you could always count on Hee Haw to be ready and waiting for us on CBS. I really believe the term "appointment television" originated in our home on Saturday nights. I'm very proud to say that watching hours of this prime time thriller is not where I got my sense of humor from. Nor did I develop my sense of style from Porter Wagoner who could be heard crooning in our home most Saturday nights. If you don't know who he is, Google him and then you will appreciate my aversion to bling.

There was always church on Sunday, for which I am thankful! In the early days, Mama would fix a yummy home cooked meal after church. As time passed and the money was really coming in, we would manage to hit the local Western Steer for a Sunday meal. We had hit the big time. Thinking back, eating lunch out after church made you feel like church had just moved to a different building and they were feeding you. These days, you walk in a restaurant around noon and you certainly feel overdressed. Times have unquestionably changed.

In my early teens, my nightlife really picked up. Finally. After the Sunday night service I was allowed to mix it up with my brother and friends from church by partaking in a little of the fine dining in downtown Graham . . . at McDonalds. You heard me right. It started with a small fries and soda and eventually progressed to a quarter pounder and even dessert; sometimes an apple pie, sometimes a sundae—always a tossup. Incredible, don't ya think? Ah, the discussions we would have in those little booths and the anticipation of who would actually show up at these little shin digs.

Summers at our home were pretty predictable, but fun. Well, most of it was fun. Back then, Daddy had a thing for big gardens. What thirteen year old do you know who really wants to spend the summer hanging out with a bunch of vegetables out in the sun? As much as I loathed the child labor, I always appreciated the benefits and I'm sure my body really misses the organic menu. A favorite memory of mine was the mornings when Mama and I would take a break from chores and watch "Dialing for Dollars." I'm sure with that name, there was money involved, but I never saw any of it. What I did see were classic old movies. I remember thinking that Errol Flynne was a good looking older man, though I didn't really know what to do with that passing thought at the time . . .

Summer also meant a week for my brother and me at Mamaw and Papaw Brown's who lived on a farm in the foothills of North Carolina.

They had dogs, cats, cows, pigs and of course, chickens. There were tractor rides with Papaw, walks to "the creek" and quality time with Ringo, their collie; running through cornfields and working in tobacco were always included in a visit.

We would always pack up our bikes and take them along with us. Mine had the banana seat along with rainbow streamers and a white basket on the front. We would use clothes pins and attach a piece of cardboard to the frame so that the spinning tire would cause it to make those really cool sounds.

Did I say the word rainbow? Unfortunately, that word brings to mind a traumatic event that occurred in my grandparent's house all over their linoleum floor in the den. You just don't say "no" to an old lady in a wheelchair! And when Great Grandma Brown kept offering me those pastel colored marshmallows, I kept eating them. Let's just say, a kid can only eat so many of those things before the rainbow is bound to find its pot of gold. But I digress.

There were no computers or electronic games; just our imaginations. Try finding *that* item on eBay these days. I'm sure it would cost a fortune.

Other than spending time with our grandparents, one of the best parts of that week was hands down Mamaw's breakfast. Her everyday breakfast menu made Cracker Barrel look like a dive: eggs, bacon, sausage, gravy, homemade biscuits, coffee, juice, milk . . . and all made with so much love you couldn't seem to push your chair away from the table. They had an old out-of-tune piano that my brother would play while Ringo and I relaxed in the middle of the floor, his paw gently laying on mine.

Summer thunderstorms were a regular occurrence in Western North Carolina. I recall one storm that was so violent that the wind forced a hunk of wood through the screen in the den window, which happened to be the window facing where we would sleep on the floor each night. It didn't break the glass, though. A lasting reminder that the Lord was always watching over our family, that piece of wood stayed right where God placed it that night until the day the house was torn down, some 20 years later.

No matter how our day started or what we did during the day, you could be sure the hot summer day would end with our tired, grassed stained bodies resting in old wooden chairs gathered on the porch and in the yard as the sound of crickets and other wild animals started singing the sun to sleep. The simplicity of it all still causes me to exhale.

These days, a power outage is likely to cause a virtual meltdown in the average home. No cable, no Playstation, no fun. But through the many ice storms that were a regular part of winter for North Carolina back in the day, it just meant exciting games of checkers and Battleship by candlelight with the sweet sound of an unplugged night in, together as a family.

Can you ever really go back? And if you could, would you? As modern as my own household is these days with large screen TV's, computers, digital cameras and other gadgets that didn't exist 30 years ago when I was growing up at home, I think about it from time to time. There is a part of me that is begging to get out because it's been packed away in a box of memories for way too long. When the stress washes over me like a rainy Monday and the "to do" lists imprison me, all I have to do is close my eyes and remember where I came from; remember the love and laughter that filled our household no matter what we had or didn't have; remember that my life has always been rich because I always had everything I needed, and a few things I didn't-like PBS being one of the only three stations we could get on the television.

Yes, with the flip of a switch and a little reminiscing, it IS possible to go back to simpler days, if only in my mind.

Mama and Me

I have often said that as a writer, I can only sit down and write when the inspiration shows me the way. It can't be forced. The heart and soul and mind come together, open up and the words begin to flow effortlessly. I am thankful the Lord has allowed me to live long enough to write about the moments in life that have meant the most to me.

It's early on a crisp and sunny Friday morning and our vehicle is packed with overstuffed suitcases and any-season beach essentials. But there is still room for our oversized smiles and our child-like spirits which are also bursting at the seams. The anticipation has been building for weeks now. Our destination: Oak Island, on our beautiful North Carolina Coast, of course.

It's Mama and me headed out for an extended weekend that has now become our own little tradition. In November of 2009 at ages 72 and 43, we began our ritual of fall and spring hops to the beach with an itinerary that rarely changes. But that's the way we like it. It's a comfortable retreat for a mother and daughter whose relationship has taken a lifetime to bloom into that perfect flower that is both colorful and pleasant; and now we are breathing in the sweet fragrance of its growth and beauty.

Take an imaginary, unassuming box and write on the outside with purpose the simple words "Mama and Me". And on the inside, fill it with moments from Southport, The Point, Blue Crab Blue, McNeill & Company, Local Call and The Christmas House. Shake the collection around a bit and you have plenty of room for spirited seagulls begging for a morsel of food yet posing long enough to have their photo taken; soft sand, crisp breezes and bright sunshine along with the healing aroma of salt air and the calming resonance of the crashing surf fill in the open spaces amongst the other gems.

Add a familiar flavor to this homemade treasure chest by tossing in a McDonald's coffee, a personal pan from Pizza Hut and a Dilly Bar from Dairy Queen. And with the right amount of chips and chocolate to munch on in the hotel room, you've got the perfect lullaby that brings our tired, wide-eyes to a close each night just after sunset.

To pull it all together, pour in a healthy dose of chatting and walking on the beach for hours while picking up seashells that others have passed over. This walk on the beach is a familiar one. Yet somehow it captivates us every time. We are seeing the scenery as if it's both our first and last time.

But what preserves the contents of this box are the miles of smiles both goofy and sincere, endless giggles that no one around would understand and the genuine love that we share not just as mother and daughter, but also as best friends.

And though we've always cherished a great relationship and experienced many special moments together, THIS is a time just for us; it's priceless. And this box of memories doesn't ever run out of room or need a fancy bow to suggest its importance or worth. Because we know what's on the inside: it's just Mama and me. And I wouldn't trade these moments for anything in this world.

Lisa and I at volleyball camp in Tampa Bay, Florida

Playing a tournament at Wrightsville Beach, NC in the
nineties

Pro Beach Volleyball tournament at Clearwater Beach, Florida

"Adventures in Paradise"—our home away from home

Family photo time at Oak Island, 2007
It would seem Mama had a common case of the
giggles . . .

Our family snapshot at Oak Island in 2011 . . .
Even the cool, rainy weather couldn't hide our smiles.
It was the first time in 10 years that we didn't make it out
onto the beach for this photo tradition.

Simply Sage

David and I containing our shivers on a blistering cold day
in front of the beautiful Mountain Lake Hotel in 2008.

mama and me

Sometimes, words just aren't necessary . . .

Perspectives

In September 2011, our family headed to the coast, once again, for our annual family beach trip. Since beginning in 2002, this tradition had instantly turned into my most favorite and anticipated time of each year. This year was our "tenth anniversary" and the expectations I had placed on these seven days were higher than in years past. I had put tradition on a pedestal. I was about to learn yet another life lesson.

Over the years we've tolerated brief bouts with bad weather such as tropical storms grazing our coast or late night thunderstorms shaking our house. These added a tad more excitement to the week. But this year, fall seemed to come a bit early. We arrived to cloudy skies and the coolest temperatures we have ever experienced for a late summer vacation. And the extended forecast wasn't looking too good.

It's easy for me to admit right away that I was a bit disillusioned from the beginning. With the fall weather looming over us, I couldn't imagine this trip resembling previous trips without the warmth of the sun leading the way. To find that magic, I would have to look elsewhere.

I was dealt another blow to my picture perfect trip when my husband injured his knee on the first evening while playing a video game with the family. With much pent up stress begging to escape, his boy-like enthusiasm in the track and field event proved to be too much. On Sunday morning, he woke up with a sprained knee that would alter his physical activity for the week as well as my expectations . . . . again.

"They" say it comes in threes. And once I realized Mama and Daddy had forgotten to bring the Scrabble game with them, I was ready to throw my hands up in the air. You don't understand. There had ALWAYS been the competitive tension of that game at the kitchen table in the evening after the sand had been brushed off our feet for the day.

I could feel my attitude taking a wrong turn at warp speed and it was time to hit the pause button and regroup. What was really going on here?

I needed to be alone with my thoughts so I set out to take a long walk on the beach. Pulling out the proverbial magnifying glass, I began to take a closer look at what was really bothering me. I believe that reflection is the beginning to gaining a fresh, new perspective. And that's exactly what I needed.

While walking down "memory lane", numerous scenes flashed before my eyes and I couldn't help but smile. But the smiles quietly disappeared amidst a cloud of shame. Reflection, as productive as it can be, also has the sobering ability to gift you with a better look at yourself. The problem all along, it would seem, was with me.

I came across a quote that laid it out plain and simple; "We don't see things as they are, we see them as we are." In life, like it or not, change is inevitable. The harsh reality is that only I am in control of how I handle change. The ugly truth was clear to me now that I had done a poor job in embracing the subtle changes that were suddenly beating me down.

You see, anything sturdy that will handle the test of time has to have a good foundation. And I had put this one week out of the year on a pedestal-a man made pedestal. No one or nothing is worthy of such a high place, except for my God. And though He had blessed me and my family with all of these years together and so many precious memories, I had failed to really see that. I seemed to be more concerned with preserving this "perfect picture" rather than savoring every moment for what it was . . . . an opportunity. A heart with no room or no tolerance for change is a heart that is void of substance. And I knew that wasn't me.

Nevertheless, I alone am responsible for inflicting this drama on myself; for tainting these memories with sadness; for suppressing the natural progression of things . . .

Over the years I have witnessed countless stimulating sunrises and breathtaking sunsets. I have seen the miracle of birth as sea turtles hatched in the late evening hours surrounded by a crowd of beach lovers like myself. I have laughed with my family until my stomach hurt and shed an internal tear at the wonder of it all. I have had quiet time under the blue skies and under the flickering stars to not only talk to the Lord, but to allow Him to talk to me. And the list goes on. I have been rich beyond what I deserve.

But fresh perspective is not typically obtained from recounting all of the good things one has experienced, but more so by the less desirable events that were simply not part of the plan.

This year, I saw two older ladies walking on the beach, one of them clearly recovering from a stroke and each step appearing to be both a struggle and a small victory for her. Yet she smiled.

With David no longer pulling out the boogie board and hitting the waves due to his shoulder surgery and having to decline the long walks on the beach due to his sudden knee injury, we found ourselves biking instead and discovering new adventures that had opened up to us. We both agreed it was the highlight of our trip.

And with the less than stellar weather joining us this year, I found myself looking inward more, seeking the warmth of the sunshine in other ways.

As hard as it is to see the coastline changing or to witness our earthly bodies breaking down and preventing us from doing the things we once did a mere five or ten years ago, I have a choice. And I choose from this point on to welcome each trip, with all of its surprises and imperfections, with open arms. I'm optimistic but I'm also realistic. I know it won't be easy. But I welcome the challenge. I have to. I won't allow myself to be defeated by my stale perspectives any longer.

This year's trip might have been our last as a family. Or, we may still have several ahead of us. Only God knows. The Bible says we are not guaranteed the next breath, let alone another year to experience such simplicities as a walk on the beach or laughter during a meal together.

My prayer and heart's desire is that September 2012 will roll around and we will once again find ourselves together for a time at that sandy little paradise making new memories to store in our collective treasure chests. I would love the opportunity to stretch the wings of my new found perspective and see where it takes me. And no matter the destination, I know that my trip will be a success as it is grounded in God's grace and shared with those I love the most in this world.

Jesus and Me

Everyone has a story to tell. And you have been reading bits and pieces of mine. But the most important story of my life is that of Jesus and me.

I was brought up in a Christian home and went to church every Wednesday, every Sunday and then some. I attended revivals, summer camps and Gospel sings. I have never walked through the doors of a public school but rather was blessed with twelve years of education at two different Christian schools. And I have been surrounded by Christian parents, grandparents, and other family all my life.

All of that is fine and good but none of it saved me from an eternity in hell. What saved me was the blood of Jesus Christ followed by my decision to accept Him as my personal savior. That is the single most important relationship one could ever have. Simple enough, you don't accept a gift and then toss it aside once you have made the choice to open it. You don't profess to love someone and then never tell them or show them.

I recall the words to a song we sang at church when I was a kid; "There really ought to be a sign upon my heart: Don't judge me yet there's an unfinished part. He's still working on me, to make me what I ought to be . . ." I am without a doubt, a work in progress. I'm not close to being perfect. But one day I will be.

Until then, I can share my story with those who will listen. And my story is simple. Jesus loves me. I may not always be eloquent when expressing the thoughts that are most important to me, but I don't have to be. If I could take every beautiful worship song, each old hymn, all good ol' Southern Gospel greats and blend them together to tell you what I feel in my heart—what I know and believe to be true—it would still fall short of the glory of God. But God knows my heart. And I love Him. I am so thankful for His many incredible blessings.

Near the top of that list are my godly parents. Mama and Daddy provided my brother and me with the most wonderful home. They made sure we had everything we needed, they loved us with all their hearts, and they led by example. They made sure we were in church, hearing the gospel and learning all about Jesus. And we did.

My daddy shared something with me via email about seven years ago. It will always be very precious to me. "When you were born," he said, "I stood outside the window at the hospital watching you and I prayed that the Lord would make you a Christian lady. As far as I can remember I've never shared this with anyone before. If I didn't tell you now you might never know. You were lying in the 'baby room' that has the big window, among the other babies, when I prayed that prayer. Please don't ever forget where you came from and keep your faith in the Lord strong. Love, Daddy."

In my first hours of life (and even before, I'm sure), my daddy loved me so much that he prayed that I would someday come to know the Lord. And do you know what's even more amazing than that kind of love? The love of my Heavenly Father! He loves me so very much, and so unconditionally. He sent His only Son to die for ME. With all the billions of people in this world, He knows me by name. He knows my every need; He even knows the number of hairs on my head. And He does not give up on me, despite my sins and my shortcomings. His mercy and amazing grace surround me every day.

It's simple. *I believe*. And it's changing me.

My prayer is that I continue to grow in the Lord. I ask for His forgiveness as I am a sinner every day, yet saved by grace. I also pray that if anyone reading this book, this story—if you don't know the Lord and want to know peace that passes all understanding, He is ready to know you!

Someday, He is coming back for me. As the old hymn says, "What a day that will be." And as another song humbly proclaims "I can only imagine." But one day I won't have to imagine any longer. Because we shall see Jesus, just as He is!

Vanilla, With Some Sprinkles Please

If you've read every word of this campfire moment up until now, you will have easily figured out at least one thing about me: I'm a simple girl who loves her simple life.

My aspirations have never been fueled by a desire for power, wealth or fame. To some, they would surmise I am void of ambition or vision. My smiles don't come from partying or jet setting. To some, I would be considered dull or boring. I obeyed my parents, I obey the rules and I stay out of trouble. Put all of these ingredients together, and most would say I am simply "vanilla".

In modern days, vanilla is more than an ice cream flavor; it is a way of describing someone who is seen as plain or lackluster; a conservative who plays it safe. Being the "glass half full" gal that I am, I have a different take on being defined as vanilla.

Pure and simple in composition, vanilla ice cream is the real deal. If I wore a label, it would read only a few ingredients, just like Breyers. You always know what you're getting and never have to wonder what's inside and still, it's all good.

Now don't get me wrong; I'm not tooting my own horn, but rather, embracing who I am and what I am. I am at peace with my "vanillaness."

There's so much I could say but let me keep it simple. I'm not meant to be a "Tooti Fruiti", a "Rocky Road" or a "Neopolitan". I simply don't need it. I need to be me. And that suits me just fine.

Let's face it; vanilla is universal. It is the foundation on which all ice cream flavors are formulated. Look at it as a blank canvas from which the most beautiful of creations can emerge. All you need are some sprinkles.

Stuff

Wow! and *sigh*. Here I am, here you are, at the end of my first (and hopefully not last) book. It most definitely is a bittersweet moment. I get only one chance to write my first book. And I'm finding it hard to let go.

When I first made the commitment to myself to write and publish a collection of short stories, I never envisioned that both the book and the journey would come to mean so much to me along the way. Yet here I sit with a light bulb dancing over my head and that look of "duh" pasted on my face.

And though I've rambled on for almost 300 pages now, can you believe I still have more I wanted to share? Really, it's like popcorn popping in my head right now. I mean, I'll be honest; I've come to know myself a lot better during this process. I understand better who I am, what I like, what I don't like, and how I feel about many different things. I've developed a greater appreciation for the simple things in life, how much I cherish them and how they are a necessary part of me. Everything in and about this book is uniquely me. And I've decided, I like me.

But there's more, you know.

What was left unwritten? Lots, I'm sure. How about that I love pastel colored curly ribbons, (lots of them), Swarovski crystals because of their sparkle, and stuffed animals. Or that the best part of my day is simply coming home! How about my favorite color. I'm not kidding. Do you have one and what makes it your favorite?

Me? I love the color blue. Baby blue, aqua blue, sea glass blue, Carolina blue . . . I see these colors and they make me happy. I think of the beach or a cozy cottage in some breezy location. They soothe me and I like to have them around me. See, I'm even smiling while I'm writing about it . . .

Do you have a favorite hobby or a preferred season? What makes those things so special for you? Do you have dreams held deep inside that you've never shared with anyone else because you thought they were silly or unimportant?

I'm not saying you need to go out and write a book, like I've done. But I would highly recommend it. Why not take a closer look at yourself and your life and embrace every little facet!

Because every detail that makes up who you are is important. And the truth is that most people go through life without ever thinking about or really pondering most of the stuff I have written about in these pages, let alone write a book about it for everyone to read. And let me tell you—they are missing out.

If you've rolled your eyes or snickered out loud or even thought once "she's lost it" while reading any part of my book, chances are you are one of the "they".

But if you've genuinely smiled, nodded your head in agreement, or had your own pondering light bulb flicker on for a minute, then you "get" me.

I love my life in flip flops and I am beyond blessed. And it's been a pleasure sharing all this sentimental, sometimes painful, maybe a little goofy, but always cool stuff with you! Actually, it's all cooler than the flip side of my pillow!

Hubby and I were having dinner at our favorite diner recently and chit chatting about this and that. I was commenting that I kept thinking of stories and tidbits that I wanted to add to my book and how I was afraid of leaving stuff out. Hubby remarked that my book reminded him of a popular movie. Momentarily flattered, I enthusiastically responded, "Really? which one?" With his irresistible charm and a genuine grin he replied, "Neverending Story."

Hey—this isn't the end, this isn't goodbye. It's simply . . .

Laterz!

About the Author

Sonja DeChene is an aspiring writer, photographer, and self-proclaimed beach bum living inland in the heart of beautiful North Carolina. She shares a piece of the American dream with her wonderful husband, David, and two precious kitties, Rumi and Sage. By day, she is an Administrative Lead within a nationally ranked healthcare system. The rest of the time, she is living the simple southern life by choice and loving every minute of it. *Life in Flip Flops* is her first literary endeavor.

Please feel free to stroll by:
www.visualbreezesphotography.com